STRANGE BUT TRUE . . .

Facts:
- Perfect rubies are more valuable than perfect diamonds.
- Not a bird in the world has fewer neckbones than the giraffe. Even the little English sparrow has 14. Credit the duck with 16. And the swan with 23. As you no doubt have read, the giraffe has only seven neckbones.

Figures:
- Three out of four homicides committed by women are committed at home.
- Crows live 80 years.

Fascinating Questions and Answers:
Q. How many earthquakes does Tokyo get every year?
A. About 1,000. Residents feel about 50 of them.
Q. How much is the Pentagon's phone bill?
A. $8.7 million a year.

Browse to your heart's delight through a bountiful collection. You may discover that the world is not what you thought it was, once you've wandered through . . .

BOYD'S CURIOSITY SHOP

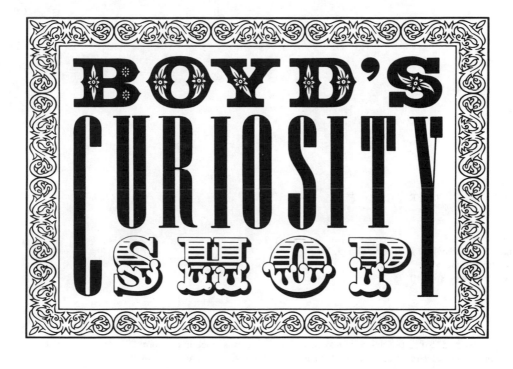

L. M. BOYD

A DELL TRADE PAPERBACK

A DELL TRADE PAPERBACK
Published by
Dell Publishing
a division of
Bantam Doubleday Dell Publishing Group, Inc.
666 Fifth Avenue
New York, New York 10103

The trademark Dell® is registered in the U.S. Patent and Trademark Office.

ISBN: 0-440-50272-1

Reprinted by arrangement with Olympic House Publishing Company

Printed in the United States of America

Published simultaneously in Canada

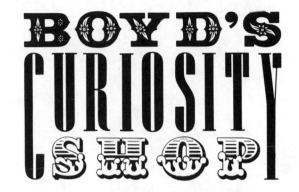

"MUSEUM" originally meant "temple of the Muses."

•

STUDENTS of ancient history, please note: Residents of Arizona's Phoenix call themselves "Phoenicians," too.

•

THREE OUT OF 10 shotgun shells are fired at rabbits.

•

IF EVERY MAN, woman and child in the United States smoked cigarets, they'd still be outnumbered by the cigaret smokers in China.

•

IT HAS BEEN written by an anonymous medical researcher: "A baby learns to smile in the womb. But it does not learn to pout until about six months after it's exposed to the real world."

•

WHAT 1930 car had 16 cylinders? That's what I asked. Those who purport to know say, a Marmon. That sound right?

ANSWER DEPT.

Q. "WHAT PROPORTION of the American people are overweight?" A. Can only tell you 67 percent think they are.

THE Philippine Supreme Court sat for months to reach this decision: A dead rooster can be declared the winner in a cock fight, if he died while on the offensive.

Q. "HOW MANY airplanes crashed in Alaska last year?" A. In 1984 — 198.

•

Q. "HOW MUCH of what does a wild wolf eat?" A. About 13 pounds a day. Average. Of flesh, hair, bones.

•

Q. "WHAT WAS the first animal featured in an animated cartoon?" A. A dinosaur called Gertie.

•

Q. "WHAT U.S. CITY has the most residents per capita listed in 'Who's Who'?" A. Princeton, N.J.

Q. "I KNOW the biggest annual fair now is the Texas State Fair in Dallas. What's the second biggest?" A. The Los Angeles County Fair in Pomona.

•

Q. "WHAT LAKE in the United States has the coldest water?" A. Tahoe, I'm told. Surprised to hear that. Thought Alaska might come up with colder.

•

Q. "A BOY and a dog appear on the Cracker Jack package. The boy is named Jack. What's the dog's name?" A. Bingo.

A HOUSE MOUSE is ready to breed when it's little more than a month old.

•

OUR WORD "giddy" comes from the old Anglo-Saxon "gyddig" meaning "possessed by the gods."

•

IT'S NOT an insect if it doesn't live inside a hard skeleton.

•

ALMOST HALF the people in Mexico get by, or try to, on less than $4 a day.

•

IN SHAKESPEARE'S day, owners of watches wore them on chains around their necks.

•

YOU DON'T find snakes on hog farms. A pig will kill a snake — zap! — just like that.

•

IN FLORIDA'S Seminole County, one out of every 20 marriage licenses is issued to partners each over age 65.

•

FORTY-NINE out of every 50 people in Arkansas are of parents who were both born in the United States.

THE SNOWS are deep at both the North and South Poles not because they get a lot of snowfall. They don't. They're almost as dry as the Sahara. But what they do get never melts.

WHEN THE Mona Lisa was exhibited in Washington, D.C., more people went to see it than had ever gone to a football game, a prize fight or a World Series.

•

NOT ALL red foxes are red, you know.

•

SOME VILLAGERS in South America's Andes speak a nearly pure Castilian Spanish no longer spoken anywhere else in the world.

AMONG FROGS and toads, the female is usually the larger.

•

YOUR GREAT grandmom probably used to flock the family Christmas tree with melted soap. Many did.

•

EVERY boa constrictor has two small spurs at the back end of its body — which prove to experts such snakes once had working hind legs.

IN JUNE OF 1948, according to court records in Oklahoma City, a man there named Never Fail filed for bankruptcy.

•

LIKELIHOOD that a scientist will marry a scientist is five times greater than the likelihood an artist will marry an artist.

•

A WOMAN is said to be more susceptible to sunburn when she's pregnant than at other times.

•

WHEN PRESIDENT Ronald Reagan makes a speech, it's immediately sent worldwide in 36 languages.

•

DID I MENTION you can get 7.5 million toothpicks out of a cord of wood?

•

ONE OUT OF FIVE neckties is sold just before Father's Day. Most popular Father's Day gift, the necktie. Second most popular is shaving lotion.

•

"MOUSE" came from a Sanscrit word for "thief."

•

A RABBIT can eat a mushroom that would kill a man.

IF YOU DON'T put on your left sock first, you don't do it the way most people do it.

ANSWER DEPT.

Q. "IF 'DRY GOODS' are dry, what are 'wet goods'?" A. Lot of early stores were run by New England merchant shippers. Their main cargoes were calico and rum. They put the cloth on one side of the store and the rum on the other.

Q. "HOW MANY babies are born every year in this country to fathers over the age of 55?" A. About 7000.

•

Q. "WHAT WAS the population of the United States at the time of Custer's Last Stand?" A. Forty million.

•

Q. "HOW MUCH of a water lily is edible?" A. All of it.

•

Q. "WHEN DID women start outliving men?" A. About 50 years ago when childbirth deaths dropped. In those few places worldwide where statistics indicate men outlive women, the childbirth deaths remain high.

•

Q. "HOW MANY Anglos survived the seige of the Alamo?" A. Two. Suzanna Dickerson and her baby. They were among at least 15 women, children and slaves who lived to tell about it.

•

Q. "WHICH OF the United States was named after Julius Caesar?" A. You must mean New Jersey. It was named after England's island of Jersey, and that's a corruption of Caesar's island.

IT IS NOT uncommon for an octopus to have one little eye to see things in sunlit waters and one big eye to see things in the dimness of the deep.

•

JULIUS CAESAR once banned a sort of football game because it was too gentle.

•

IF YOU JUST have to blame a woman for something, blame her for one out of every 10 violent crimes.

•

IN THE WINTER, 35 percent of the body content of that living thing known as the "eastern tent caterpillar" turns into anti-freeze.

•

YOU WASTE as much energy when you throw away an aluminum can as you'd waste if you poured out half a can of gasoline, it's claimed.

•

"AMPHIBIOUS" comes from Greek words meaning "double life."

•

IT'S NOW KNOWN the sperm whale sometimes dives as deep as two miles.

BIG BEAVERS 6000 years ago almost but not quite wiped out the forests of northern Europe.

CURRENT FAD in Sweden: Artistic manicurists paint miniature pictures on the fingernails of ladies with the wherewithal to pay for same.

•

A HUNTING TIGER reportedly succeeds in only one kill out of every 20 attacks.

•

ENGLISH thatchers expect a foot-thick thatched roof to last 70 years.

•

FOUR BITES a second is about as fast as any person can chew.

IF YOU WERE born earlier than 1952, you got here before the word "automation" ever appeared in a dictionary.

•

MORE CARS are stolen in the United States annually — aren't we great? — than are manufactured in the Soviet Union.

•

LOS ANGELES city officials think there are about 50,-000 homeless street people there now.

•

GRASSHOPPERS have white blood.

MIDDLE EAST pack camels are outfitted with phosphorescent harnesses. Am told they look weird out there on the sand, glowing in the dark.

•

IF WE DIDN'T get niacin in our food, we'd all be insane within a year, the doctors say.

•

THAT SILENT-FILM mogul William Fox — you know, "20th Century-Fox" — hardly ever set foot on his theater stages or saw any of his productions. Wasn't interested.

•

PEOPLE ARE said to think and play and work at their best when the 24-hour temperatures average between 63 and 73 degrees F.

•

THE SUICIDE rate among retired men over age 65 is 12 times that of those in the same age bracket who go on working.

ANSWER DEPT.

Q. "WHICH ORGAN needs the most energy — the heart or the brain?" A. Neither. The inner ear. Surprisingly.

MOTHS LIKE night flight, butterflies day.

Q. "IN INDIAN talk, what's 'chiefing'?" A. That's the current Cherokee vernacular for putting on a fancy feather headdress and posing — reluctantly — for tourists' snapshots.

•

Q. "WHAT IS IT that makes goldfish stay small in a bowl but grow much bigger when turned loose in a pond?" A. Theory is they secrete a substance that inhibits growth when concentrated but doesn't when diluted. Shrug.

Q. "ARE POSSUMS immune to snake venom?" A. To rattlesnake venom, yes. And to copperhead and cottonmouth, too. But not to cobra venom. Only poisonous snakes that don't live where possums live can kill possums.

•

Q. "HOW DO jungle natives know what's edible and what isn't?" A. If they see any animal eat it, they figure it's okay.

•

Q. "WHY DO roots grow downward?" A. Gravity. It draws the calcium on the root caps.

•

Q. "WHERE'D we get the word 'scalawag'?" A. From the name of the undersized, temperamental ponies raised on Scalloway in the Shetland Islands.

•

Q. "WHEN DIVORCE breaks up a one-car couple, who gets the car?" A. The wife, almost invariably.

•

Q. "WHY DID the lawmakers in Mobile, Ala., make it illegal to wear high heels on that city's streets?" A. To keep women in high heels from suing the city if they fell.

"**G**OLD" must've been of some interest to the ancients. The word turns up in the Bible more than 400 times.

•

CUCUMBERS, too, get tumors.

•

AM TOLD acid rain through shallow wells has corroded copper plumbing in Sweden, and a lot of Swedish blonds now are running around with green hair.

•

NO, FLYING FISH don't flap their fins.

•

DIP THAT fertilized chicken egg in estrogen and you'll get a hen. Dip it in androgen and you'll get a rooster.

•

WAS A TIME in college football when it was against the rules to gain more than 20 yards with any one forward pass.

•

YOU CAN BUY plastic-wrapped frankincense in Oman markets now for about $3 a bag.

"PASS the butter" — in three out of four U.S. households — means "Pass the margarine."

YES, SCIENTISTS have indeed performed brain surgery on cockroaches.

•

OLDEST ball game? Handball, no doubt about it.

•

EIGHTY-SIX percent of the women in Muslim countries are illiterate. The law doesn't work, evidently. Islamic law provides for equal education of women.

•

AMONG the Islamic Rashaida of the Sudan, females start wearing veils at the age of 5.

ONE international border is more fortified than any other on Earth now. Name it. All right, the front between North and South Korea.

•

ONLY PART of the human body that can't repair itself is the tooth.

•

FUMBLERS such as you and I lost 100,000 tons of silver coins in the first half of this century. Or so say the government accountants.

•

COSTS $1 million-plus to train a U.S. Navy jet pilot.

CIGARET smokers in Iran now are paying about $5 a pack.

•

FRANCE'S PARIS has some parking problem. Police say a third of all the cars not in motion are parked illegally.

•

ORIGINAL TITLE of Joseph Heller's "Catch-22" was "Catch-18." He evidently ran across four more.

•

THAT publication called Woman's World contends full-time homemakers work 99.6 hours week.

•

EXPECTING, my dear? Consider this: The red bat gives birth to as many as four young at a time, "and their combined weight may exceed that of the mother."

•

EIGHTY YEARS ago, the New York City Foundling Asylum kept a blanket-lined receiving basket on its front doorstep

•

AM NOW TOLD The Who is the world's loudest rock outfit. One decibel beyond the point of pain.

DURING a typical rainstorm about five million drops of water — count 'em — fall on an acre.

ANSWER DEPT.

Q. "WHO FOUGHT in the first televised prizefight?" A. Lou Nova knocked out Max Baer — heavyweights — in the first round. In 1939.

Q. "WHAT DO the British Columbians mean by 'green jellybean day'?" A. A loggers' joke, that one. It's told that when some loggers, gone all week, fly home weekends, they scatter bagfuls of green jellybeans all over their green lawns. This keeps youngsters outdoors while loggers say hello to moms.

•

Q. "SAYS HERE marijuana is the nation's second largest cash crop. Second to what?" A. Corn.

•

Q. "OKAY, friend, what do these have in common: GI Joe, Poker, Snowball, Navy Blue, Homerun, Daily Double, Airflow, Boomerang and Cowboy?" A. All were cigaret brand names once.

•

Q. "IN 1968, Bertha Van Der Merwe of Capetown, South Africa, was kept awake by her doctors for almost 12 days, I've just read. What was her condition at the end of this time?" A. She was sleepy.

•

Q. "IS THERE a Tennis Hall of Fame?" A. There is. On Bellevue Avenue in Newport, R.I.

ROBOTS in Japan pay union dues. All right — at the Fujitsu Panuc factory, robots replaced some employees. The union screamed. The company ponied up robot dues.

•

IN ROMANY, the language of the European gypsies, a clan brother is called a "phal." It's where we got the word "pal."

•

AMONG sperm whales, females both babysit and wet-nurse the offspring of other females.

•

WERE YOU aware that the southernmost point in Canada is in the same latitude as Northern California?

•

DEER on the Keys of Florida are about the size of collies.

•

"COPENHAGEN" means "Merchants' Harbor."

•

THE BEAUTIFUL apple orchards of Tasmania got their start from three trees planted before the famous mutiny by none other than Captain Bligh.

YOU KNOW that bullring cheer "Ole"? Dates back to hundreds of years of Islamic rule in Spain. Originally, it was a shout of the devout: "Allah!"

IN ANCIENT Athens, every third man worked with marble.

•

THE U.S MARINE Corps started out as a British army unit.

•

GROWNUPS outnumber kids three-and-a-half to one at Disneyland.

•

AM TOLD a good hamburger franchise can bring in $15,000 a day.

•

JAPAN'S national anthem has only four lines of lyrics.

IF YOUR NOSE were as sensitive as the sniffer of a shark, you could smell edibles all the way across town. Two-thirds of the shark's brain does that only: detects aromas.

•

THAT Hollywood Oscar weighs 6 pounds, 12 ounces.

•

PLACER MINERS wash 250 tons of gold a year out of Siberian streams. The Soviet Union is second only to South Africa as the world foremost gold producer.

•

A CUBAN land crab can outrun a horse.

TWO COMMON phrases reportedly coined by Franklin D. Roosevelt: "cash and carry" and "breathing spell."

•

THE SINGLE most complex instinct in the animal world, some say, is the building of dams by beavers.

•

THE WEEK of the Aztecs lasted 20 days.

•

WHEN YOU hear comment about "the right kind" and "the wrong kind" of cholesterol, bear in mind that without cholesterol you'd have no sex hormones.

•

FIJI CRABS climb trees.

•

MORE THAN half the people in Nevada live within 50 miles of Las Vegas.

•

GORILLAS go to bed about 6 p.m., if typical.

ANSWER DEPT.

Q. "HOW COME black sheep are being bred out of existence?" A. Their wool can't be dyed.

NEVER heard of anybody who suffered from "fear of walking," but there is such a dread, evidently. Its technical name: "basiphobia."

Q. "ISN'T IT TRUE that the first female FBI agent was a nun?" A. One of the first two, anyhow. She was Joanne E. Pierce, 31. The other was Susan Lynn Roley, 25, a former U.S. Marine.

•

Q. "WHAT'S the oldest of the fast-food hamburger chains?" A. White Castle. Started in 1921.

Q. "ISN'T the elephant the only animal that can be taught to stand on its head?" A. Except for man, that's right.

•

Q. "WHO INVENTED the original one-armed bandit?" A. The famous Liberty Bell nickel slot machine? A German immigrant named Charlie Fey. He sold his first one to a San Francisco saloon keeper in 1895.

EIGHTY-ONE out of every 100 women in their 70s are convinced that men excel in science and math. But only 5 out of every 100 teenage girls believe it.

•

SUICIDES peak in the spring. So do conceptions of babies. When I grasp the pattern there, I'll pass it along.

•

REALTORS, please note: The male bluebird, too, picks out three or four nesting sites and shows them to the female — then she decides.

•

SALVAGE crews have recovered capped bottles of varnish from sailing ships sunken centuries ago — to find the varnish perfectly usable.

•

NEARLY ALL the signs used in writing music are of Italian origin.

•

UNHATCHED chickens dream. So do newborn kittens with eyes still closed.

•

NINETY-NINE percent of the universe is nothing.

THE BROOKLYN Bridge originally charged a toll of a nickel a cow.

CHEDDAR — called the "American cheese" — originated in England.

•

QUICK, what was the first outdoor game in which women competed on equal terms with men? Say croquet.

•

SOME CREATIVE character invented a lens. Then it was 300 years before another creative character put a lens in front of a lens to invent a telescope.

•

IF YOU BET the fellow on the next stool that the first subway in America was in Boston, you'll win.

THE MONEY counters say we'll have spent as much by 1990 on computers as we have spent over the last 200 years on textbooks.

•

THE CORVETTE is 19 times more likely to be stolen than is the average car.

•

THREE MILLION miles — that's how much closer the sun is to Earth in mid-winter, January 1, than in mid-summer, June 1.

•

IN AREAS where waterbeds are sold, one household in every four has such.

BABOONS chew tobacco. No, sir, real baboons. Yes, sir, real tobacco. And on purpose. They develop a craving for the nicotine.

•

A DRAGONFLY generates three times more lift than the most advanced man-made aircraft.

•

RAPID REPLY: No, the possum that plays dead isn't acting. It really passes out.

•

ONLY THREE out of five people ever develop wisdom teeth.

•

THE PELICAN'S pouch is so elastic that the bird can pack said pouch with the weight of more fish than it can lift into flight.

•

MOST SUICIDES are arranged so the person the victim wants to punish finds the body.

•

CHESS, it's said, is the only game without an element of chance.

•

IF YOU LIKE fine distinctions, please note that penicillin does not kill germs, just stops their reproduction.

Q. "IS 'FEAR of dogs' common enough to have a scientific name?" A. It is. Cynophobia.

NEWBORN babies have ulcers. Some babies, anyhow. Not many.

ANSWER DEPT.

Q. "AREN'T DOGS and cats color-blind?" A. Dogs, yes. Cats, not quite. You won't see any demonstration of this at intersections, but it's now known that cats can indeed distinguish red and green.

•

Q. "HOW MANY U.S. families live with quintuplets now?" A. 11. At this writing.

Q. "BEAVERS MATE for life, you said. Who's boss?" A. They devote virtually all their time to fixing up their home. She is.

•

Q. "WOULD a spaceship in orbit ever get dusty out there?" A. Presumably. About 1000 pounds of cosmic dust falls to Earth daily, at any rate.

•

Q. "WHAT WAS the name of the world's first moving-picture theater?" A. It had no name. One Thomas L. Tally set it up as part of a carnival on April 2, 1902, in Los Angeles.

FOR THOSE who care, please note Ronald Reagan is an Aquarius and Walter Mondale is a Capricorn.

●

YOUR BRAIN was almost but not quite its full size on your seventh birthday.

●

ELDERLY impoverished black people are said to be the most disadvantaged group in the nation. They have the lowest suicide rate.

●

CATHOLIC UNIVERSITY in Washington, D.C., offers a master's degree in lobbying.

●

ON THE ISLAND of Lan Yu near Taiwan, the husband alone is blamed, disgraced and divorced if the wife fails to have a baby. ●

AMONG THOSE retirement-age Americans who move, one out of four moves to Florida. ●

WHEN the beaver builds the subsurface exits of its hut, it takes into account how thick the ice will be next winter. The beaver is rarely wrong. But how does the beaver know?

WHEN FALSE teeth were made of inflammable celluloid, history records one man's mouth caught on fire while he was smoking.

THE RUSSIANS in Moscow outnumber the Norwegians in all of Norway.

●

THE EMPEROR Penguin can't fly, doesn't sing, won't build a nest. As a bird, all he's got are feathers.

●

ENGLAND'S Royal Family in 1983 spent $112,000 on upkeep of horses and carriages but only $82,000 on upkeep of cars. ●

THE MONEY authorities say $60 million worth of pennies gets lost every year.

WHAT IMMIGRANTS see first upon entering New York Harbor is not the Statue of Liberty, but the roller coasters of Coney Island. ●

DEATHS related to the weather — more are reported in Texas than in any other state. ●

NEW ZEALAND'S Lake Wakatipu rises and falls three inches every five minutes. Why? ●

IT'S "BAGPIPE," not "bagpipes," says our Language Man. Yea, even though a bagpipe has five pipes.

IN IRELAND'S Limerick County are more than 400 medieval castles. Nowhere else has that many, surely.

•

A 400-YEAR-OLD MUSHROOM may be a rarity, but you can't say nonesuch exists.

•

BY NEXT YEAR, if the prognosticators have it right, women will own 10 percent of all the farms nationwide.

•

ICELAND'S telephone directory lists people in order by their first names, not their surnames.

ANSWER DEPT.

Q. "WHEN Senator John Glenn piloted bombing missions over Korea, who was his co-pilot?" A. None other than that heavy hitter of baseballs, Ted Williams.

•

Q. "WHAT USED to be on the site of the White House Rose Garden?" A. A greenhouse, or a vegetable garden, or an ice house, or a stable and or a milk house, at one time or another.

DID I tell you the housefly hums in the middle octave, key of F?

Q. "IS THERE any place on earth where men and women dress exactly alike?" A. Ladakh. That's India's mountain province. They wear long, heavy sashed robes and embroidered stovepipe hats.

•

Q. "WHY IS that little channel in your ear called a Eustachian tube?" A. Because it was first identified by a 16th century Italian physician named Bartolomeo Eustachio.

Q. "WHO WAS the most famous female impersonator of all time?" A. Pal, I'd guess, the dog most frequently seen as Lassie.

•

Q. "HOW MANY ticker-tape parades have been held in New York City?" A. Only 27. At this writing. Last one before the 1984 Olympic medalists' was the 1980 parade for the hostages back from Iran.

•

Q. "WHICH IS higher in wild-card poker, a royal flush or five of a kind?" A. Five of a kind, unless house rules say otherwise.

•

Q. "ALL RIGHT, can you name a 2-year-old who made more than $1 million in two minutes?" A. Aha! You mean "Nihilator." The colt that won the Woodrow Wilson Pace for pacers and promptly picked up $1,080,500. How much is that per second?

•

Q. "DIDN'T actor Humphrey Bogart get his lisp in combat?" A. An accident when he was a helmsman aboard a troopship during World War I. It was his father, Dr. Belmont Bogart, who surgically repaired the damage, might mention.

NEVER SNEAK up behind a platypus. That's where its spurs and venom are. Behind.

•

ANOTHER PLANT or animal life form is said to become extinct every 10 minutes.

•

DURING Prohibition, a woman could buy shoes with vials in the high heels wherein she could carry a little liquor for emergencies or whatever.

•

NEPAL used to charge climbers $900 each to go up Mt. Everest. Inflation hit. Nepal now charges $3300.

•

SIR, IF you're typical, your ability to handle hard physical labor declines by 9 percent between the ages of 45 and 55.

•

IN ITALY, the tax on gasoline is higher than the price of it.

•

BEE VENOM is pure protein. That's why people put meat tenderizer on stings. The papaya enzyme in it breaks down protein.

ONE OUT of five high school dropouts has an IQ of 130 or higher. That's bright, sometimes brilliant.

SIX NEW lakes are created in the United States every day.

•

ALBANIA outlaws chewing gum.

•

NINETY percent of the elderly in Florida were born outside the state.

•

ESKIMOS have more than 100 words for ice.

•

SCALES on the feet of birds give them "fingerprints" as unique as those of people.

FORTY-SIX percent of all movie tickets are sold to people under age 21.

•

THE YEAR 2000 is not that far off, is it? Our Chief Prognosticator forecasts these costs: Average house, $150,000. Hamburger, $4.50 a pound. Daily newspaper, $1.

•

ON THE Seminole reservation in Florida, an Indian husband with a white wife can live on the reservation, but an Indian wife with a white husband cannot.

NO YEAR can have more than three Friday-the-13ths.

•

ON SOME construction sites in Alaska, oil company crews drill holes in the frozen ground, set pilings in them, then pour in a sand-and-water slurry that freezes, holding the pilings in place as solidly as concrete.

•

IF BOTH you and your spouse are left-handed, you're more likely to have twins than right-handed offspring.

•

IN NAHUATL, the ancient Aztec language, the word for "wife" was a set of syllables that translate "one who is owner of a man."

•

INTERIOR designers will tell you the first thing that registers on you when you enter a strange room is color.

•

IT'S NOT extraordinary for a tennis player to lose five pounds during a match.

•

RAPID reply: Yes, a riled Texas horned toad can indeed squirt blood from the corners of its eyes.

AMERICAN Indians had never heard of prostitution before European settlers showed up.

ANSWER DEPT.

Q. DOES anybody know how many men Al Capone killed? A. Had killed on his orders? More than 500, if the crime historians have it right.

•

Q. IN THE song "Waltzing Matilda," an Aussie sees a "jumbuk" come down to take a drink of water. What's a "jumbuk"? A. A sheep.

Q. IN POLICE talk, what's a "mooner"? A. "A mentally disturbed person who is activated during a full moon." This definition is printed in an official publication of the New York City Police Department.

•

Q. WHAT COUNTRY has the most golf courses per capita? A. The Bahamas.

•

Q. WHATEVER happened to Black Jack, the riderless horse that walked behind the coffin of John F. Kennedy? A. He was put to death at age 29 on Feb. 2, 1976.

•

Q. DOES ANY animal have a better sense of smell than a bloodhound? A. Not any domesticated animal.

•

Q. AREN'T WE rapidly running out of 18-to-24-year-olds? A. You might say that. By 1995, the number of U.S. citizens in that age bracket will be down by 23 percent.

•

Q. OF ALL the literature ever produced in this country, what book best typifies the American way of life? A. The old Sears, Roebuck and Co. catalog, I'd guess.

ON PERMANENT exhibition at Yale University is a massive replica — 22 feet high, 1¾ tons, mounted on tank treads — of a lipstick.

•

BIRDS, TOO, have weight limits for flight. About 35 pounds is tops. A turkey or swan may get that heavy. But from there up, flight isn't possible.

•

AMONG WEARERS of contact lenses, the women outnumber the men by seven million to three million.

•

ANY SINGER who wants to improve rhythm and breath control ought to take up the hobby of juggling. So recommends a juggler of lengthy experience.

•

HOW DO YOU suppose the ordinance-makers in Atlantic City, N.J., propose to enforce their law that forbids the smoking of cigarets there in the kitchens of private homes.

•

THE KILLER in 11 out of 100 murders is identified within a few days.

HER "BEAUTY SLEEP" was what the woman of yesteryear called that sleep she got before midnight, if any.

WHEN a gentleman met a lady in public, he was supposed to kiss her, not on the lips, not on the cheek, but on the neck. That was the custom 200 years ago in France.

•

EIGHTY PERCENT of the diamonds sold in this country pass through offices on New York City's 47th Street between Fifth and Sixth avenues.

•

AN ELEPHANT grows six sets of teeth, including tusks, in its lifetime. That better be enough. If and when the last set fails, the elephant starves to death.

NOBODY knows how many Philippine islands there are.

•

A NEWBORN baby's body is only 20 percent of its grown-up size, but its brain is already 90 percent.

•

DON'T JUST SAY aluminum weighs more than concrete. Say a cubic foot of aluminum weighs 168.5 pounds; of concrete, 145 pounds.

•

THE TRUE Indian peace pipe was a short, straight clay. That long, graceful pipe adorned with feathers was dreamed up for the movies.

A BABY BORN in Singapore or Hong Kong has a better chance to survive its first year, statistically, than a baby born in the United States.

•

BUSINESSMEN of Japan's Osaka are noted for turning a profit. The traditional greeting in that city is not "Hello" or some such, but "Are you making any money?"

•

SPAGHETTI and tomato sauce, a twinned natural, right? Not in the beginning. Italy got its spaghetti from China 200 years before it got its tomato sauce from America.

•

ITEM NO. 92177A in our Love and War Man's file labeled "Travel" reads: "When in Turkey's Ankara, don't kiss a girl while in a taxicab. The driver will throw you out."

•

THE JAPANESE idiom for motorcyclists translates "underbreed."

ANSWER DEPT.

Q. "QUICK, name the only U.S. president who'd graduated from Annapolis." A. Jimmy Carter.

THAT TYPE of baldness most common among American men is "the haircut with the hole in it."

Q. "HOW LONG does marijuana stay in the body after smoking?" A. About a month, according to the medics who study such.

•

Q. "AMONG WOMEN divorced before they're 30, what proportion never marry again?" A. More than one out of four — 26.7 percent, precisely.

Q. "DON'T MOST heart-attack victims survive the first attack?" A. Almost but not quite. Annually, the first attack kills 650,000 Americans, but another 600,000 survive the first.

•

Q. "HOW MANY girls age 14 or under in this country get pregnant every year?" A. About 30,000. And 12,000 have live births.

•

Q. "PRIMITIVE tribespeople in Africa keep good hearing until much later in life than do most Americans. Why?" A. It's quieter there.

•

Q. "METEOROLOGISTS mark Jan. 31, 1977, as a unique day in U.S. history. Why?" A. It was the first occasion all 48 contiguous states had snow on the ground at the same time.

•

Q. "WHO WAS the first black woman to serve as adviser to a president?" A. Publicly? Mary McLeon Bethune. Curiously she'd be relatively unkown today were it not for the football players who made names for themselves in the pros after coming out of the college she founded — Bethune-Cookman.

HAVE YOU eaten your typical five tons of aspirin today, America?

•

IT WAS AT Colgate University that psychologists learned that students seemed best able to solve math problems while lying down with their feet propped slightly higher than their heads.

•

THREE out of four homicides committed by women are committed in their own homes.

•

IN THE LINGO of the great railroad era, those men who checked out the freight cars for hoboes were called "knockers."

•

CURIOUS, isn't it, that the quickest way to get to the back of the church is to walk in through the front door?

•

IF YOU'RE over age 55, mister, it's almost a cinch you're buying a size larger shoe than you bought 30 years ago.

•

RABBITS AREN'T rodents, but porcupines are.

STUDIES SUGGEST women who like literature tend to be better cooks but poorer drivers than women who like math.

WHALES LIKE ice cream, the water-park people report. Where do you get a cone for a snacker with a four-ton tongue? •

WORLDWIDE, land equal in size to Idaho turns into desert each year, I'm told.

•

THE REAL Pilgrims who had windows customarily threw their garbage out same. It was the thing to do.

•

THE GLUE on Israeli postage stamps is certified kosher.

DO YOU cook with wine? In a conventional oven, the alcohol evaporates, but not in a microwave oven.

•

THE WESTERNMOST part of Alaska is farther from the easternmost part of Alaska than San Francisco is from New York City, I'm told.

•

ONE-SEVENTH of the general population is left-handed. But one-fifth of the mathematicians are left-handed. Why this difference?

"WHEN MY feet hurt, I can't think," said Abraham Lincoln. You never see it on plaques in shoe stores. Why not?

●

WILL YOU BUY an expert's claim that at least one out of every 10 high-stakes poker games is played with marked cards?

●

THE MOST VISITED national park playground nationwide is . . . ? Ask around. Answer is the Great Smokies. Second most visited? Cape Cod National Seashore.

●

NO, A BIRD with a temperature of 108 degrees F. does not have a fever. That's normal.

●

LADLES ARE older than spoons.

●

YOUR HAND is wide if it's wider than its third finger is long. Got that? The finger's length and the hand's width are about the same on the average hand.

●

WHERE WOULD YOU go to learn how to fish? Bear in mind, Harvard's library contains more than 10,000 books on fishing.

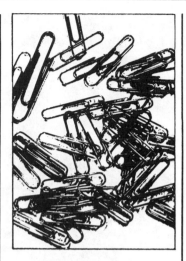

ONE OUT OF every 10 paper clips manufactured is bought by the U.S. government.

ANSWER DEPT.

Q. "WHO WAS the king alluded to in the phrase 'chicken a la king'?" A. England's King Edward VII. He is said to have fancied the recipe.

●

Q. "WHAT'S the average interval between the births of twins?" A. Ten minutes is typical.

Q. "WHERE'D WE get the expression 'passing the buck'?" A. An old card game term. A marker called a buck was put in front of the player whose turn it was to deal.

●

Q. "WHAT proportion of the nation's doctors are women?" A. 14.8 percent. And rising.

●

Q. "IN BYGONE days, what was the difference between an able-bodied seaman and an ordinary seaman?" A. Experience versus no experience. Or reliable versus not so reliable. Or troubleless versus troublesome.

●

Q. "WHAT'S the insect that cooks its food?" A. You mean the Dalmatie ant? It chews grain, forms it into patties, and bakes them in the sun. Pretty close to cooking.

●

Q. "GENERAL George Armstrong Custer has been characterized as every sort of a fool. Did he ever do anything right?" A. Must have. His widow, Elizabeth, loved the man deeply and continued after his death to devote more than half a century to the defense of his honor. How's that for a memorial?

ABOUT 250,000 cakes of soap a year are used to draw X's on the windows of buildings wherein construction men labor.

•

LIST BOSTON as that U.S. city where car thieves are most active.

•

IN BASEBALL, volleyball and tennis, a ball that hits the line is "in." In basketball, football and soccer, it's "out." Why this difference?

•

SCHOLARS SAY they've never found a human tribe without a legend to explain the origin of fire.

•

SOME VIOLETS bloom both under the ground and above it.

•

THE FIRST ear rings were ear plugs, actually, and scholars say they were worn as body ornaments even before stone weapons were devised.

•

ORCHIDS BLOOM longer than other flowers. Any other flowers.

THE ORIGINAL "heathen" was anyone who lived in wild uncultivated heath.

IF YOU USE a map of California for your dart board, chances are one out of every four darts will land in a desert area.

•

THE GREEK words "oikos" meaning "house" and "nemein" meaning "manage" gave us the word "economics" — household management.

ALWAYS BUY bathing suits and toothbrushes two at a time, if the budget allows. Resting such makes them last longer. That's the advice of the experts.

•

ALL OUR LIVES we've been told that sports build character, but can anybody prove it?

HOW MIGRATORY birds can forecast the weather 12 hours in advance still isn't understood, but it's known that they do.

A LADY who gardens in her backyard keeps the birds away from her newly planted seeds by throwing an old coonskin cap in the center of her plot. They think it's a cat, she says.

IF YOU, sir, are an average man, you've got 66 pounds of muscle and 40 pounds of bone. To say nothing of 3.25 pounds of brain. I don't like the ratio.

GIRLS WALK two weeks earlier than boys do, generally.

MOST WOMEN think all wives lie to their husbands, pollsters say.

STRAIGHT PINS are precisely pointed, not too dull, not too sharp. On purpose. So they'll pass between the threads, not penetrate them individually.

WHEN YOU get good at slipping fortunes into fortune cookies, you can do about 1200 an hour.

THERE ARE house mice in Asia that sing like canaries. Sort of.

ANSWER DEPT.

Q. "HOW MANY U.S. presidents really were born in log cabins?" A. Four — Lincoln, Fillmore, Buchanan and Garfield. No, dummy, Garfield was a president.

Q. "WHAT DO the Canadians do with the guns they confiscate along the U.S. border?" A. Run forensic tests on them for crime evidence. Then ship them off to Ottawa for scrapping.

Q. "WHO WAS the first person to refuse the movie world's Oscar?" A. George Bernard Shaw. In 1938.

Q. "HOW LONG does it take a sponge to grow to 'bath size'?" A. About 50 years.

Q. "WHAT'S the most popular name for housecats?" A. Tiger.

Q. "WHERE DID cucumbers come from?" A. Northern India, probably.

Q. "WHAT WAS the first car to be air-conditioned?" A. A Packard, exhibited on Nov. 4, 1939, in Chicago.

Q. "ARE DOGS and cats mentioned in the Bible?" A. Dogs, yes. Cats, no, curiously.

Q. "HOW DID Ogden Nash describe 'The Perfect Husband'?" A. "He tells you when you've got on too much lipstick . . . and helps you with your girdle when your hips stick." Or something like that.

TWENTY-ONE days of unrelieved bed rest will age your body by 30 years. Or so say the medicos now. Fortunately, it's reversible. Once up and about, you'll "youth" again.

•

WHAT ANIMAL has the longest tail? Men have been known to win bar bets with this query. Hardly anybody says, rightly, it's the male giraffe, with eight feet of aft appendage.

•

IF YOU GO by the rules of the Professional Rodeo Cowboys Association, you can't stick your thumb up the nose of a steer.

•

LOOKING FOR a job? Emphasize your dependability. Hiring executives say that's the No. 1 qualification now.

•

SORRY, our Language Man cannot explain how it came to be that the idiom has us park in the driveway and drive in the parkway.

•

DID YOU KNOW most Boston Terrier puppies have to be delivered by cesarean section?

POLLSTERS have proved that the great majority of New Yorkers can't name the only state in the union that ends with the letter "k."

NINETY PERCENT of the tourists from Finland to this country go straightaway to Lake Worth, Fla. No other city nationwide has more residents of Finnish extraction.

•

ALMOST but not quite one out of every five American women between the ages of 18 and 44 has had a legal abortion. Or so estimate those who study such matters.

•

AM TOLD our jet airplanes use more energy than all our farms put together.

PEACHES, too, started in China.

•

MICHAEL JACKSON has his own Zip Code.

•

BY CHEWING, the beaver sharpens, not dulls its teeth.

•

BANANAS grow wild in Southeast Asia. But their seeds are too big. People thereabouts eat the flowers but throw away the fruit.

•

A TENTH of Boston is city park.

THE FOUNDATION under Egypt's Great Pyramid is about as big as 10 football fields.

•

EVEN THOUGH two-thirds of New Jersey is farm and forest, the state statistically is more densely populated than Japan. They really jam up in the cities.

•

THE WORD "anxiety" comes from the Latin "to choke."

•

ONE OF the British Virgin Islands is called Dead Man's Chest, and 15 men thereon is not really all that crowded.

•

CALL IT dubious, this claim that William Shakespeare would not sit at a table where salt was served. But maybe so.

ANSWER DEPT.

Q. "WHAT WOULD I see if I scraped paint off the White House?" A. Plain brownstone and a Secret Service agent.

•

Q. "HOW BIG is the biggest sort of fish?" A. About the size of a city bus. The whale shark. Maybe 40 feet long at 13 tons.

AM TOLD there exists a patent on a device called the American Egg Marker, which, when strapped to a hen, automatically dates each egg as it's laid.

Q. "WHEN DID Nevada legalize gambling?" A. 1931. At the start of the Great Depression. Seasoned citizens will tell you an Eastern mobster named Bugsy Siegel kicked off the Las Vegas boom with the first luxury hotel on the hot sand thereabouts.

Q. "ALL MANX cats are born without tails, right?" A. Not right. Tailless Manx can have Manx with tails. Manx with tails can have tailless Manx.

•

Q. "DID Christopher Columbus visit all the places that are now nations in the Caribbean area?" A. All but two. He missed the one named after him, South America's Colombia, and the United States.

•

Q. "DID THE LATE Walt Disney live in Disneyland?" A. No, but he stayed sometimes in his secret apartment over the Disneyland firehouse.

•

Q. "SAY A HOUSE is built exactly on the city limits between two towns. How is it decided which town gets to tax the householder?" A. By the placement of the master bedroom.

•

Q. "YOU REPORTED Delmonico's in New York City was one of the first of the world-famous American restaurants. What was the first price of a meal there?" A. 12 cents — for soup, steak, half a pie and coffee. On Nov. 25, 1834.

SURVEY-TAKERS asked 9000 husbands if they would marry their wives again, and 2000 said no. Why not? Nagging was the No. 1 explanation.

•

GRIZZLY BEARS won't live where no huckleberries grow. Or so the scholars now say.

•

MORE GOLD goes into class rings every year nationwide than into anything else.

•

MAYBE YOU didn't know the literal meaning of "Bethlehem" is "House of Bread."

•

IF THE AVERAGE worldwide temperature were to drop only 6 degrees F, you could expect another ice age.

•

ONLY BIRD with its nostrils at the tip of its bill is the Kiwi.

•

THE JAPANESE now take shark liver oil for as many reasons as your granddad took cod liver oil.

OLD SPANISH proverb: "It's better to be a mouse in the mouth of a cat than a man in the hands of a lawyer."

IF A CRANBERRY grower's cranberries won't bounce, he throws them out.

•

THE MEDITERRANEAN Sea dried up completely, at least once, maybe several times.

•

HALF THE SILVER ever mined was mined in this century.

•

THE ARABIAN Bedouin has 160 words for "camel." No, "cigaret" isn't one of them.

IT'S NOT JUST desirable but mandatory to the Hmong homeowner in Laos to be able to see the mountains from both the front and back doors of the house.

•

THE ELECTRIC EEL of South America can generate enough electricity to stun a horse or drive a small motor. Whichever comes first.

•

TO PICK the feathers from a live goose is not only humiliating for the goose — in California, it's illegal.

EARLY FOOTBALL had no halves, no quarters. Players just took a break after every score.

•

WHAT YOU DO in a shark attack is turn the shark over on its back. In this position it goes limp and motionless. Remember that,

•

FAMOUS feminists in history generally have lived extraordinarily long lives. Much longer than the average of their times. No explanation comes to mind.

•

POLICE in Finland's Helsinki rarely give parking tickets. They just let the air out of the tires.

•

NO CHINESE surname has more than one syllable.

ANSWER DEPT.

Q. "WHAT proportion of the married couples chooses sterilization as a means of contraception?" A. Forty-one-point-four percent. In 26 percent, it's the woman. In 15.4, the man. Sterilization is now the most common method of birth control.

THE ANCIENT Greeks chewed gum, too.

Q. "SAYS HERE sugar substitutes are taking over in all markets except one. Which one?" A. Baking.

•

Q. "HOW MANY kinds of insects die after stinging?" A. Only one — the honeybee.

•

Q. "WHAT'S the average life expectancy of the American Indian today?" A. Slightly over age 44.

Q. "HOW LONG would it take a cloud — if it didn't dissipate — to circle the Earth?" A. Ten, maybe a dozen days. If you lose your little red balloon, young fellow, come back in a week and a half.

•

Q. "WHAT authority published the claim that there are more stars in the universe than grains of sand on all the world's beaches?" A. Hayden Planetarium. Some claim, what?

•

Q. "WHO COINED the term 'acid rain'?" A. An English chemist in 1852. Robert Angus Smith, by name. Later, he wrote a 600-page book about it. But hardly anybody read it.

•

Q. "CAN A GIRAFFE outrun a horse?" A. In a short sprint, maybe, but not in the long run. Lung capacity of a horse is 33 quarts of air. Of a giraffe, 13 quarts.

•

Q. "HOW COME icebergs are white instead of clear like some ice cubes?" A. Because the accumulation of snow layers packs little ice bubbles into the bergs.

IF YOU'RE running short of things to drink to, might as well drink to William Phelps Eno — clink! — inventor of the one-way street.

•

THE MILITARY order "Present arms" originally was a directive to offer weapons for the taking, a disarmament command.

•

THE LANGUAGE of the African Bushmen depends as much upon gestures and grimaces as upon words. Bushmen don't talk after dark.

•

THE GALAPAGOS tortoise will eat any food that's red. So zookeepers always put a tortoise's medicine in a tomato.

•

ALL CITRUS fruits, it's believed, derived from the Chinese orange.

•

TWO out of three towns nationwide depend entirely on well water.

•

HEAVY DRINKING raises the blood pressure. Medical records of 95,000 people prove it.

OBSERVED humorist Robert Benchley: "In America, there are two classes of travel — first class and with children."

THE SUN only looks 12 times brighter than the full moon to the naked eye, but the sun is, in fact, 100,000 times brighter than the full moon.

•

RADIO newscasters speak more swiftly than TV newscasters.

•

A BOWLING ball outweighs a ping pong ball by 2800 to 1, about.

•

A TON of iron turns into three tons of rust.

MAYONNAISE makes a good hair conditioner. You rinse it out. Skim milk makes a good wave set. You don't rinse it out. So says a beautician of lengthy experience.

•

IN DETROIT, it's claimed, the guns outnumber the people by 1.5 million to 1.2 million.

•

AN ELEPHANT'S eyelashes are four inches long.

•

ON VENUS, it rains sulfuric acid all the time.

DIVORCE among retired people has doubled in the last 15 years.

•

IN VERMONT, it's against the law to whistle underwater. No, surely don't know what brought on that weird legislation. Will check further.

•

IN ANCIENT ROME, the time between sunrise and sunset was divided into 12 equal hours. Never mind the season. Winter hours were a lot shorter than summer hours.

•

MANY IS the African who collects discarded aluminum cooking pots, which are hammered into body ornaments.

•

IT IS ACCURATE to say the giant panda is not a bear, but "a deviant raccoon." Nuts to accuracy.

ANSWER DEPT.

Q. "WHERE'D that Australian giant bird, the emu, get its name?" A. From the Portuguese "ema," meaning "ostrich." Fast of foot, that bird. If you can't run at least 40 mph, don't chase it.

ONE BABY bat a year is top production for a mama bat.

Q. "HOW DID the Ozarks get that name?" A. Arkansas Indians lived there, so the French called it "aux Arcanas." Anglos cut it to "aux Arcs." It just kept getting tightened up, finally into Ozarks.

•

Q. "SAYS HERE the John Wayne Airport in California's Orange County is the fourth busiest in the nation. Where are the first three?" A. Chicago, Long Beach and Atlanta.

Q. "WRONG, Dummy — The number 9 occurs 19 not 20 times in the numerical sequence from 1 to 100. Fix that!" A. Still say 20 times, though you and numerous others say not so. 9, 19, 29, 39, 49, 59, 69, 79, 89, 90, 91, 92, 93, 94, 95, 96, 97, 98, 99. Did you count the two 9's in 99?

•

Q. "ISN'T FINLAND'S Helsinki the world's most northerly capital?" A. Next to Iceland's Reykjavik, it is. Speaking of Helsinki, might mention that a traffic ticket fine there is based on the income of the finee.

•

Q. "WHERE DO the people of Venice, the city of canals, bury their dead?" A. First, on the cemetery island of San Michele. For a decade or so. Then the older remains are moved to an ossuary farther seaward.

•

Q. "DON'T ALL mammals have bellybuttons?" A. All except platypuses and spiny anteaters. The egg layers. Never saw the navel of a great blue whale, but imagine it's a beaut. Vampire bats have navels, too.

GOOD MORNING, how are your 22 head bones today? That's how many you've got, you know — 14 facial and 8 cranial.

•

THE WORD "diaper" comes — by way of a bachelor, I believe — from the Greek "diasporos," meaning "pure white."

•

ACCORDING TO the U.S. Department of Health and Human Services, you're a "drinker" even if you drink only one glass of wine a month.

•

DO YOU KNOW your astrological sign? No, it's not a ridiculous question. One out of four Americans doesn't know.

•

MORE THAN a million women over 35 years old are back in school.

•

THE FIRE ANT has no natural enemy but man.

•

FORTY-FIVE out of every 100 Americans don't read books. Newspapers, yes. But not books.

LAST I HEARD, 76 retired generals were living in Colorado Springs.

DO YOU HAVE an "arctophiliac" in the family? Probably. It's "a lover of stuffed bears."

•

THERE WAS a time when the hogs in the middle of this continent stood 5 feet tall at the shoulders.

•

TAKES an American auto factory 31 hours to build a car, typically. Japan's robot-equipped Zama plant can do it in nine hours.

•

DID YOU KNOW the meat of some sharks is poisonous? More people have died from eating sharks than from being eaten by same, in fact.

GRASSHOPPERS sing only by day, katydids mostly by night.

•

THE DUPONTS own Coke, too.

•

THE U.S. ARMY contracted some time back for combat boots soled to leave tracks that looked like those of Vietnam peasants.

•

TAKES 110 silkworm cocoons to make a good necktie.

•

THERE HAS never been a human society that didn't tell stories.

A TRUTH about pasta: "A minute in the mouth is a lifetime on the hips."

•

THE MENDERES River twists and turns through much of Asia Minor before it flows into the Aegean Sea. Used to be called the Maeander River. Whence, our verb "meander."

•

ONE OF Jupiter's moons, Io, is in a tidal tug between two other moons, Europa and Ganymede. Io's ground surface, therefore, billows, heaving up and down 328 feet every 36 hours.

•

WHALES HAVE no sense of smell. Or so some sea scientists now believe.

•

CUSTOMS inspectors on the Maldives, islands off India, are looking for four things when they check out tourists' luggage: liquor, dogs, pigs and graven images.

ANSWER DEPT.

Q. "WHAT STATE as a territory was first called Jefferson?" A. Colorado.

ARE THERE any "Dial-a-Bird" telephone numbers still in service? Doubt it. In numerous U.S. cities a dozen years ago, you could dial certain advertised numbers to hear bird calls plus the voice of a scholar to identify same.

Q. "WHAT'S the difference between a snowstorm and a blizzard?" A. It's just a snowstorm until the temperature drops below 20° F. and the wind goes past 35 mph. Then, sir, it's a blizzard.

Q. "WHY IS the cocker spaniel called that?" A. The woodcock was its original game.

•

Q. "WHAT DO the English mean when they say you're 'longheaded'?" A. That you're witty.

•

Q. "MAGICIANS pull rabbits out of hats. Why rabbits instead of some other animal?" A. Rabbits don't make any noise that could botch up the act.

•

Q. "DO PANDAS eat meat?" A. If they can catch it. Mostly they can't, so they settle for bamboo shoots.

•

Q. "IN WHAT U.S. city are the most Rolls Royce cars sold?" A. Newport Beach, Calif., I'm told. Only England's London moves more Rolls.

•

Q. "DOES 'tortoiseshell' actually come from tortoises?" A. If real, it does. Or used to. From one species, the hawksbill. Sliced into thin sheets and heated, it can be molded in a marvelous manner.

IT'S A MATTER of record that the federal government once commissioned a $27,000 study to find out why inmates want to break out of jail.

•

OUR LANGUAGE MAN is appalled by the report that one hospital substitutes for the word "death" what it thinks is a better term: "negative patient care outcome."

•

THE LATE Nathan Pritikin, much acclaimed diet authority who thought about food all the time, said fat calories made cheese the most dangerous food he could think of.

•

THOSE OF US not in jail at the moment wouldn't call this country a "police state." It's a fact, though, that the United States has more police per capita than any other nation.

•

LAST AVAILABLE count of Dolly Parton's wigs was 410.

•

MORE PEOPLE live in North Carolina than live in any of half the member countries of the United Nations.

IT'S not only rude and crude to cuss out an umpire in Massachusetts — it's downright illegal.

IN THE LINGO of England, a performer does well, not poorly, if he "bombs."

•

"HIDE AND SEEK" is not so much a learned game as a game of nature, evidently. Otters play it. So do young deer.

•

YOUNGSTERS from age 10 through 17 commit half the serious crimes nationwide.

YOUNG LADY, if a Southerner tells you your "cotton is low," that means your slip is showing.

•

"A LA MODE" means "in the manner of." Had nothing to do with ice cream, originally.

•

WHEN COIN flippers ask, "Heads or tails?" nine out of 10 people say "Heads."

IF YOUR LAWN is average, I'm told, it's home to as many as 100 different kinds of animals big enough to be visible.

•

IN A BATTLE between a shark and an octopus of like size, the octopus wins, according to those who study sea critters.

•

THE ONLY RODENT that will eat onions is the groundhog.

•

IN PRINT of late is a statistic mighty difficult to verify. Namely, that U.S. government agencies pay at least 148,000 spies.

•

NO LAW compels members of Congress to attend House or Senate sessions all of the time, part of the time or even any of the time.

•

THE GRIP of that bird called the swift must be tremendous. It has been seen to take naps upon the wings of airplanes in flight.

•

WHITE-COLLAR folk in China typically work from 8 a.m. to 8 p.m. — with a two-hour lunch break — six days a week, 52 weeks a year.

EIGHTEEN NAPS a day is just about average for a rabbit.

ANSWER DEPT.

Q. "WHICH OF the United States has lost the largest proportion of its young men in this country's wars?" A. West Virginia.

•

Q. "WHY IS IT the professional baseball teams still won't use aluminum bats, which don't break and hit farther." A. That's why. The ball parks aren't big enough. Aluminum in the hands of the heavy hitters could make a lot of parks obsolete.

Q. "WHAT ARE 'The Seven Summits'?" A. The highest peaks on the seven continents. Asia's Everest, 29,028 feet. Australia's Koscusko, 7310. North America's McKinley, 20,320. South America's Aconcagua, 22,834. Africa's Kilimanjaro, 19,340. Europe's Elbrus, 18,510. And Antactica's Vinson Massif, 17,000.

•

Q. "WHY DO porpoises leap out the the water when they swim?" A. Speed is thought to be the motive there. They're faster when in the air.

•

Q. "THOSE WAGON trains of the old West — how fast did they move?" A. A mile or two an hour, maybe 100 miles in a seven-day week.

•

Q. "DOES QUEEN Elizabeth of England own her own home?" A. Buckingham Palace? Windsor Castle? No, sir, they're owned by the state. So's the royal yacht. And owning same, the state has to pay for the upkeep, please note.

•

Q. "WHAT'S the greatest physical force on Earth?" A. That phenomenon known as the hydrologic cycle — vapor into rain, rain into rivers, rivers into oceans, oceans into vapor. Or so say the experts.

THOSE WHO snort cocaine most often do so through a rolled-up currency bill. That bill goes into circulation. Toxicologists in Miami ran some random tests on the paper money there. Ten out of 11 bills tested had traces of cocaine.

•

IT'S NOT a wharf if it doesn't run parallel to the shoreline.

•

AN IRANIAN husband has the legal right to kill his wife if he finds her with another man.

•

EVERY DAY, about 10 truly catastrophic earthquakes shake some place on Earth, out of a daily total of about 2700 quakes.

•

A BABY under 6 months of age — like most other mammals of any age — breathes only through its nose.

•

IN OLD England, beer was also a sort of breakfast food.

•

ONLY ONE insect can turn its head without moving its body — the preying mantis.

THE DANES steam pleats into their skirts at village bakeries, but they hang their fish out to dry on clotheslines.

ONE OF King Henry VIII's complaints about Anne Boleyn had to do with how much money he spent on bows and arrows for her. He solved the problem, though.

•

IN THE ANCIENT tombs of Egypt, archeologists found honey — still edible.

•

A WHALE'S lip grooves are as individual as human fingerprints, and it's now believed whales recognize other whales by that distinctive characteristic.

TO GET a visa to Tahiti you need a round-trip ticket. Tahitians want visitors, not settlers.

•

SOME PEOPLE say they lost their desire to smoke when they became vegetarians.

•

THE ELDERLY in Vietnam were brought up to believe it barbaric to shake someone's hand.

•

CLASS RINGS originated at West Point.

VINEGAR softens porcupine quills. So if you want to disarm a porcupine, soak it in vinegar, right? Something like that.

•

IN THE AMERICA of 1683, a pound of coffee beans was worth about as much as four acres of land.

•

THE HARD statistical fact is the United States averages 50 times more gun murders per year than do Great Britain, West Germany and Japan combined.

•

A NEW ZEALAND law requires any dog owner there to walk said dog once every 24 hours.

•

KEY WEST is closer to Havana than to Miami.

•

BEHIND the elephant's toe is a pad of flesh that raises its heel off the ground when it walks. That's why the elephant always walks on its tiptoes.

•

ANOTHER WAY to get to the Panama Canal is fly due south from Pittsburgh, Pa.

LACK OF SLEEP doesn't darken the circles under your eyes. It makes the surrounding skin paler, so the circles just look darker.

IT IS NOT on the dark back streets where most muggings occur, but on the main drags near bus stops.

ANSWER DEPT.

Q. "ARE ALL lobsters red?" A. No, sir, only cooked lobsters. The uncooked are variations of blue, white and brown.

Q. "HOW MANY Russians did Josef Stalin's regime execute at the height of the terror over there?" A. About 40,000 per month. During the 1937-38 purge. Total unknown. Footnote: The earlier czars executed an average of 17 a year.

•

Q. "DIDN'T Benjamin Franklin swim the English Channel?" A. No, but he talked about doing it. Using a huge kite as an aerial towboat. Franklin probably could have made it. He was a strong swimmer.

•

Q. "HAVE the New England states ever had a serious earthquake?" A. Not since the last Ice Age.

•

Q. "WHY DO supermarkets always put the milk at the back of the store?" A. Can only tell you milk is about the most frequently purchased product, and shoppers have to walk past a lot of enticing shelves to get to it.

•

Q. "WHERE'S the Philadelphia house where Thomas Jefferson wrote the Declaration of Independence?" A. Gone. Replaced by a hamburger stand.

THIRTY-SIX out of every 100 American men change jobs each year. Only 26 out of every 100 women do that.

•

BENJAMIN Franklin spent much of his life in Pennsylvania, but no building still stands there where he ever lived or worked.

•

YOU'LL GET more juice out of that lemon if you'll zap it for a few moments in the microwave.

•

COMPUTER operators and broadcast announcers are among those who switch jobs most frequently.

•

AM TOLD the policy at Goodyear is always to use the word "inflate" and never the words "blow up."

•

WHAT KILLS the most people in hurricanes is not the high wind but the high water.

•

"AGAINST every great and noble endeavor stand a million mediocre minds," said Albert Einstein, morosely.

ONE LOUISIANA law specifically upholds your right there to grow as tall as you can.

THE PEACOCK is a sort of pheasant.

•

NINETY percent of the waiters in the United States are waitresses.

•

THERE really is a gravestone in Pennsylvania with this inscription: "Here lies the body of Jonathon Blake. Stepped on the gas instead of the brake."

•

ALL THE SNAKES in Tasmania are poisonous.

•

YOU CAN'T take a pig to the Island of Skye off Scotland. No pigs allowed there.

ONE OUT of five professional athletes needs glasses of some sort. Of these, four out of five wear contacts.

•

TAKES HALF again as much gas to cover a mile if there's deep snow on the road.

•

TWO OUT of three American geologists are looking for oil.

•

THE OLD Route 66 westbound from Albuquerque started out as a camel trail.

•

"SHEENA" is the Scot's version of "Jeanne."

DOUBTLESS you've never seen just one smithereen. Or one measle. Or one annal. Nobody has, nobody, nobody.

•

ANY GROWNUP who starts out healthy should be able to go for a month without eating. Or so say the medicos.

•

A MOSQUITO never sings solo.

•

MORE THAN HALF the pending cases in the civil courts are divorce actions.

•

DOES ANYBODY in your family spend 19 hours a week in taverns? That's said to be the average of the typical habitue.

•

THERE IS NO age bracket in which the men's clothing bills on average are higher than the women's.

•

YOU COULD READ the Sherlock Holmes stories in Eskimo, if you knew Eskimo.

•

THREE out of four of the people in jail have been there before.

FOUR CENTS a mile was typical pay for the Pony Express rider. The horse didn't do that well.

THAT PALOMINO horse wouldn't be so described today had not Cortez in 1519 given one such in Mexico to a fellow named Juan de Palomino.

ANSWER DEPT.

Q. "WHAT, pray, is a 'dingbat'? A. Any distinctive typographical symbol — &, *, /, $ or whatever — used in print shops to start or separate paragraphs. Cartoonists draw dingbats in place of unprintable epithets.

•

Q. "DO FROGS have ears?" A. Sort of. The hearing nerve is directly behind the eye. They hear with their eyes, as it were.

•

Q. "DON'T ALL the states now have publicly funded kindergartens?" A. All but Mississippi.

•

Q. "DO BATS eat fish?" A. Some bats, some fish. The fishing bat of Monos Island, Ecuador, does. Flies low and scoops fish out of the water.

•

Q. "WHO INHERITS the title of Prince of Wales next?" A. Nobody. It's always conferred by the Crown.

•

Q. "HOW DO lobsters catch food?" A. They dig a hole, back into it, then just sit there, waiting for a comestible to saunter by.

•

Q. "IF ALL the diamonds ever mined in this world were fused into a cube, how big would it be?" A. About 10 cubic feet.

THE SUN is getting smaller. It's lost about 250 miles of radius in the last half century.

•

"STICK TO the first model," said the original Henry Ford. This wasn't about cars. He said it to explain his secret for happy marriage.

•

WHEN YOUR youngster reahes about 66 pounds in weight, expect a growth spurt. That's when it usually starts, according to the medicos.

•

KING HENRY IV of France observed the order of his own priorities when he said: "There are only two beautiful things in the world — roses and women."

•

IF IT'S a perfect knuckle ball, it makes only half a revolution on its way to home plate.

•

ALBERT EINSTEIN didn't talk until he was 4 years old.

•

THAT ANIMAL with the finest hair is the bat.

IN THE FAR EAST, the yak is to the animal world what bamboo is to the vegetable. Used for everything. Tails of dead yaks are made into fly swatters.

MAYBE YOU'VE seen pictures of the stiff blue capes worn by the police of Paris. Lot of those capes are lined with lead weights. They're weapons of a sort, when swung at rioters.

•

WHEN ICEBERGS calve off heavy glaciers, the broken faces are always blue. Great weight compresses the ice crystals so they absorb all the colors except blue.

•

CANADA'S east coast is closer to London than to Victoria, B.C.

KING KAMAHAMEHA once offered to cede to Great Britain the island of Hawaii, but Great Britain turned it down.

•

"LAMPOON" originally was the cry of French students in taverns. It meant: "Let's drink!"

•

STAFFERS on "People" refer to their magazine as "Peephole."

•

SAID NIETZSCHE: "He who has a 'why' to live can bear almost any 'how.' "

HOW ARE your arteries doing, sir? It was almost two centuries ago that the French physician Pierre J. G. Cabanis said, "A man is as old as his arteries."

•

THAT WORD "trampoline," too, started out as a brand name.

•

CLAIM IS one out of every 20 expectant fathers mimics the symptoms of his wife, craving oddball foods, if she does so, and suffering morning sickness, if she does that.

•

JEAN NICOT was a 16th-century French foreign ambassador who first took tobacco to France. Maybe he shouldn't have. It's in his dubious honor that we got the word "nicotine."

•

YOU DON'T SEE Plato quoted much in the women's periodicals. You remember Plato. He was the fellow who said, "A woman is only a lesser man."

•

LANGUAGE experts say there's almost no place in the world now where the locals don't understand the American word "striptease."

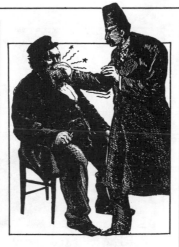

DANGEROUS TIME, Saturday afternoon. Particularly between 3 p.m. and 5 p.m. That's when the most people are bitten by other people. Or so show the computer runs on health-agency records.

A CAMEL has three eyelids on each eye.

ANSWER DEPT.

Q. "WHAT'S the difference — in Dutch cheeses — between Gouda and Edam?" A. Gouda is fatter.

Q. "WHERE'D WE get the expression 'kick the bucket' to mean dying?" A. What, you've not yet heard that one? Yesteryear's most common suicide stood on a bucket, strung himself to a rafter with a rope, then kicked the bucket.

•

Q. "WHAT'S the largest member of the deer family that ever lived?" A. The Alaskan moose. Ask me the smallest: the Chilean Pudu, about the size of a rabbit.

•

Q. "HOW DID the first skywriter produce the smoke that came from his airplane?" A. Major John Savage of England was the fellow. In 1922. He piped a light oil spiked with paraffin through the plane engine's exhaust.

•

Q. "FIRST motion picture theater charged a nickel, right?" A. Twice that much. The first movie house — the Electric Theater, which opened April 2, 1902, on Main Street in Los Angeles — charged a dime.

•

Q. "HOW COME you never see beer in square bottles?" A. Square bottles are too weak at the corners to hold the pressure.

ONE MEDICAL scholar, who believes the common cold is prompted by emotional conflict, says you oftentimes can prevent an oncoming cold simply by having a good cry.

•

WHY SINGLE MEN as a group have a bad reputation: They comprise 13 percent of the population over age 14 — and 60 percent of the criminals who commit 90 percent of the violent crimes.

•

CLAIM IS Adolf Hitler during his last 10 years constantly took amphetamines.

•

ALL THE NEWS in a half-hour network telecast would fit neatly into less than a column of type on a typical newspaper page.

•

IN GETTING across a stretch of water, a motorboat is about five times more efficient than a duck. Hydrodynamically speaking.

•

EVERY BIG city in the Soviet Union has its own circus.

THERE ARE rare people who know a face is a face when they see one but don't know whose face it is, even the face in a mirror. The disorder is called "prosopagnosis."

SUN VALLEY'S original chair lift — the first such device at ski resorts — was patterned after a conveyor to load bananas on ships.

•

THE BEAVER gulps air before it dives. Underwater, it gets about half a mile to the gulp.

•

A LOT OF Wisconsin lakes have the same names. Lumberjacks named them after girlfriends. Some had the same girlfriends.

OCEAN WAVES — they're not just on the surface — sometimes go 1000 feet down.

•

IN Steamboat Springs, Colo., each school child gets two hours of ski lessons a week. Part of the regular curriculum.

•

THOSE WHO study the crayon art of children claim all normal youngsters worldwide draw the same things at the same age in the same way.

AS YOU GROW older, your bones fuse together and some disappear — from infancy up, you lose 144.

●

DO YOU KNOW anybody named Chang? If not, maybe you don't get out much. People named Chang worldwide outnumber the combined populations of Great Britain and Canada.

●

THE LAW in London, England, makes it illegal there to drive a car with a dent in the fender.

●

WHY PEOPLE with high blood pressure should give up licorice I don't know, but that's the current claim of the medicos.

●

YOUR first cousin once removed is a closer relative than your second cousin.

●

"THE WORDS in this sentence average 4.78 letters long." That's too long. Average length of English words in general use is 4.5 letters.

●

THE BEST tennis players most often come from small families, the best wrestlers from large families.

NO rooster is ever henpecked.

OFFICE HOURS in Yugoslavia are 7 a.m. to 2 p.m.

●

YOUR BLOOD has to travel through your whole body to get from one side of your heart to the other.

●

STUTTERERS don't stutter when they whisper.

ANSWER DEPT.

Q. "AIDS KILLS 100 percent of those who get it. What proportion did the bubonic plague kill?" A. About 40 percent.

●

Q. "DO flamingos breed in captivity?" A. Only in southern Florida.

Q. "HOW FAST can the good paddlers move their canoes?" A. About 7 mph.

●

Q. "DID YOU say the poet Joyce Kilmer invented baby powder?" A. No, it was his father, Fred. For Johnson & Johnson.

●

Q. "THAT Japanese wine called sake — does it have vintage years?" A. No, sir, the fresher the better. Tends to lose flavor when stored overlong.

●

Q. "WHY ARE some babies so scared of the dark? Instinct?" A. Not according to the experts. Dark is what happens right after they're put down and left alone. They learn to fear and hate it.

IF YOU'RE a deep and constant thinker, 2 percent of your body weight — your brain — uses 20 percent of your energy.

•

KETCHUP originated in Southeast Asia. However, the French historically have blamed the English for it. For it, and syphilis.

•

BEFORE Sean Connery is filmed in short-sleeved shirts, the makeup artists do a camouflage job on his forearm. Tattooed there are "Scotland Forever" and "Mum & Dad."

•

IN SOME of Japan's supermarkets, robots slice meat. Thinly, usually.

•

MOST POOR people don't shop for bargains. Most rich people don't shop for bargains. But most of the people in the middle do shop for bargains.

•

THOSE WHO visited the Lama of old Tibet always took off their eyeglasses. Courtesy thing.

•

BIRDS don't sweat.

WHY "strong as an ox"? A camel can carry twice as much weight as an ox.

GREEK HISTORY records that Socrates sometimes drained a half-gallon jug of wine in one long pull.

•

IN THE DIGGING of their homes, some ant colonies move up to 40 tons of dirt.

•

MEADOWLARKS are blackbirds, actually. Of a sort.

•

ITALY has had 44 governments since World War II.

TAKES 24 separate hand drawings for each second of a TV cartoon. A 30-minute show can chew up 30,000 such drawings.

•

THE FACES of astronauts bloat in space, and their legs shrivel a little. At zero gravity, body fluids rise to the head.

•

"BEST THING about the future," said Dean Acheson, "is it only comes one day at a time."

THE SECOND graduate of Harvard built London's famed No. 10 Downing Street. What the first graduate of Harvard did is not in the record at hand. Will check further.

•

IN PENNSYLVANIA, it's against the law to hurt a skunk.

•

AN unemployment rate of 80 percent is just normal — in Actors' Equity.

•

TWO out of three rapes occur between 10 p.m. and 4 a.m. Liquor figures in one out of five cases.

•

THE WOLF walks among the caribou. If its head is high, they browse unafraid. If its head is low, they take off.

•

AT A TENNIS tournament in imperial Russia early this century, according to the sports historians, the ballboys returned the tennis balls on silver trays.

•

AM TOLD there are more motorcycles in Kansas than in California.

•

ENGLEBERT Humperdinck was born in India.

THAT SORT of human most likely to get a headache, according to the categorizers, is the young, well-educated woman.

NEED $2000? Skin a polar bear. A good pelt can bring that much.

ANSWER DEPT.

Q. "WHERE'S the world's longest subway tunnel?" A. London.

Q. "HOW COME chicken pox is called that?" A. The old English word "gican" meant "itch." The ailment started out as itching pox.

•

Q. "THE Atlantic Ocean is choppier than the Pacific, right?" A. Choppier, true. But the Pacific is bulgier. Sea swells are higher in the Pacific.

•

Q. "A PROFESSIONAL hockey team was named after a song? What song?" A. Same song that once served as the battle hymn of the Ethiopian army. "The St. Louis Blues."

•

Q. "DIDN'T the Viking sailors of old sleep in hammocks on their boats?" A. No, sir, each was assigned two sealskin sleeping bags — one for his gear and one for himself.

•

Q. "WHAT HAPPENS if a queen gives birth to twin sons? How can it be known which is to inherit the throne?" A. Such royal births are always attended by official witnesses to identify the first born.

•

Q. "WHAT TRAIN is named after a composer?" A. The Chopin Express? Runs between Warsaw and Vienna.

THERE ARE three times as many "adult" bookstores nationwide as McDonald's restaurants.

•

NINETY percent of the scientists in the history of the world are still alive.

•

THE GOVERNMENT of Austria — right there at the edge of the Soviet Bloc — spends more money on the Vienna Opera than on national defense.

•

NOT MANY would guess Indiana is the state most likely to be hit by tornadoes. And even fewer would guess Massachusetts is next most likely.

•

DID I mention 21 percent of all major-league baseball players are left-handed?

•

ANTS CAN see ultraviolet light, but I don't know what good it does them.

•

IT IS ALSO true that one thoroughbred can wear out four new shoes in a single horse race.

SWISS CHEESE with big holes sells better than Swiss cheese with little holes, the market researchers have learned.

WHAT YOU and I might call fat was considered beautiful to the early Hawaiians, and any lady who weighed 300 pounds was approaching perfection.

•

TWENTY CARS a day are abandoned in New York City. Nationwide, the junked-car count is 20,000 a day. Not to mention 4000 trucks and buses.

•

EXPERTS NOW say you perform a lot better on the job — tell your boss — if you take not just one but two, even three rest breaks each morning and each afternoon.

IT'S ILLEGAL in China Grove, N.C., to snore, to gargle or to spank children.

•

TOP SPEED of the passenger elevator is 19 mph.

•

DID WE THINK 98.6 degrees F. was the normal human body temperature? No, sir. Among those over age 65, a temperature of 97.7 is average.

•

A SILK FIBER is triangular. It reflects light much as does a prism. That's why silk cloth shines.

MOST WOMEN who play harps are married to men who play violins.

•

THE DIFFERENCE between the "firefly" and the "glowworm," in that order, is the difference between male and female.

•

THE LAW in Spain's Seville permits two people together to climb the 320-foot Giralda Tower there, but never one person alone. An anti-suicide measure.

•

DETROIT and Pittsburgh combined have fewer factory workers than Brooklyn.

•

"THE YOUNG sow wild oats while the old grow sage," said Winston Churchill, sagely.

•

YOU KNOW those plants that trap insects? What they crave is nitrogen. They usually grow in dirt where heavy rains leach out all the nitrogen.

ANSWER DEPT.

Q. "CAN TWO hurricanes collide?" A. No, one gets weaker, and they rotate past each other.

Q. "IF mushrooms aren't the fastest-growing vegetable matter, how come they pop up overnight?" A. Rain can swell them 100 times their dry size. They're right at the surface, then the rain hits them.

Q. "WHAT COLOR is the inside of the sun?" A. Black. Take my word for it. I took somebody else's.

•

Q. "WHAT'S the strongest expletive in the Bible?" A. "The Devil take you."

•

Q. "HOW COME the quickest, niftiest runners in football are the little men?" A. The bigger the muscle, the more time it needs to stretch and contract. Same reason leopards are swifter than giraffes.

Q. "WHO WAS the first author to make $1 million solely on writing?" A. Jack London. Dead at 40 in 1916.

•

Q. "HOW MANY earthquakes does Tokyo get every year?" A. About 1000. Residents feel about 50 of them.

•

Q. "ALL OIL floats on water, right?" A. Not right. Oil of cloves doesn't. Nor oil of wintergreen. Some oils are heavier than water, that's all.

SEVENTEEN out of every 100 wives tell the survey-takers they know their husbands have been unfaithful.

●

MOST COMMON major operation in the United States now is the coronary bypass. Surgeons do 500 a day. About.

●

IN ANCIENT Rome, the death penalty was decreed for female adultery and female alcoholism.

●

THE MONEY managers move about $500 billion a day across international borders.

●

IF YOU THINK your skin shows signs of age, you ought to see your innards. No, maybe not. But the point is skin ages better than any other organ in the body.

●

THERE ARE 350 varieties of sharks, even without counting loan and pool.

●

NOW, 33 percent of the law students, 14 percent of the lawyers and 17 percent of the judges are women.

NEW YORK landlords during the Great Depression evicted about 17,000 tenants a month.

A SKILLED inspector with the U.S. Customs can look at 50 different makes of zippers and identify the country in which each was made.

●

BRANDY CAPITAL of the world now is Hong Kong.

●

LAKE ERIE differs from the other Great Lakes in that its bottom is above sea level.

●

CLAIM IS it takes 17 muscles to smile and 43 to frown.

DEATH WAS the prescribed punishment in ancient Germany for tree mutilation.

●

A FLY needs meat. Feed it nothing but sugar and it can't lay eggs.

●

YOUR TYPICAL new book will have a shelf life of about 30 years before its paper will deteriorate so badly it will fall apart when you open it.

●

MOST PEOPLE have at least 25 moles. Start counting.

SNAILS PAIR OFF to fertilize each other, and then both lay eggs.

•

THOSE WHO know all about alligators say this country has about a million of those wild rascals.

•

THE PEOPLE in Portofino along the Italian Riviera can't even paint a shutter on a window without showing a sample of the proposed new paint to the city council for approval.

•

THE WATER in Florida's Everglades is not stagnant. It's a great river, moving steadily toward the Gulf of Mexico.

•

A FEW mountain roads in Peru are so narrow that the haulers have an understanding: Traffic goes one way Mondays, the other way Tuesdays, so on.

•

"PAGODA" isn't a Chinese word. Portuguese sailors took it to China from Persia.

•

THE WORLD'S largest moth — the Hercules, with a 14-inch wingspan — lives only 14 days and never eats anything.

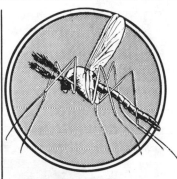

SAID A Yellowstone ranger of mosquitoes: "They're the only wildlife in the park you're allowed to feed."

EXACTLY a quart of water and exactly a quart of alcohol, when combined, make less than two quarts of whatever you want to call it. Those molecules mingle.

ANSWER DEPT.

Q. "HOW COME pearls come in different colors — white, blue, pink, yellowish, greenish?" A. Nobody knows.

•

Q. "IS THERE any society that has never used stimulating drugs?" A. Not anymore. Used to be true of the Eskimo, however.

Q. "WHAT'S the most widely manufactured product in the world?" A. The colas.

•

Q. "IN COFFEE talk, what do we mean by 'mocha'?" A. An allusion, that, to the port town of Mocha, Yemen, where coffee supposedly originated. People in Mocha don't drink coffee, might mention. They drink tea.

•

Q. "WHERE'S the fastest train ride now?" A. The Tokyo-Osaka run, 212.4 miles, average speed 105 mph.

•

Q. "WHEN DID we get the first kidney dialysis machine?" A. Early in World War II. It was made from an old bathtub, spare auto parts and some sausage casings.

•

Q. "ARE THERE a million millionaires in this country?" A. Almost. Will be in 1986.

•

Q. " 'FROM THE Halls of Montezuma' — I mean the Marine Hymn — was it an original piece of music?" A. No, sir, it came from Offenbach's opera "Genevieve de Brabant."

A STUDENT of matrimonial matters says nine out of 10 marriages in which the women proposed have been successful.

•

IN COLONIAL times, gold bullion was heavily taxed, but gold jewelry was not. So the rich carried a different sort of travelers checks. Gold chains with links that could be broken off one at a time for cash.

•

SOME PEOPLE are born with a slightly abnormal ear structure that causes them to go through their whole lives listening to their own heartbeat.

•

FOUR out of five Texans live in cities.

•

PERFECT RUBIES are more valuable than perfect diamonds.

•

FOUR YEARS is the average career longevity of players in NFL football, NBA basketball and NHL hockey. But the major-league baseball player on average stays at it for seven years.

IF THE STATISTICS hold up, at least five women in this country will commit murder today.

YOUR BRAIN uses 10 times more oxygen than the rest of your body.

•

NEW YORK CITY doctors called upon to treat bites inflicted by humans are required to report same to the police.

•

OUR Chief Prognosticator thinks most blood tests now done in laboratories eventually will be done with do-it-yourself kits in homes.

•

THE FACE of an ordinary ant, greatly magnified, looks like the face of a rabbit, floppy ears and all.

ONE BIRD eats nothing but leaves. The South American hoatzin. It has claws on its wings. Nests above swamps. Escapes predators by diving into the water.

•

RESEARCHERS claim sex relieves arthritis, too.

•

THE FASTEST Ping-Pong balls aren't as fast as the fastest tennis balls.

•

IF THE MARRIAGE lasts one full year, its next most difficult years are the fifth and ninth. Such is the claim of the matrimonial researchers.

IF YOU FAIL to save any money out of your wages, you're in the same category as two out of five nationwide, the statisticians report.

●

ALL ACROSS this country are movie-house owners who'd be completely out of business if it weren't for popcorn.

●

WHAT DO you do when you get nervous? A kangaroo licks its forearms.

●

"HILARIOUS laughter" is outlawed in Helena, Mont. Understandable, maybe, if it's a public nuisance. But why is it illegal just to frown in Pocatello, Idaho?

●

AM TOLD you can take some makeup marks off some clothing by rubbing the spot with a slice of bread.

●

WITH TODAY'S electrode implants, Helen Keller could have been made to hear, doctors say.

●

THE SOCIAL SECURITY system is a so-called sacred cow, politicians say, because four out of five people over age 65 vote.

POSSUMS keep on growing as long as they live.

ANSWER DEPT.

Q. "WHO invented stilts?" A. Can only tell you their regular use probably originated in southern France. Early sheepherders strapped on such to negotiate the marshes around the Bay of Biscay.

●

Q. "HOW MUCH of what's now the United States used to belong to Mexico?" A. A fourth.

●

Q. "HOW MANY active volcanoes are there?" A. On Earth? About 500.

Q. "DOES the world produce as much as a bushel basket of diamonds every year?" A. About 75 bushel baskets, in fact. And 73 of them come from Africa.

●

Q. "HOW LONG would it take me to look at every painting in The Louvre?" A. About three hours, walking non-stop, if you glance but not gaze.

●

Q. "HOW LONG can a rat tread water?" A. That's entirely a matter of morale. With hope, three days. Without hope, maybe an hour.

TOLD YOU the Eskimo has dozens of words for varieties of snow. But did I mention there's only one Eskimo word for tree?

•

GIRL BABIES smile more than boy babies do.

•

RAPID REPLY: Yes, sir, a "spermologist" is a collector, all right, but a collector of trivia.

•

TINY VEINS in the neck of the Turkmene horse of Central Asia break when the animal overheats, and it literally sweats blood.

•

HAWAII and Australia are getting closer to each other by 2.7 inches a year. And both are moving away from South America.

•

GIRAFFES always give birth standing up. It's a five-foot drop. Thud! Ah, Mom!

•

ON A TRAIN trip over the breadth of the Soviet Union, you'll pass through 11 time zones. But you'll only need one watch. All the trains stick to Moscow time.

WHEN VIKINGS sailed to Iceland, they mistook the geothermal steam there for smoke, so named the capital, "Reykjavik," meaning "Smoking Bay."

TWO out of five military recruits catch colds within a couple of weeks after they join up. You can say something similar for kindergarten kids.

•

MASAI tribesmen of Africa need salt, too. So they get it in blood they draw from their cattle.

•

IN SAUDI ARABIA, a gallon of gasoline costs 31 cents. A watermelon costs $16.

•

AM TOLD by one who claims to know that it takes 65 hours of real work to handcraft a good bamboo fly rod.

BIRDS, TOO, ice up and lose altitude.

•

TYPICAL firetruck now costs $100,000.

•

AMONG hypochondriacs, the men outnumber the women.

•

ASK YOUR family physicist, "What's the speed of dark?"

•

THE FISH HAWK is a far better hunter than the lion. That bird comes up with a fish in nine out of 10 strikes. The lion fails to get its prey in nine out of 10 attacks.

AMONG unmarried men and women over age 55, the women earn more money than the men, typically.

•

IRATE authorities are still hopping on me about the bayonet. It was invented in Bayonne, France, early in the 17th century, not shortly after the Civil War, as erroneously reported here.

•

COST OF an abortion in Czechoslovakia — legal there — is about $20.

•

IN WINTER, woodpeckers do indeed use their beaks as icepicks.

CLAIM IS unhappy people don't eat popcorn.

ANSWER DEPT.

Q. "IS IT TRUE people are more inclined to act with reckless abandon in a room decorated in red?" A. It's what the experts believe, true or not. Most gambling casinos are decorated in red.

•

Q. "IF DIAMONDS can only be formed 80 miles beneath the Earth's surface, how do they get up to where we can find them?" A. Volcanic action. Explosions, sort of. They're shot toward the surface almost like shrapnel.

Q. "WHAT happens to the old buffalo bulls that can't cut it anymore?" A. They go off. To live alone. Or with a few other oldsters in a similar fix.

•

Q. "IF YOU TRY to quit smoking and fail, doesn't that make it even harder to quit the next time you try?" A. On the contrary. Makes it easier the next time, according to the psychologists. It starts to build the foundation.

Q. "HOW WIDE does the Mississippi River get?" A. Up to 80 miles. In a flood.

•

Q. "DIDN'T the Vatican ban the crossbow as too deadly a weapon even for war?" A. Except against Moslems, yes. In 1139, it so decreed.

•

Q. "DO BRAZILIANS drink coffee?" A. Some. Not all that much. Six pounds each a year. U.S. citizens drink 16 pounds each a year.

AN OLD murderer is not much to be feared, but a young murderer is. That, from scholars who've studied the criminal mind. A third of the convicted murderers under age 30 murder again.

•

SURGEONS in the United States operate on the knees of about 45,000 football players every year. Astounding.

•

REMEMBER, says our Language Man, you may "sneer" with the mouth, but you "leer" with the eyes only, and if it isn't lascivious, it's not a leer.

•

A FLY that eats nothing but sugar will never lay eggs.

•

THE LAW of Wisconsin specifically forbids a railroad conductor from kissing a passenger.

•

SEA LEVEL worldwide has been rising a foot a century. Don't build too close to the beach.

DEEP-SEA divers who've had flesh wounds 50 feet underwater say their blood at that depth is green.

AVERAGE married man lives 6 years, 7 months longer than the average never-married man.

•

IF THAT firefly is flying, it's a male.

•

NEW MEXICO law states any wife there can go through her husband's pockets whenever she wants to.

•

GREENLAND is closer to the Soviet Union's Moscow than is the town of Yakutsk in Siberia.

THERE'S NO "goodbye" and no "hello" in the language of the Eskimo.

•

A LIGHT RAIN speeds up the roller coaster track by at least 10 mph.

•

FRENCH playwright Edmond Rostand wrote most of "Cyrano de Bergerac" while sitting in a bathtub.

•

NITPICKERS will tell you that top judicial dignitary is the chief justice of the United States, not the chief justice of the Supreme Court.

ICELAND'S Reykjavik outlaws dogs.

•

PEOPLE milked horses before they rode them, please note.

•

AMERICAN cuckoos don't cuckoo, they cluck.

•

"WHALE harassment" is a federal crime punishable by a $10,000 fine.

•

A STEEL BALL will bounce higher than a glass ball, and a glass ball will bounce higher than a rubber ball.

•

COLONISTS WHO fought for the British outnumbered colonists who fought against the British during the American Revolution.

•

AN IRANIAN woman doesn't shake hands with an Iranian man, not in public.

•

REALIZE it doesn't look that way along the side of the road, but it's a scientific fact that dirty snow melts faster than clean snow.

THE THREE inanimate things that figure most frequently in injuries are bicycles, stairs and footballs.

ANSWER DEPT.

Q. "IN THE hospital, the more I slept, the more I wanted to sleep. Why?" A. Carbon monoxide builds up in the blood, then begins to work as an anesthetic.

Q. "IN DIAMOND talk, what's a 'point'?" A. A hundredth of a carat. Average diamond is two-fifths of a carat — 40 points.

•

Q. "IN WHAT age bracket is a woman most likely to be on a payroll?" A. From 45 to 55.

•

Q. "NAME THE ONLY sort of animal with bones sticking out of its head." A. Deer. Trick query, sort of. Antlers are bone, horns are skin.

•

Q. "WHY DID Albert Einstein refuse to wear socks?" A. He didn't refuse. Socks were just too much trouble. His big toes kept poking holes in them, he said.

•

Q. "VIKING SAILORS had no lemons, limes, oranges. How come they didn't get scurvy?" A. They ate sauerkraut, I'm told. That's pretty fair anti-scurvy grub.

•

Q. "HOW LONG is a guitar string supposed to last?" A. Forty hours of playing is average.

•

Q. "WHAT creature has the best vision of all?" A. Hawks.

ARE YOU one of those who daily sits in an office chair with casters on it? If so, please note, that chair travels eight miles a year, typically.

•

MADAME, did your appearance improve after you got married? When pollsters put that query to a sizable sampling of ladies nationwide, most said yes.

•

THREE out of four people in bathtubs lather their stomachs first.

•

YOU KNOW those students who get college degrees in agriculture? Only 14 percent of them go back to the farm to use same.

•

IN A PHILIPPINES bullfight, two bulls fight each other.

•

AM TOLD the favorite food of goats is poison ivy.

•

A MOST appropriate place to hold the Sunday picnic 100 years ago was in the cemetery.

HAVE YOU as yet enlarged your vocabulary to 50,000 words? No? Wait. In your lifetime, you will, if typical.

"THE LORD'S PRAYER" appears variously twice in the Bible, but nowhere therein is it called "The Lord's Prayer."

•

ELEPHANTS, too, get flat feet.

•

ONE HORSERACE in three, about, is won by the favorite.

•

FOUR out of five people who wear glasses are nearsighted.

A SURVEY in British driving schools turned up this consensus: Teachers are the hardest to teach to drive.

•

EITHER the wife kills the husband or the husband kills the wife in one out of every 10 homicides.

•

IN OLD ROME, silk sold for its weight in gold.

•

AVERAGE Japanese man moves five times in his life. Average American, 14 times.

GLACIERS have growth layers. Cores show what the atmosphere was like over centuries. It has changed. When coal mining and cattle raising boomed a couple hundred years ago, the air's methane content jumped.

•

DISNEY WORLD at last report needed 138 telephone operators to handle reservations. Do believe that place might make it.

•

IT'S A MATTER of record that the First National Bank of Scotia granted a four-year loan to Wendy Westfall, a former teller there. Purpose was to pay back the money she'd been convicted of embezzling from that bank.

•

LONE SOULS live in half the households in Stockholm.

•

MOSQUITOES sing. That's been known for a while. The males listen to the females, but the females don't listen to the males.

•

WERE NO strictly female names in ancient Rome, only feminized male names: Claudia, Julia, Cornelia, Lucretia, so on.

TELL the fellow on the next stool that the medicos now know that barley — whence cometh much beer — cleans cholesterol from the blood.

ANSWER DEPT.

Q. "HOW DO you account for the fact that more people are killed by lightning in Florida than in any other state?" A. More people are outdoors there year-round, that's all.

•

Q. "WHAT'S the fish that hunts on land?" A. The mudskipper? It loiters at the water's edge, its bulging eyes periscoping for insects ashore. Every now and then it flips itself onto the beach, snaps up some bug, then wiggles back into the water.

Q. "WORD experts know we get 'thug' from the name of a sect of criminals in India. What crimes did they commit?" A. They strangled to rob. Their headquarters were in the city of Mirzapur on the Ganges about 175 years ago.

•

Q. "WHAT'S the oldest fermented liquor?" A. Toddy — from the sap of the palmyra palm, dating back to 800 B.C. in India. When the British installed the word "toddy" in English, they put "hot" in front of it to label any warm, spicy alcoholic drink.

IF ALL the people in U.S. prisons lived in one place, they'd make a city almost as big as San Diego.

•

CHINA HAS more horses than any other nation, yet Taiwan, right off its coast, has none. Or almost none. Two are kept on display at the Taipei zoo.

•

EVERY TIME there are Northern Lights, there are Southern Lights.

•

FLOODS have diluted Great Salt Lake. Now you can sink in it.

•

TIME IS everything, isn't it? The female lobster is fertile only six hours a year — that's it.

•

ESKIMO matrons at Barrow occasionally charter airplanes to fly to Wainwright for afternoon tea.

•

ORDER a fried egg for breakfast in the Falkland Islands and the egg will cover the platter. An albatross egg, probably.

BIRD hunters will tell you geese are smarter, not dumber, than ducks.

MOST WORD mechanics like "citadel" but not "kremlin." Yet they mean exactly the same.

•

PEACHES grown against a sheltered wall are always bigger and juicier than those grown out in the open.

•

THE SPANISH soldiers of old decked out their Great Pyrenees dogs in armor and turned them loose in battle to make their enemies' horses shy.

THE COATING on fake pearls is made from the scales of little herring.

•

EARTHWORMS are 72 percent protein and less than 1 percent fat. If they were prescribed as the only food in your diet, you'd lose weight, sure enough. Starve, maybe.

•

NO DOUBT you'll want to keep your books in the refrigerator. Bookworms go dormant below 70 degrees F.

YOU DON'T get spectacular fireworks displays on the Fourth of July in Alaska. No night. Sky is too bright.

•

AM TOLD that those who know their crystal can estimate the percentage of lead in it by the tone it gives off when flicked with a fingernail.

•

SOME EVIDENCE suggests that a chimpanzee is smarter at birth than a newborn human baby.

•

SUNGLASSES as we know them — not the slitted ivory frames the Eskimos carve — have been around for 100 years now.

•

A LION fell in love with a squirrel, according to Chinese legend, and thus came into being the first Pekinese.

•

PERFECT temperature for fleas — they come out in swarms — is said to be 75° F.

•

MANY, maybe even most, of Canada's lakes still haven't been named.

•

A WEED is any plant that's unwanted, that's all.

I FEEL sorry for that beautiful French actress Catherine Deneuve. Market research reveals she doesn't sell as well in TV commercials as does Bugs Bunny.

THIS ALSO can be reported about Los Angeles: In no other city in the world do more men buy hand lotions, body creams and hair sprays.

•

RUSSIAN ICE cream is not just better but much better than American ice cream, the correspondents claim.

ANSWER DEPT.

Q. "WHAT'S THE most popular main dish in the United States?" A. Fried chicken.

•

Q. "RUSSIA HAS two traditional drinks. One is vodka. What's the other?" A. Tea.

•

Q. "HOW MANY people who go through bankruptcy do so again?" A. Not even one in 100.

•

Q. "WHAT'S THE standard maternity leave for payrolled wives in the Soviet Union?" A. 112 days at full pay plus a year without pay.

•

Q. "WHAT'S THE oldest team sport?" A. Polo, research reveals. I'd have guessed tug-of-war.

•

Q. "HOW MANY jumps can you get out of a good parachute?" A. About 100.

•

Q. "DURING World War II, some male American marines wore skirts, I've read. Who?" A. A battalion of Samoans.

JUST STANDING still at the equator, you're moving 1040 mph because of the rotational velocity — that's 1.7 times faster than the world's land speed record.

•

TWENTY-TWO out of 25 people put on the right shoe first.

•

GOLFERS AT Yellowknife in Canada's Northwest Territories always start one annual tournament on June 21 — in the sunshine at exactly midnight.

•

LOOK CLOSELY at the next child you see who stands less than 5 feet tall and weighs about 85 pounds. That was the typical size of earliest man.

•

THE PESKY BEARS keep turning off the lawn sprinklers at Canada's Jasper golf course. A hired man follows the bears around and turns the sprinklers back on. Or did. Last I heard they were working on bear-proof valves.

•

THE THUONGS of Vietnam like roast fowl, too, but they leave the feathers on.

BATS ARE more closely related to humans, biologically, than to mice.

IN ENGLAND, a rock band staged a benefit concert for prisoners in Northumberland's Acton jail. But the prisoners walked out to protest the foul language.

•

IN SOME communities in the Himalayas until recently, a wife, to show respect for her husband's guests, greeted them with her breasts bared.

•

SOME RATS kill some mice.

•

STEAM is invisible until it cools a little.

ICE WORMS live in glaciers. They do all right in the cold. But when the temperature rises above 68° F, they disintegrate.

•

IN AUSTRIA, a ski teacher earns twice as much as a school teacher.

•

GREATER TOKYO is a little bigger than Connecticut.

•

BET THE fellow on the next stool that if he's ever struck by lightning, he'll live. Two out of three so struck do indeed survive.

MORE THAN 3000 puppies will be born in this country in the time it takes you to say "three thousand pups."

•

DOCTORS still aren't sure why blond women in particular tend to bruise easily.

•

NOTHING IN the Constitution qualifies justices of the U.S. Supreme Court. No age limits, no legal requirements, no nothin'.

•

DIVORCE LAWYERS say joint custody must work — only 6 percent of the fathers with joint custody default on their support payments.

•

FEWER PEOPLE look at TV during July than during any other month. February is when the most watch.

•

FIFTEEN PERCENT of the payrolled wives earn more money than their husbands.

•

IT WAS THAT Scottish writer James M. Barrie who said, "Nothing is really work unless you'd rather be doing something else."

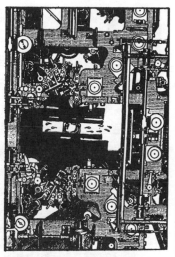

COMPACT an ice cube under 600,000 pounds of pressure and it thereafter won't melt in boiling water. Won't float in it, either.

ANSWER DEPT.

Q. "HOW LONG does it take mice to make love?" A. Five seconds.

•

Q. "THE WHITE shark never gets sick, I've read. Why not?" A. Mysterious antibodies make it immune to all known bacteria.

Q. "WHERE WAS IT in this country that a youngster over age 16 at one time could be executed for cursing a parent?" A. New Haven, Conn. During the Puritan era.

•

Q. "IS THE TENDENCY toward high blood pressure inherited?" A. More often than not.

•

Q. "HOW CAN those ancient pine trees survive high up on rocky mountainsides?" A. The needles of conifers absorb moisture from the clouds and minerals from the winds.

•

Q. "HOW COMMON is divorce in Japan?" A. At one divorce every 3 minutes 11 seconds, pretty common. One marriage in five so ends. Japan copied its divorce laws from the United States.

•

Q. "IN WHAT ORDER does a walking horse lift its hooves?" A. Left front, right hind, left hind, right front.

•

Q. "BIGGEST money maker for the casinos in Las Vegas is nonetheless the game with the best odds for the players. Name it." A. Craps.

TWO OUT OF five homicides nationwide are wives killing their husbands or husbands killing their wives.

•

SO HUGE is the Grand Canyon, you could put 100 Great Salt Lakes in there. Such a project has not been written into the federal budget, however. Not yet.

•

DIVORCED MEN over age 50, if they marry again, tend to match up with women who on average are four years younger. Only one over-50 divorced man in 25 marries a woman 20 years younger.

•

NO HOTWIRE hooligan with pride in his craft should overlook the historical fact that it was in 1905 in St. Louis where the first car was stolen.

•

YOU HANG women's slacks by the waistline, men's by the cuffs. Why this difference?

•

PRICE OF brides in the United Arab Emirates has gone up to about $50,000. The men there say that's way too high, so they're importing.

ALASKANS eat more ice cream than residents of other states. Explain the why of that.

YOUR EDUCATION is what you've learned. Your culture is what you've got left after you've forgotten what you've learned. So say the sages.

•

SNOW DOME in Canada's Jasper National Park is unique — North America's triple divide. Its waters flow to the Pacific, the Atlantic and the Arctic oceans.

•

THE HONEYBEE is totally deaf.

IT'S REPORTED that Americans spend about $10 billion a year on games of chance. Not counting weddings and elections.

•

SCHOLARS STILL debate why Christopher Columbus always signed his name as "Xpo Ferens."

•

YOU CAN GET sugar from dahlias, too. And it's said to be far better sugar than the sugar you get from cane or beets.

PENGUINS WILL walk right up to anything. They look fearless. They're not. They're nearsighted.

•

"FOSSIL" is from the Latin for "dug up," that's all.

•

ROLLS-ROYCE termite-proofs its dashboard wood.

•

BIRDS DON'T like strawberries.

•

WHITE SHRIMP feed by day. Pink shrimp feed by night.

•

EXPECTANT mothers on the island of Fernando de Noronha off Brazil long paid a standard fee for complete maternity care — one chicken.

•

EARLY EGYPTIANS believed in the confessional, too. Except they confessed sins they hadn't committed, even. To build up good will in the afterlife.

•

PITCAIRN ISLAND people — descendents of the Bounty mutineers — are all Seventh-day Adventists.

THEY DON'T make pretzels the way they used to. That's good. They used to make them big enough to wear around your neck.

ANSWER DEPT.

Q. "NEXT TO the United States, what country has the most Baptists?" A. The Soviet Union.

•

Q. "WHAT WAS the first American car to come out with seat belts?" A. Nash Rambler in 1950.

Q. "WHAT'S the best-selling sort of nut?" A. The almond, research reveals. Peanut doesn't count, evidently. Not a real nut.

•

Q. "WHAT PROPORTION of the cigaret smokers who sign up for those quit-smoking programs actually do quit?" A. One in four, research reveals.

•

Q. "ONE TIME every member of the U.S. Congress wore a white rose. Why?" A. On Jan. 30, 1946, that was, the anniversary of Franklin D. Roosevelt's birthday. The name Roosevelt means "field of roses," please note.

•

Q. "WHAT ARE 'incunabula'?" A. Books printed but not handwritten before 1501.

•

Q. "ARE cattails edible?" A. Are indeed. In fact, at some time during a year, all parts of the cattail are edible — shoots, leaves, bloom spikes, root stalks, all.

•

Q. "DOES ANYBODY know what the Pilgrim ship, the Mayflower, looked like?" A. Not exactly. In its time, there were 19 vessels of English registry called "Mayflower."

MARYLAND law makes it illegal for a woman to go through her husband's pants pockets while he sleeps.

•

"AUNT JEMIMA" started out as a hit song in an old vaudeville show. Cereal maker Chris L. Rutt thought it had such a nifty ring that he named his pancake mix after it.

•

FLAT FACT: English has more words than any other language in the world.

•

DOCTORS who study the way the human body is supposed to function say the only natural swimming stroke for people is the dog paddle.

•

ABOUT 25 feet a day is the normal brousing speed of a snail.

•

WHO DESTROYED the reeds at Acapulco? And why? Nobody knows. All that's known is that the name "Acapulco" comes from "Acatl Poloa Co" meaning "in the place where the reeds were destroyed."

SAID William Wrigley: "When two men in a business always agree, one of them is unnecessary."

INDIANS SAY: "If the whites won, it was a battle. If the Indians won, it was a massacre."

•

WHEN YOU SAY "lousy," please note, you're quoting Shakespeare. Likewise when you say "laugh it off."

•

THE AMISH don't sue and, if sued, don't contest.

•

ELEPHANTS do not fight over territory. In this, they're most unusual animals.

THERE'S a name for everything, isn't there? Hang a chain loosely between two hooks. Its sag is called an "inverted catenary."

•

IT WAS that golf fanatic Mary, Queen of Scots, who decided "Stuart" looked better than "Stewart." Before then, all with that name spelled it "Stewart."

•

DICTIONARY editors report one of the most frequently misspelled words in English is "commitment."

OREGON'S Corvallis has a curious ordinance that makes it illegal for young ladies there to drink coffee after 6 p.m.

•

OF THE 350 earthquakes that shake California every year, about 45 actually can be felt by the people.

•

THIS WAS the contention of that French moralist Jean de La Bruyere: "Most men spend the first half of their lives making the last half miserable."

•

THE MAYOR of Augusta, Wis., reportedly wants a law to require horses there to wear rubber galoshes.

•

THE HEARTS of the astronauts get smaller in outer space.

ANSWER DEPT.

Q. "IN WHAT city worldwide are the most aircraft built?" A. Wichita, Kans.

•

Q. "DO ANY two people have identical handwriting?" A. Undoubtedly not. Odds against that are said to be less than one in 68 trillion.

I'M SICK IN BED WITH A HIGH FEVER, A NASTY FLU, AND MY FOOT HURTS!

IT HAS BEEN proven that many — even most — people who can't comfortably tell lies face to face are able to prevaricate freely when talking on the telephone.

Q. "WHAT'S a 'baby-waker'?" A. A firecracker. In the vernacular of the Virginians.

•

Q. "HOW FAST is the pulse of a killer whale?" A. At the surface, 60 beats a minute. Underwater, 30 beats a minute.

Q. "CAN a prize-winning cow really produce 30 calves a year?" A. Conceivably, yea, conceivably. If her embryos, sometimes split, are implanted in other cows, with a breeding every two months, yes.

•

Q. "WHAT DOES the name 'Tokyo' mean?" A. "Eastern capital." When it was first founded in 1603, it was called Edo, meaning "Door of the Bay." A feudal lord so named it when he decreed the town was his headquarters.

•

Q. "WHO WAS president when the White House got its first car?" A. William Howard Taft. It's also a fact that he was the last president to keep a milk cow on the premises. Her name was Pauline.

•

Q. "WHAT'S an 'English flute'?" A. A wind instrument more commonly called a "recorder." Said to be the easiest instrument of all to learn to play.

•

Q. "THERE'S ONE place where the United States flag flies at full staff 24 hours a day without ever being raised or lowered and without ever being saluted. Where?" A. The moon.

TAKE a wide-awake rabbit. Inject it with some blood just taken from a sleeping rabbit. The wide-awake rabbit immediately falls asleep. Explain that.

•

MOST POPULAR name for newborn baby girls nationwide now is Ashley.

•

DID YOU start smoking before you were 14 years old? If so, you can expect twice as much trouble in trying to quit as will be encountered by smokers who started later. Or so say medical researchers.

•

AM TOLD Kleenex started out in World War I as a gas-mask filter.

•

COCKROACHES once were four inches long.

•

NO, NOT ALL male lions have manes.

•

ANOTHER pronouncement by Admiral H.G. Rickover: "A child is being properly educated only when he is learning to become independent of his parents."

IT WAS the custom for centuries in Istanbul to light the harem quarters with candles fastened to the backs of wandering tortoises.

SEVENTEEN out of 20 people worldwide have brown eyes.

•

RAPID REPLY: Yes, bee stings are deadlier than shark bites, statistically.

•

THE AFRICAN violet is no violet, please note.

•

NO PLACE in Greece is more than 85 miles from the sea.

•

AVERAGE AGE now in this country of the first-time bride is 21.8.

AQUAFARMERS can grow one-pound lobsters in one month. In the sea, it takes six years for a lobster to get that big.

•

IF YOU WANT a pet elephant, remember, you've got to give it 50 gallons of water a day.

•

TO THAT lengthy list of commonplace things first designed by Leonardo da Vinci, add the self-closing door.

•

CAN YOU contradict the claim that there have been no child-prodigy playwrights?

AMONG BABY MICE, the males start to fight with one another right after they're born, but the females don't.

•

THE MAN, typically, is likely to wait until the gas tank is nearly empty, but the woman, typically, is inclined to fill it up at about half.

•

THERE ARE 31,557,600 seconds in a year.

•

THE WORD "Ye," as in "Ye Old Sweete Shoppe," was always pronounced "Thee," never "Yee." Got that?

•

MAN'S SKIN is thicker than woman's.

•

MUST BE a lot of old hand-held calculators lying around in rarely opened drawers. Americans buy 65,000 new ones every day.

•

COMPUTER studies show June marriages have the highest divorce rate.

•

EVERY TIME you say something, your blood pressure goes up.

POLLSTERS say they've proved that women generally spend more time in bed than men do.

ANSWER DEPT.

Q. "WHY IS bubble gum pink?" A. Because that's the only food coloring Walter Diemer had at hand when he invented bubble gum in 1928.

•

Q. "HAVE WE whipped malaria?" A. Not yet. Four new cases turn up nationwide every day.

Q. "WHY IS influenza named Asian or Hong Kong?" A. Flu viruses circle the Earth in a westerly-to-easterly arc. In pursuit of cold climate, actually. The strains are named for the places where they first show up.

•

Q. "WHAT WAS the first man-made object to get to outer space?" A. A rocket launched at Peenemunde, Germany, on Oct. 3, 1942.

•

Q. "WASN'T IT Shakespeare who coined the phrase 'Butter wouldn't melt in her mouth'?" A. Close, but no. Just a few years before Shakespeare's prime, an English playwright named John Heywood said it.

•

Q. "IS THERE any sort of bird that can fly the moment it's hatched from the shell?" A. Only one, insofar as I know — Australia's mound builder bird.

•

Q. "HOW MANY people have been executed in this country? And how many of them were women?" A. Since 1608, the count at this writing is 14,400, including 300 women.

CATS STARTED OUT as desert animals. Their fur evolved to deal best with hot, dry air, not rain or snow. The scholars say that's why they don't like to get wet.

•

BARROOM BETTORS also win a few on the motto of the U.S. Postal Service, which is, in fact: "Certainty, Security and Celerity."

•

AZTEC EMPEROR Montezuma didn't drink the water, either. History records he drank nothing but chocolate.

•

HOW LONG have you been driving your car? Britain's Prince Charles drove his Aston-Martin convertible for 14 years.

•

SLEEPWALKING runs in families.

•

HOLLYWOOD records indicate movies released in December and May are more likely to be hits than movies released in other months. But nobody knows why.

•

NEARSIGHTED? If so, you're one out of every three.

NINETY PERCENT of this year's new wine, worldwide, will be drunk within 12 months. Or so the wine experts think.

JUST BECAUSE the elephant's brain weighs five times more than yours or mine, doesn't mean said elephant is five times as smart.

•

IN THE SLAVERY years, Louisiana, the only state with a law on the subject, stipulated that a slave owner could work a slave 21 hours a day every day.

•

A 747 JET burns 185 gallons of kerosene a minute on takeoff.

OKLAHOMA IS twice as big as all of New England. All of New England has four times as many people as Oklahoma.

•

THOSE WHO purport to know claim 40 cents of every $1 spent on car repairs is wasted.

•

BOTH THE STUDENTS and the teachers perform better when the principal of the school is a woman. Or such were the findings of the Education Testing Service.

THE RATTLESNAKE can strike at something directly over its head, but the cobra can't.

•

IF YOU'RE drinking, you can't legally ride a horse, either. Not on a public place, at any rate. Yes, a horse is a vehicle.

•

COYOTES wag their tails, too.

•

THE COCKROACH has never been linked with any epidemic of human disease.

•

IF YOU HAVE 30 billion fat cells in your body, you're just average. Any more than that is too many. Sell off some.

•

YOU CAN figure another 210 U.S. citizens will observe their 100th birthdays this week.

ANSWER DEPT.

Q. "WHERE'S the world's longest ski run?" A. Jackson Hole, Wyo.

•

Q. "WHICH STATE has the highest proportion of its population in jails?" A. Florida.

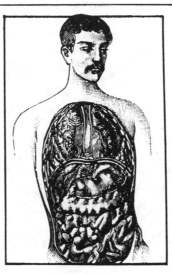

TO VISIT Tibet now, you're required to pass a heart and lung examination to prove you can handle yourself at 12,000 feet.

Q. "WHAT WAS considered the most important sport in ancient Greece?" A. Boxing. Because it doubled as basic training for soldiers.

•

Q. "WHO GOT the first Medicare ID card?" A. No. 1? The late Harry S. Truman. In 1966.

Q. "I KNOW the odds are with the house on all casino gambling games, but which game gives the best odds to the player?" A. Roulette, according to the math majors.

•

Q. "WHERE'D WE get the phrase 'to win hands down'?" A. From horse racing. When a horse was so far ahead it couldn't possibly be beaten, the jockey of old dropped the reins, hands down, to give the horse its head.

•

Q. "WERE the first blacks to reach this country slaves?" A. About the same as. Indentured servants, actually. More than 20 came ashore in Virginia in 1619. Slavery wasn't legalized there until 1661.

•

Q. "WHAT'S the difference between 'flotsam' and 'jetsam'?" A. Flotsam becomes junk when it slips into the sea by accident. Jetsam becomes junk when it's tossed overboard to lighten the load.

•

Q. "BESIDES the atomic bomb, what was this country's most closely guarded military secret of World War II?" A. The Norden bombsight. Everybody knew about it. But only a few knew how it worked.

THOSE WHO know the drug store business say the words "elixir" or "tincture" on a label usually are synonyms for "alcohol," nothing more.

•

A CENTURY ago, it was against the law of Brazil to execute white men. So before going to their deaths, whites convicted of capital crimes were dyed indigo.

•

OVERHEARD: "That kid's got hangups about everything but his clothes."

•

DELAWARE LAW was written in such a manner that it enables a husband there legally to cuss out his wife. Other states don't have such enabling legislation.

•

ALMOST 100 colleges offer rodeo scholarships.

•

COLOR EXPERTS insist their research shows students stay more alert in classrooms with yellow walls.

•

HALF OF India's Bombay is built on landfill.

ACCORDING TO the pest controllers, mice love chocolate — snap! — unfortunately for the mice.

DOCTORS SAY they can't cure colds. One out of five patients goes to the doctor because of a cold.

•

WHERE IS France? In the Indian Ocean is a French island called Reunion. It is as much a part of France — with full political status — as Hawaii is part of the United States.

•

HALF the country's illegal aliens live in California.

A "FLUKE" is any happy accident now, but originally it only meant a lucky billiard shot.

•

TEXAS CHANGED the whereabouts of its state capital at least 15 times.

•

HOUSEFLIES understand English, don't they? At least, some English. They always understand, "Hand me the swatter," know that.

IT WAS Christopher Columbus, too, who brought in pickles.

•

THOSE WHO profess to know claim donkey flesh is far tastier than horseflesh.

•

HALF THE PEOPLE in South America, almost, live in Brazil.

•

DO LIZARDS get bored? If not, why not? They devote 90 percent of their lives to lying absolutely motionless.

•

THE SUICIDE rate nationwide remained just about the same during the Great Depression as during the previous decade.

•

NINE OUT OF 10 cancers are on the face.

•

MONTREAL HAS a restaurant for every 230 people there.

ANSWER DEPT.

Q. "WHY DO OLDER women gain more weight when pregnant than young mothers do?" A. Older everybody gains more weight than younger everybody.

IN BOSTON'S Fenway Park, if a baseball hits a pigeon, the ball is dead. Don't know about the pigeon.

Q. "WHAT OTHER sort of animal is the closest, biologically, to the elephant?" A. A furry little beast about the size of a rabbit called the hyrax.

•

Q. "HOW FAST does the wind have to blow to close the airport?" A. 46 mph. That's gale speed, 2 mph shy of storm speed.

Q. "WHAT HAPPENS if I put mothballs in my gas tank?" A. You clog up your carburetor, that's all. The theory that mothballs boost gas mileage has been around a long time. But it's bunk.

•

Q. "HOW COME you gain weight when the temperature drops?" A. You sweat less.

•

Q. "HOW MANY U.S. towns called Pittsburgh are there, anyway?" A. One only spelled thataway. But there are Pittsburgs in California, Kansas, Kentucky, New Hampshire, Oklahoma and Texas.

•

Q. "WHY IS a baseball pitcher and catcher together called a 'battery'?" A. Comes from the military. Before the turn of the century, soldiers referred to it as a battery when they worked two artillery pieces together as a unit.

•

Q. "WHICH WAS the first baseball team to wear pinstripes?" A. The Yankees. By 1925, Babe Ruth had ballooned to 260 pounds. Owner Jacob Ruppert, disgusted, ordered new uniforms for the team — pinstripes to make Ruth look thinner. Turned into a tradition.

CONTRARY TO what you've always heard, the safest holiday of the year for car drivers — statistically — is New Year's.

•

EINSTEIN SLEPT a lot. Edison didn't. So you see?

•

A GALLON of wine weighs less in the summer than in the winter.

•

UNDERSTAND the bed experts say the mattress is supposed to be seven inches longer than the sleeper. Too bad. No fault of the mattress, though. I just sleep too long.

•

SHORT-HAIRED dogs shed more than long-haired dogs.

•

DID YOU know you get more vitamin C in strawberries than in oranges?

•

IF A NATIVE in Madagascar says yes to your question, that's not the answer. It only means your question is understood.

THE TYPICAL Arabian camel driver now carries extra water in an inner tube fitted neatly over the camel's hump.

SAFEST TIME to drive is on a Monday or Tuesday in January, I'm told. A national statistic, that one.

•

THOSE advice-to-the-lovelorn columns have been around a long time. First of same turned up in London's Athenian Mercury almost three centuries ago.

YOUR CAPILLARIES expand when you sleep. Thus they speed the spread of nutrients. It's one reason children grow faster while asleep than while awake.

•

THE WORD "republic" comes from a set of Latin syllables meaning "the people's thing."

IF A TV station wanted to broadcast everything in one Sunday edition of the New York Times, it would have to transmit 60 minutes an hour, 24 hours a day, seven days a week, for more than a month.

•

THE COLONIAL custom was to serve meals not hot, but lukewarm. It was an offense then to set out food that might burn the tongue.

ANSWER DEPT.

Q. "WHAT WAS Erle Stanley Gardner's first mystery story with Perry Mason?" A. "The Case of the Velvet Claws" in 1933. Gardner's publisher suggested Mason might make a good series hero. So Gardner recycled him.

•

Q. "HOW MUCH is the Pentagon's phone bill?" A. $8.7 million a year.

•

Q. "DIDN'T ONE pope have a son who also became a pope?" A. Yes. Pope Hormisdas, 514-523, was the father of Pope Silverius, 536-537. The first 37 popes weren't committed to celibacy.

YOU DON'T just double a street's capacity by making it one-way, but triple or even quadruple it.

Q. "HOW MANY coups d'etat has Bolivia had?" A. At this writing, 189. That's since 1825, when it got started as a sovereign nation.

•

Q. "WHY WAS the Brooklyn Dodger pitcher Sal Maglie known as 'The Barber'?" A. He threw fast balls close to batters' heads.

Q. "IN COMIC books, who was 'The Alchemist'?" A. Superman. It was an alias the writers created in 1961 for a scenario wherein Superman and Batman teamed up.

•

Q. "WHAT'S THE longest tunnel in the world?" A. That non-vehicular tube, the Delaware Aqueduct in New York State. It goes 105 miles.

AN AVALANCHE does not necessarily slide down a mountainside. It can fly down. It can create a vacuum above and an air cushion below and fly, literally fly, at twice the speed of a sky diver in a free fall.

•

TEACHERS GET more Valentines than mothers.

•

DIAMOND hunters look for garnets. When they find garnets near the surface, they say, they'll probably find diamonds buried a little more deeply nearby.

•

PEOPLE who visit Hong Kong spend 65 percent of their time shopping.

•

LARGEST POLISH population in the world — except for Warsaw — is in greater Chicago.

•

"DRACUL" in Romanian means "devil," so in that real province called Transylvania the name "Dracula" means "son of devil."

•

WHY DON'T YOU shine your shoes with the inside of a banana peel? That works.

YOU GET 68 percent alcohol in a lot of cough syrups, pain relievers and sedatives. In most whiskey, you only get 40 percent.

IF NEW YORK CITY had the same ratio of residents per square mile as Alaska, there'd be 14 people in Manhattan.

•

AVERAGE professional burglar — we're not counting teenage experimentalists here — is said to be 27 years old. More often than not, he has been to college.

•

"MOSCOW" comes from a Finnish word meaning "waterway."

BOWLING statisticians say a perfect game of 12 consecutive strikes occurs once in every 450,000 games, about.

•

YAKS get sick at sea level.

•

THAT INDIANA town called Santa Claus once saw fit to outlaw gossip. Couldn't make it stick, though.

•

THE FEET of eagles are not just yellow, but bright yellow.

ITEM NO. 883C in our Love and War Man's file: Seven out of every eight really intimate letters are written after 10 o'clock at night.

•

PSYCHOLOGISTS say most gifted youngsters get so bored they routinely perform about three grades below their potential.

•

PICASSO defined art as "a lie that lets us see the truth."

•

UPDATE: Among military, officers retire at an average age of 46, enlisted personnel at 42.

•

ONE OUT OF 10 Americans speaks some language other than English at home, and of these, seven out of 10 speak Spanish.

•

GROWNUPS' headaches occur on weekends, moreso than on weekdays. With children's headaches, it's the other way around.

•

ENGLAND'S chimney sweeps work from the bottom up. U.S. chimney sweeps work from the top down.

IF THAT butterfly doesn't warm its body to at least 81 degrees F, it can't fly.

ANSWER DEPT.

Q. "HOW COME the Chinese are such whizzes at table tennis?" A. The late Chairman Mao half a century ago decreed it ideal exercise for the Communist Chinese Army. Cheap equipment. Not much space. It turned into the No. 1 sport there.

Q. "BEST-SELLING car of all time was the Model T Ford, right?" A. Until the Volkswagen Beetle passed it in 1972, it was.

•

Q. "DO MOST of the Indian reservations permit bingo games?" A. Not most but many. About 80 of the 290 reservations are making money with bingo. The Seminoles in Florida reportedly get almost $20 million a year out of it.

•

Q. "WHO WAS the movie cowboy who had both a dog and a horse with the same name as the cowboy himself?" A. John "Duke" Wayne had a dog named Duke in several films and rode a white horse named Duke in 1932-33 pictures.

•

Q. "BY HOW MANY years has President Ronald Reagan outlived his original life expectancy?" A. By 25 years at this writing. When he was born in 1911, his predictable span was 48.2 years.

•

Q. "TWO MEN in the Baseball Hall of Fame never really had anything to do with baseball. Name them." A. Bud Abbott and Lou Costello, the comedy team. For their "Who's on First?" routine.

PEOPLE OVER the age of 65 have fewer nervous and mental disorders than people in any other age bracket. Or so report the medical statisticians.

•

ALL OF SWEDEN has fewer people than the city of Tokyo.

•

EVERY YEAR about 2500 men nationwide kill women they used to sleep with.

•

DID YOU take biology? Maybe you can explain how aphids go on multiplying even though all aphids are born female. All the daughters are pregnant even before they're born, might mention.

•

WHAT'S "CHARM?" That French literary light Albert Camus said, "Charm is a way of getting the answer 'yes' without having asked any clear question."

•

AVERAGE temperature worldwide now is only four degrees warmer than during the Ice Age, I'm told.

IF YOU hear "5,6,7,8" on your shortwave radio, better report it. U.S. scientists some time back broadcast "1,2,3,4" into outer space, and they're waiting for some logical reply.

CAMBODIANS give each day its own color and each month its own gender. A bride might schedule her wedding for a red day of a female month, a particularly lucky combination.

•

OUR LANGUAGE MAN keeps up with change. The standard biblical punishment for adultery, he notes, was to be stoned in the marketplace or wherever, and about half the national population now thinks that sounds like fun.

COSTA RICA is no bigger than West Virginia, but it has more kinds of birds and mammals than the continental United States.

•

THAT RENOWNED Greek philosopher Epicurus calculated the sun was approximately two feet in diameter.

•

IF YOUR lifetime runs average, you'll shed 40 pounds of skin before you're through.

DANDELIONS are sexless.

•

AM NOW told a cat will lose its balance if you cut off its whiskers. Is that right?

•

SIR, if you can read 200 words a minute, you're doing that thing in a manner typical of the American business executive.

•

THE FLAMINGO eats with its head upside down. Try that.

•

A MARBLE FACTORY turns out 200 marbles a minute, typically.

•

YOU CAN GET enough paper out of one cord of wood to print 942 books.

•

IN A WALKING contest between a swan, a goose and a duck, bet on the goose.

•

LABORATORY experiments prove you can keep your dentures clean by soaking them in bourbon. No, take them out.

•

MOST GENIUSES have been short. Very short.

SCARE an elephant and its ears will stand up straight.

ANSWER DEPT.

Q. "WHAT happened to the slaves who fought with the British during the American Revolution?" A. A lot of them were taken to Nova Scotia so they wouldn't be re-enslaved at war's end.

•

Q. "HOW LONG would it take you to read one day's issue of the Congressional Record?" A. About 60 hours, if your reading speed is average.

Q. "WHERE'D WE get the line, 'Close but no cigar'?" A. Can only guess it goes back to carnival booths where gamesters tossed coins, pitched rings or threw baseballs for small prizes such as cigars.

•

Q. "WHO WAS the first woman named 'Athlete of the Year' by Sports Illustrated?" A. Billie Jean King. In 1972.

•

Q. "WHAT KIND of meat has the least cholesterol?" A. Turkey.

•

Q. "HOW MANY of the original Seven Wonders of the World still exist?" A. Only one, the Sphynx.

•

Q. "WHERE'S the largest freshwater port in the world?" A. Philadelphia.

•

Q. "WHAT DID these famous Americans have in common — Henry Ford, Robert Fulton, Eli Whitney and Paul Revere?" A. All had been clockmakers.

•

Q. "DOES ANY bird of prey sing?" A. Only the South African Chanting Goshawk. None other even hums.

DO YOU HAVE arthritis? If not, you will, probably. Ninety-seven percent of the people over age 65 have sufficient arthritis to show up on X-ray films, doctors say.

•

MANY A WOMAN in Greece on election day even now is merely handed an already marked ballot by her husband or her father.

•

IF YOU SEE the lightning, it missed you.

•

EVEN IF YOU don't count today's reruns, "M*A*S*H" endured at least three times as long as did the Korean War.

•

IN SAUDI ARABIA, marriage "beneath one's station" is a crime, punishable by death.

•

FORTY-THREE percent of the convicts in state penitentiaries tell researchers they were drinking at the time of the crime.

•

USED TO BE a sort of hippopotamus on Madagascar about the size of a dog.

DEEP IN the tin mine at Camborne in England's Cornwall, the water that oozes from the rock walls is so hot the miners can make instant tea with it. And do.

TRUE, 85 percent of all divorced people marry within five years, but only 40 percent of these second marriages survive.

•

FROM uric acid, the chemists got barbituates, so named because their discovery occurred on St. Barbara's Day.

•

TWO out of five women with one child tell the surveytakers they don't want another one.

THE TEMPERATURE of your toes reveals the rate of your metabolism. Or so claim some medicos. Cold feet, low metabolism. Hot feet, high metabolism.

•

CLAIM IS the United States spends less on the Voice of America than the Soviets spend on jamming it.

•

WHAT, you can't name the first U.S. president born outside the original 13 states? Abe Lincoln, Abe Lincoln.

ONE OF the most brilliant thinkers of the Middle Ages was a scholar named John Duns Scotus. But scoffers in the 16th century ridiculed his name to give us our word "dunce."

•

A SWEDISH traffic researcher checked out 31,000 auto collisions to learn the car color least likely to be seen in such smashups was pink.

•

NO PERSON named Guppy was named after the fish, but the fish were named Guppy after a person — R. J. Lechmere Guppy, to be specific. He gave some to the British Museum.

•

ZANE GREY wrote three novels a year for 29 years.

ANSWER DEPT.

Q. "WHAT ARE the statistics on who pays the bills every month, the man or the woman of the house?" A. In 66 percent, the woman. In 31 percent, the man. In 2 percent, both the man and the woman, if they manage to stay together.

•

Q. "ARE THERE any skunks in China?" A. No, none anywhere in Asia, nor any in Australia, Africa or Europe, either.

IN Kitchener, Ontario, is a domestic bird breeder who's growing 70-pound turkeys. He thinks there will soon be 100-pound turkeys.

Q. "WHERE'S 'The City of Carousels'?" A. That's another name for Portland, Ore.

•

Q. "WHERE DO most of the people on Cape Cod get their money now?" A. No. 2, Social Security payments. No. 1, tourists.

•

Q. "THE OLD MAN says he doesn't know where he got his favorite word — 'pipsqueak.' Do you?" A. Hand-made toys that squeaked when squeezed — called pipsqueaks — were very popular a century ago.

•

Q. "I KNOW Los Angeles means The Angels. How does Las Vegas translate?" A. The Plains.

Q. "THOMAS A. EDISON said his invention he liked best was the phonograph, but did he ever say why?" A. He told associates it was absolutely original. Nobody had ever before thought of anything like it.

•

Q. "HOW MUCH money did Noah Webster get for compiling the first dictionary?" A. No money. At least not from the book. His publisher went bankrupt. He did all right on the lecture circuit, though.

•

Q. "COULD I break a bone in my face by trying to stifle a sneeze?" A. It happens occasionally.

YOUNG SLOTHS are so inept they sometimes think their own arms are tree limbs, grab ahold of same, and so come tumbling down.

•

IF STANDARD OIL of Indiana carved up its land into four states of equal size, each would be bigger than New Jersey.

•

IN BELT, MONT., it's illegal to dance the "angleworm wiggle," whatever that is.

•

A SHRIMP'S heart is in its head.

•

WHICH OF the states has the most boats per capita? Nobody guesses this one. Arizona.

•

THE MALDIVE Islands off India are Moslem. It's considered unseemly there for women to appear in the streets during daylight. So the girls have to go to school at night.

•

BOTH LEMON PEEL and tinfoil are commonly used as bait by the fishermen of the Aegean Sea, and they do well.

HEAD counters say 17.2 million people visited Manhattan last year, but they didn't say why.

CHINA NOW — even after birth control and death are reckoned in — adds to its population 25 people every minute.

•

A PAIR of eyeglasses at the time of the American Revolution — all such were imported then — cost the equivalent of two or three years' wages.

•

JAPANESE etiquette is precise. When served to you, the teacup's design is toward you. Before you sip, you turn the design toward your host.

THE TIDES at Tahiti vary less than a foot.

•

THE BIBLICAL rose of Sharon was a tulip.

•

ON BROADWAY, you know the play is about to start when the lights go dim. In Japan, you know it's time when you hear wooden blocks clacking.

•

THE COCAINE experts say three out of five users eventually turn into sellers.

DAIRY checker-uppers say far more boys than girls drink milk at school.

•

IF A PYTHON is a huge snake, what's a pythoness? No, sir, that's a witch.

•

NO PLANT cultivated in ancient Mexico was known anywhere else in the world then. That includes tomatoes, sweet potatoes, avocados and red and green peppers. Toss in chili. Add vanilla.

•

VIRGINIANS will tell you that Roanoke started out as a settlement called "Big Lick."

•

CHILDREN rarely blush before age 4. You can say the same about grownups over 50.

•

IF YOU WANT to add a little zest to your life, put an orange or lemon peel in your drink. That's still the No. 1 meaning of "zest" in most dictionaries — orange or lemon peel for flavor.

•

GUIDE DOGS never watch the stop-and-go lights, only the traffic itself, I'm told.

DEBATE GOES ON over the origin of the expression "mind your Ps and Qs." Most widely accepted notion is it started out in the 1700s as tavern talk where Ps and Qs meant pints and quarts as standard measures for ale.

ANSWER DEPT.

Q. "WHO WAS 'Silence Dogood'?" A. Benjamin Franklin's first pen name.

Q. "DO STORES in Russia have names?" A. Not anymore. Just numbers. Book Store No. 15 or Grocery Store No. 9 or Drug Store No. 3. Like that.

•

Q. "WHAT FEMALE mammal has nipples not in front but along her backbone? And why?" A. That great water rodent called the nutria. The curious configuration lets her nurse her young while she swims.

•

Q. "HOW LONG is a newly hatched alligator?" A. About nine inches.

•

Q. "IN WHAT show did Lee Majors get his first acting job?" A. "The Big Valley," 1965. The day he walked on that set was the first day he'd ever acted in anything. He'd been a playground instructor.

•

Q. "WHAT'S the race track name 'Hialeah' mean?" A. "Pretty prairie." In Seminole.

•

Q. "TO WHOM did Abraham Lincoln bequeath his estate?" A. He didn't. That was one lawyer who left no will.

IF IT WAS a jerkwater town, the train didn't stop there. Between the tracks in towns so called were water troughs. Slung under the train tender was a scoop, lowered as the train passed over, to "jerk" the water upwards into holding tanks aboard.

•

YOU CANNOT be sent to prison for tax evasion in Switzerland. Fined, yes. Imprisoned, no. It's not a criminal offense there.

•

"WILBUR" IS an old Saxon name. Meant "wild boar." Get the spelling right.

•

THE STATUE of Liberty tape-measures 35 feet around the waist, and the refurbishers are not doing anything about that, not a thing.

•

TO THE TYPICAL Britisher, that ground around the house is the "garden," never the "yard."

•

A MAIN DISH no longer eaten around these parts was in antiquity thought to be the finest of delicacies: roast puppy.

FARMERS refused to use the first iron plows. The metal would poison the soil, they said.

GRIZZLY BEARS, male and female both, are wildly promiscuous. Beasts.

•

THE GOLF caddies of Sri Lanka think it's undignified to stoop. They pick up golf balls with their toes.

•

ON THE SUN, sir, you'd weigh two tons, while you lasted.

•

"SHAMBLES" used to mean "slaughterhouse."

•

BRUNETS tend to get gray earlier than blonds.

TAKES A FIFTH of a second to blink your eyes, and if typical, you blink them 25 times a minute. So, on a 10-hour trip at 50 mph, you'd drive 42 miles with your eyes closed.

•

IN NORTH DAKOTA it's against the law to serve pretzels with beer.

•

NO ANIMAL on earth was ever much more than half as big as today's biggest whales.

•

IN SAUDI ARABIA, the pages of the Koran are supposed to be free. What you pay for is the binding.

EXPERIENCED jungle hunters say the tiger always kills from behind. It won't attack if it sees you looking at it, and if you fall face up so you can look straight at it, it won't eat you. I've not tested this.

●

NORTH AMERICA has only five Olympic-size hockey rinks, and Alaska has three of them, two in Anchorage.

●

ALMOST ALL animals stop growing right after they hit puberty, but not the male kangaroo. That numbskull doesn't get the signal, evidently. It just keeps on growing all its life.

●

"NASTURTIUM," for evident reason, comes from two Latin words meaning "nose" and "twist."

●

THE VENOM of the Black Widow spider is about 15 times more potent than the venom of a rattlesnake.

●

THE FIRST mahogany seen by the people of England was on the rudder of Sir Francis Drake's "Golden Hind." He'd repaired said rudder with it in the West Indies.

TELL YOUR youngster to draw a picture of Dad as though the man were some kind of animal. Most children so directed in a California project sketched their fathers as lions.

ANSWER DEPT.

Q. "WHAT DID the early American Indians do with their garbage?" A. Covered it with dirt. Even in their caves, sod huts, domiciles of whatever sort, when the trash collected on the floor, they spread it around and heaped soil on it, raising the floor level by that much.

Q. "HOW COME owls fly silently?" A. Their wingtips are feathered with down.

●

Q. "WHAT WAS the early Eskimo diaper before civilization shipped up ready-mades?" A. A piece of fawn skin edged in fur and lined with disposable moss.

●

Q. "IT'S SAID of Philadelphia: In no other big city in the world do so many people ride through on trains without getting off. Why?" A. Because it's so close to New York City. Nowhere else worldwide are two such metropolises so close together.

●

Q. "HOW DO YOU play the violin 'collegno'?" A. Scrape the strings with the back of the bow.

●

Q. "WHICH IS the only one of our states that's growing in physical size?" A. Louisiana sometimes is credited with that distinction.

●

Q. "HOW LONG does an iceberg adrift in the Atlantic last?" A. Up to three years, unless it floats into the Gulf Stream, in which case it melts in two weeks.

MINOR offenders aren't jailed in Yemen. They're locked in leg irons and turned loose in the streets — to do what they do, clank, clank. Even children get this chain reaction.

•

SWISS BANKS had cash machines years before U.S. banks installed same.

•

APPLE BLOSSOMS are sweeter than other blooms, aren't they? Indeed. Apple blossom nectar may be as much as 87 percent sugar. Other nectars average only 35 percent sugar.

•

QUICK, name three things Marco Polo introduced into the Western world from China. You've got it if you say fireworks, spaghetti and ice cream.

•

A FELLOW of sad experience writes to our Love and War Man: "Marriage is the process of finding out what sort of husband your wife would have preferred."

•

FOOD MARKETS get hit harder by shoplifters than any other kind of store.

HEADS YOU WIN, TAILS I LOSE...

IN THE restaurants of Richmond, Va., you can't legally flip a coin for the check.

ON MAPS of the Sahara is a spot called "Tree of Tenere." Nothing is there but one scrawny acacia tree. There's no other tree within 100 miles.

•

IS SALT an "emotional stimulant"? Some medical researchers so aver, though they don't elaborate on what they mean by emotional stimulant.

•

OUR Chief Prognosticator thinks the medical researchers one day will figure out why rats don't get infections in open wounds, and that should make a considerable difference in doctoring.

MOST POPULAR food in the world is still rice. But it's no longer No. 1 in Nepal. The imported potato has taken over there.

•

WHAT A BABY swan needs more than anything else, I guess, is persistence — takes 24 hours to peck its way out of its shell.

•

WHERE CITRUS trees grow, the colon cancer rate is less than half the national average.

•

AMONG SNAKES, there are no vegetarians.

JANE FONDA'S family tree has not been traced all the way back to when her family lived in it — but it has been traced as far back as that American Revolutionary leader Samuel Adams.

•

THE SHE snakes are bigger than the he snakes.

•

SAID Mark Twain: "Good breeding consists of concealing how much we think of ourselves and how little we think of the other person."

•

ONLY THREE out of five grizzly bear cubs live more than a year and a half.

•

FASTEST of the whales is the big blue, at about 25 miles per hour.

•

THAT RUSSIAN word "Bolshoi" means "grand."

•

ONE YOUNGSTER in six sleepwalks.

•

WILLIAM JAMES said forgetting is as important as remembering. Do you buy that?

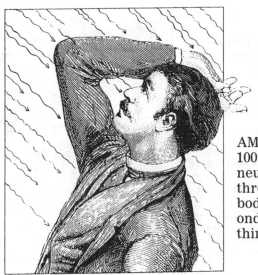

AM TOLD 100 trillion neutrinos shoot through your body every second. Feel anything?

ANSWER DEPT.

Q. "WHY in the world were the San Diego pro football players called 'the Chargers'?" A. That's not "charge" as in Light Brigade but charge as in Fly-Now-Pay-Later. Their onetime owner, Barron Hilton, owned Carte Blanche charge cards.

•

Q. "Wasn't Jacqueline Kennedy Onassis at 31 the youngest First Lady ever?" A. Almost, but not quite. Julia Taylor was 24, Frances Cleveland 21.

Q. "WHERE'S the hottest, driest place in the world?" A. Death Valley. Some places are hotter and some places drier. But no place is both-er. Little wonder it's so dry. Evaporation rate is 200 inches a year, the rainfall less than two inches.

•

Q. "WHAT'S the most common nightmare about?" A. Falling.

•

Q. "EXACTLY how much gold was actually found in King Tut's tomb?" A. 2448 pounds of it.

THE ODDS are with you if you bet the fellow on the next stool that his toothbrush is blue. Blue is the American preference for toothbrushes generally, and the great preference of American men.

•

PICTURE half a walnut with a small pearl in it. That's just about the same as a hummingbird's nest with an egg therein.

•

THE WORD "gin," as in "cotton gin," started out as nothing more than slang for "engine."

•

IF YOU are 58 years old, you've been around just about as long as pay phones.

•

BOOK PUSHERS in the Library of Congress every year — to make room for the new stuff coming in — move what's on 37 miles of shelves.

•

YOU'RE typical if you write 24 personal checks a month.

•

SWANS FIGHT to the death.

GLACIERS over Greenland's west coast kick about 7500 icebergs a year into the North Atlantic.

THE WRISTWATCH telephone is just around the corner, says our Chief Prognosticator. Don't believe I'll turn there.

•

WHEN YOU trace the origin of the word "Caribbean," you get to the origin of the word "cannibal."

•

THE RATIO of maple sap to maple syrup is 40 to 1.

AVERAGE hip measurement among the current New York models is still 33 inches.

•

BEFORE MATING can occur, the male porcupine must soften the female's quills with urine. So much for X-rated wildlife.

•

GERANIUMS on the Isles of Scilly off Cornwall, England, grow seven feet tall.

ALL RACES of man are physically equipped to make all the sounds in all the languages.

•

PLAIN black pepper, too, has been seen to cause cancers in mice. University of Kentucky researchers who discovered this say it's meaningless.

•

OF THE 50 MILLION eggs a female oyster spawns at a single setting, only two can be expected to survive.

•

YOU KNOW that musical "West Side Story"? Originally, it was called "East Side Story."

•

IN IRAN, glaciers of salt move downward on high ground just as do ice glaciers elsewhere.

•

MUCKLE JOHN in the reign of Charles I was the last royal fool of England, unless you want to get nasty about it.

ANSWER DEPT.

Q. "WHICH COUNTRY in Asia was first to get television?" A. Thailand. In 1955.

MICE sing. High notes. Very high.

Q. "IS IT TRUE Benjamin Franklin had a family of 13 illegitimate children?" A. Doubtful. Only onesuch is known, a son, who was raised by Franklin and his wife. Nobody has ever found out who the mother was.

•

Q. "MAN'S FIRST use of fire was cooking, right?" A. Not quite right, sir. Nor was cooking man's second use of fire. Heat was the first, theorists believe. Then came the discovery that fire scared off wild animals, its second use.

Q. "THAT mixed drink called the 'Mai Tai' — what does the name mean?" A. "The very best." In Tahitian.

•

Q. "AREN'T ALL mammals hairy?" A. All except whales and porpoises. And even they have whiskers.

•

Q. "YOU SAID yellow fire trucks have fewer accidents than red fire trucks. Why?" A. Credit that phenomenon called the "Purkinje shift," which makes red appear black at night. Yellow does not shift this way.

•

Q. "WHY ARE 'M & M's' called that?" A. Because they're made by Mars and Murray.

•

Q. "WHAT VEGETABLE is most widely used worldwide?" A. The onion.

•

Q. "BOXING RINGS come big and small, but what's regulation?" A. 20 square feet.

•

Q. "HAS AN ACTOR of Chinese extraction ever played Charlie Chan?" A. Not in the movies.

HERE'S TO Saxon King Edgar — clink! — who in A.D. 958 ordered no work be done from Saturday noon to Monday dawn, and thus invented the weekend.

•

THE POET Carl Sandburg flunked out of West Point, according to the record, because of deficiencies in English.

•

THE ZERO was invented in India. So was the concept of infinity.

•

FLIES GET athlete's foot, too.

•

THAT HUGE plaza in front of the Kremlin was called "Red Square" at least 100 years before the word "communism" was coined.

•

PILOTS ALOFT can still pick out the wagon tracks of the old Oregon Trail, they say.

•

A BOLT of lightning goes 20,000 miles a second.

•

MOST COMMON physical ailment of moose is arthritis.

MALE MOSQUITOS are vegetarians.

SUNNY SPAIN is pretty far to the north, actually. Madrid lies roughly across from New York City. Our Canadian border is about as far south as some of Spain's northern coast.

•

CURIOUS, but on lists of Thomas A. Edison's inventions, you almost never see the flashlight, which he dreamed up in 1914.

•

"THE DEEPEST urge in human nature is the desire to be important," said John Dewey, importantly.

•

CAREFUL with those begonia seeds. By weight they cost 100 times more than gold.

YOU'RE AWARE, are you not, that a giraffe's neck, though long, is not long enough to reach the ground.

•

JAMAICANS don't say "goodbye." They say "walk good."

•

IF THE GRAPES are dusty, that's good. In France. Shoppers there think the dust proves the grapes have been snipped carefully from the vines, untouched by human hands.

•

AN OLD LAW lets Indians pass back and forth between Canada and the United States without restriction.

HOW CAN YOU call yourself an expert on basketball if you've never heard of Bert Loomis, the man who invented the dribble.

•

THE SCORCHED cub that later came to be known as "Smokey the Bear" originally was called "Hot Foot Teddy."

•

TO PAY parking fees for a year in mid-Manhattan now, you need about $4900. Not so long ago, the price of the car itself, that.

•

PRIVATE PLANES carry 50 times more passengers than the scheduled airlines.

•

A CHILD, if typical, has numerous nightmares; a grownup, only about one a year.

•

REMBRANDT painted 62 self-portraits.

•

THE PRESIDENT and vice president of the United States aren't permitted to travel together.

THE RIGHT TUSK of the elephant is almost invariably larger than the left.

ANSWER DEPT.

Q. "HOW MANY test tube babies are there now?" A. At this writing, about 700. Claim is one in every seven couples is a candidate for the procedure.

•

Q. "IF THE Three Wisemen were Magi, what was one Wiseman?" A. A Magus. Means hereditary priest.

Q. "HOW MANY of the usual dinner vegetables are perennials?" A. Only two come to mind — rhubarb and asparagus.

•

Q. "WHAT ARE the three most common last names in Russia?" A. Ivanov, Vasiliev and Petrov.

•

Q. "WHAT BONE in the human body is most frequently broken?" A. Collarbone, research reveals.

•

Q. "HOW MANY slaves did Confederate General Robert E. Lee own?" A. Not a one. Didn't believe in it, he said.

•

Q. "DO FROGS and toads have teeth?" A. Frogs, yes. Toads, no.

•

Q. "WHAT BROTHER combination in baseball hit the most home runs? The DiMaggios? Alous? Boyers?" A. Try the Aarons. Hank, 755. Tommy, 13. That's 768.

•

Q. "WHAT'S the best-selling liquor label in the United States now?" A. Bacardi rum.

THE MOST dangerous modern occupation now — because of so much mechanization — is farming.

•

CAN YOU envision six square miles of human skin? Neither can I. But that's how much new skin Americans altogether grow on any given day.

•

THOUGH MANY women are convicted of passing worthless checks, forgery is almost exclusively a man's crime.

•

IF YOUR family gets back a tax refund of $700 or more, you can call your bunch average in that matter.

•

THE NUMBER of Americans of Irish ancestry outnumber the Irish in Ireland by 12 to 1.

•

A WELL-FED lion can sleep 18 hours at a stretch.

•

TEXAS LAW of 1945 makes it legal there to horsewhip one's wife but not one's horse, I'm told.

IN MEDIEVAL TIMES, the lion was called a "Leo," the unmarked panther a "Pard." This combo was the origin of the word "leopard."

CREDIT the philosopher Friedrich Nietzsche with the observation: "It is not lack of love but lack of friendship that makes unhappy marriages."

•

THE MEN of ancient Egypt wore mascara, too.

•

FIRST CARS permitted in Yosemite Park in 1913 were required to honk at every curve in the road.

IT WAS the Arab sailors from the wrecked Spanish Armada who taught the Scots how to weave wool tweeds.

•

NINE OUT OF 10 readers of science fiction are male.

•

"TROUBLE WITH being a housewife," writes a wistful lady, "is when you don't feel well enough to go to work, staying home doesn't help."

AMONG Catholics, women who go to confession outnumber men by about two to one.

•

MEXICO City sinks 10 inches a year.

•

HALF THE fruit of the date palm is sugar.

•

TWO OUT of three people struck by lightning survive.

•

IF THEY ate parsley, they wouldn't get drunk. So thought the ancient Greeks. They were wrong.

•

IF THE weight of saltwater is 28 percent salt, no more salt will dissolve therein.

•

TAKES FIVE times more heat to turn boiling water into steam than to bring freezing water to a boil.

•

GOLDSMITHS' Hall in London was where articles of silver and gold were assayed and officially stamped as genuine. For many a moon, if it wasn't stamped on silver or gold, it wasn't a "hallmark."

THOSE WHO tan the skins of fish say it takes two salmon to make a pair of shoes.

MORE THAN half the whales in the oceans are less than 15 feet long.

ANSWER DEPT.

Q. "DOES THE skunk have a six-shooter?" A. That, or a five-shooter, or four-shooter. If the first shot misses at 12 feet, the skunk fires again. Did I mention a skunk fires tracers? The spray gives off an eerie phosphorescent glow.

Q. "NOT EVERY language can be written down. True?" A. Of the 3000 different languages spoken, only about 150 have a written form.

•

Q. "WHAT WERE Pablo Picasso's dying words?" A. "Drink to me."

•

Q. "WHAT'S the average weight of newborn baby girls around here now?" A. 7 pounds 7 ounces.

•

Q. "DO ANY animals have pink teeth?" A. Could be. All I know is some elephants have rose-colored tusks.

•

Q. "WHAT DO the historians say made George Washington sterile?" A. Malaria.

•

Q. "WHAT'S THE oldest edible vegetable cultivated by man?" A. The cabbage, some say. History records some ancient peoples ate it even before corned beef.

•

Q. "IF THE ancient Romans didn't have toothbrushes, what did they use to clean their teeth?" A. Little balls of wool dipped in honey.

A SURVEY of secretaries indicates 53 percent of them think they're smarter than their bosses. The bosses weren't surveyed.

•

A REGULAR user of cocaine doesn't build an immunity, evidently. Takes less of a dose, not more, to be fatal, the medicos say.

•

THE MEDITERRANEAN Sea near Messina, Sicily, is the only place in the world where swordfish breed.

•

ANCIENT Egyptians manufactured plywood. That craft is almost as old as beer brewing. But not quite. Did I tell you it was the Egyptians who invented sourdough bread?

•

CHEER UP, young lady. A producing dairy cow is pregnant 75 percent of the time.

•

THOSE HASH BROWN potatoes you buy cost about twice as much as those you make, if typical.

•

SAND RUNS about 10,000 grains per handful.

THE "GREENS" of golf courses in Saudi Arabia are "browns." Not grass. That takes too much water. They're packed sand and oil, both of which Saudi Arabia has aplenty.

SOME ALBANIANS have pet dogs or cats, but those who do are generally regarded there as quaintly old-fashioned and a bit silly.

•

IN MASSACHUSETTS, a young lady can marry at age 12, but her husband better be at least 14, or it's illegal.

•

IN THAT matter of breakfast cereals, even after all these years, nothing sells better than corn flakes.

POLAND GROWS more potatoes than the United States does. So there.

•

SURE, you knew Texas is the biggest cattle state, and Oklahoma is the second biggest. But did you know Florida is the third?

•

CLAIM IS your brain has more than 100,000 miles of nerve fibers, called dendrites, to connect your brain's billions of cells.

NO, SIR, snakes don't blink. No eyelids.

•

IN SPAIN, the tourists over one full year outnumber the Spaniards there, I'm told.

•

AMONG COLLEGE undergraduates, the women now outnumber the men.

•

YOU CAN TELL the age of a clam, too, by counting its rings. Those on its shell.

•

THAT RULE of 80-20 holds true in supermarkets, too. Eighty percent of the profits are derived from 20 percent of the inventory.

•

REACTION TIME of the cockroach — 54/1000ths of a second — is about as fast as any in the animal world.

•

YOU MAY TELL the family poet that "gossamer wings" are just cobwebs, that's all.

•

NO, a regulation boxing ring is not 20 square feet — as typoed here — but 20 feet square.

THE BLOOD of lobsters is blue.

THREE OUT OF 10 soap-opera viewers are men.

ANSWER DEPT.

Q. "DID BLONDIE in the comic strip ever hold down a job?" A. That she did. At the outset she was a stenographer.

•

Q. "YOU SAID either bamboo or kelp was the fastest-growing vegetation. What's the fastest-growing animal?" A. The whale. Goes from a tiny egg to a 15-ton, 23-foot-long baby in 11 months. Then to a 65-ton, 65-foot-long yearling. The whale puts on 2.3 tons a month.

Q. "IS IT TRUE that most of the missing persons are teenage runaways?" A. No, sir, most are grownup men with money problems.

•

Q. "WHAT'S the Polynesian 'hongi'?" A. That greeting wherein two, when they meet, close their eyes, press noses and murmur, "Mmmm-mm."

•

Q. "DO PEOPLE who lose thumbs and fingers ever grow them back?" A. Children under age 10 have done so. Surgeons at Mt. Sinai Hospital in New York have documented two such cases.

•

Q. "WHAT'S a 'nosocomial disease'?" A. Any ailment you pick up in the hospital while you're there for treatment of some other disease. The New England Journal of Medicine says 36 percent of all hospital patients get those dreaded nosocomial diseases.

•

Q. "IS IT TRUE the Mormons were the first to dig irrigation ditches?" A. The first Anglo-Saxons, anyhow. They won that distinction when they rerouted City Creek in 1847 to water the Salt Lake Valley. Others elsewhere, though, were irrigating before recorded history.

"COVER YOUR fires," said William the Conqueror. Actually, he said it in French: "Couvre feu." And we wound up with "curfew."

•

HALF THE lawns and gardens nationwide are kept up by women.

•

DO YOU realize that 45 out of every 100 Californians were actually born there?

•

ALONG WITH Saudi Arabia, add Bolivia (Simon Bolivar) to that lengthening list of nations named in honor of individuals. And Colombia (Christopher Columbus) and Israel (Jacob) and The Philippines (King Philip II of Spain) and El Salvador (Jesus). And China, certainly (Emperor Chin — 221-210 B.C.). Not to mention home — the United States of America (Amerigo Vespucci).

•

ACTRESS MERYL Streep's first name is a run-in version of Mary Louise.

•

WIDOWS outnumber widowers by 5.3 to 1.

WEASELS AND leopards have this in common — they kill for joy.

THOSE ILLICIT types who ship outlawed vegetable matter across international borders deal in rare foliage. Just one fernlike tropical plant called a Cycad — a holdover from the dinosaur days — is said to be worth $70,000.

•

NOBODY HAS been able to link up the Australian aborigines with any other living race. Where their ancestors came from remains unknown.

•

HOW DOES a blind man build and fix TVs and stereos? Ray Charles does it. It's his hobby.

TRUE BELIEVERS in old Tibet rescued fish endangered by winter freezes and summer droughts and tried to preserve their lives in pails of water. To those people, it was a violation of their religion to let any living thing die, if such death could be prevented.

•

ITEM NO. 699C in our Love and War Man's file labeled "Intimate Surveys" reads: "Three out of four American men can be accurately described as two-minute lovers."

•

NOBODY knows what ice worms eat.

A DOG has 42 teeth, a man only 32. A letter carrier told me that.

•

"AIN'T NO man can avoid being born average, but nobody's got to be common." Satchel Paige said that, too.

•

AVERAGE work week shortly before the Civil War was 66 hours — six 11-hour days.

•

NOT ALL bees sting. Some bite. The Royal Mayan bees bite.

•

IF YOU TAKE 23,040 breaths in the next 24 hours, you're typical. Keep track.

•

PENNSYLVANIA used to give a $50 bounty on bobcats. Now it gives a $50 fine for killing one.

ANSWER DEPT.

Q. "ARE PLAYING cards found in all the world's nations?" A. All so-called civilized nations, anyhow. If the country has paper, it has playing cards.

A FARM is a dangerous place. Or can be, anyhow. Accidental death rate for people on farms is half again as high as the accidental death rate for everybody everywhere.

Q. "IS THAT club called the Irish shillelagh supposed to be made of some particular kind of wood?" A. All I know is Ireland's town of Shillelagh is renowned for its oak trees.

•

Q. "TO BE an Arab, of what race, religion and nation must I belong?" A. None of the above. An Arab is one who speaks Arabic, that's all. Arabs are of numerous races, religions and nations.

Q. "WHY DO historians insist Nero did not play a fiddle while Rome burned?" A. Because the violin bow wasn't invented until the Middle Ages, centuries later. A lyre was responsible for that tale.

•

Q. "THE BIBLE says you can't serve God and Mammon. What's Mammon?" A. Name of the Chaldean or Syrian god of worldly possessions.

97

TAKES 4½ months to replace a fingernail from quick to tip.

●

STRONG SILENT types are admirable, but in real life, people who talk the most make the most decisions, according to the students of such matters.

●

THAT PASTRY you and I call a "Danish" is referred to in Denmark as "Vienna Bread."

●

WOULD TAKE more than a million fireflies to crank out as much light as a 60-watt bulb.

●

AMONG WILD animals, the flesh eaters lap water, the grazers and browsers sip it.

●

NO, YOU CAN'T tell the age of a deer by the prongs on its antlers, but yes, you can tell the age of a mountain sheep by the rings on its horns.

●

SEASONED citizens around here saw trains first, then planes. But all over the world are people who've seen planes but not trains.

WORMS IN southeastern Australia can grow three-fourths of an inch in diameter. You can hear their gurgling, sucking sounds as they move underground. Their eggs look like big olives. Four feet in length is typical. Some have reached 12 feet.

THREE-FOURTHS of the earth is covered with water.

●

WHAT'S THE average annual rainfall around your place? Death Valley's is 2 inches. Antarctica's, 4 inches.

●

DIRECT exposure to hot sunshine in Southern California's deserts can kill a rattlesnake in nine minutes.

●

THREE OUT OF four American women are married by age 23.

AD AGENCY copywriters have influenced the language, all right. Take the word "economy." Means "large" in soap flakes and "small" in cars.

●

IN THE FIRST half of this century, one out of every four of the families that moved to Arizona did so because some family member was ill.

●

A COMPUTER sort of the nation's public thoroughfares always ends with the name of a place in the Mojave Desert — Zzyzx Road.

THE OFFICIAL flag of one state and only one — Ohio — is in the shape of a pennant.

•

"MORAL indignation," said H.G. Wells, "is jealousy with a halo."

•

ONE STATE and only one, Maryland, has an official state sport — jousting. Jousting?

•

SOUTH DAKOTA raises more geese for the dinner table than does any other state.

•

DESIGNERS SAY: Vertical lines create formality. Horizontal lines suggest comfort. Ovals convey daintiness. I'd like it dainty, my dear. Leave the football on the mantel.

ANSWER DEPT.

Q. "WHAT IS there about shark liver oil that makes it so valuable to the manufacturers of lipstick?" A. Temperature changes don't congeal it in extreme cold nor thin it overmuch in heat.

•

Q. "WHERE'S the 'golf capital of the world'?" A. California's Palm Springs. With more than 50 courses thereabouts.

THE MAINE municipality of Waterville once saw fit to make it illegal there to blow your nose in public.

Q. "WHAT'S the median age in the United States now?" A. For whites, 31. For minorities, 24.

•

Q. "WHAT'S the average weight of women in their 40s?" A. 140 pounds.

Q. "ANY DANGER that the $2 bill will be decreed unacceptable someday?" A. No, sir. All currencies and coins ever issued by the U.S. Government are legal tender. In perpetuity. Congress so provided.

•

Q. "WHAT DID they do to the man who murdered Wild Bill Hickok?" A. Jack McCall? Hanged him.

•

Q. "WHERE'S the most gold in one spot?" A. In a vault at the Federal Reserve Bank of New York in Manhattan. That 12,600 metric tons of it is the property of 80 different nations.

•

Q. "WHAT'S meant by the claim that celery has 'negative calories'?" A. Chewing of it burns more calories than it contains.

•

Q. "WHEN and where did the word 'humongous' first appear in print?" A. In 1973. In a student newspaper at the University of Denver.

•

Q. "DON'T some men in Japan continue to work after age 65?" A. Not just some but 45 percent of them do.

IN 1790, blacks made up 19.3 percent of New York City's population. Today, it's still about 19 percent.

•

MEXICO WON'T let foreigners buy land within 31 miles of its coast.

•

THE BEAN STALK climbs the bean pole from right to left.

•

IF A BEETLE were as big as a horse — and proportionately that much stronger — it could pull a 100,000-pound load.

•

NO STATE of the union has suffered as many battle casualties per capita in recent U.S. wars as has Puerto Rico.

•

THE ONLY cats that live in groups are lions.

•

WHEN the English describe somebody as "cuckoo," they mean crafty, not crazy. The cuckoo, they know, is an exceedingly crafty bird.

LONDON shop sign: "Official Sausage Maker to Queen Elizabeth II. God Save the Queen!"

LANGUAGE scholars say the Japanese generally find it more difficult to learn English than the Chinese do.

•

FIGURE the ball speed of a good golfer's drive at 170 mph. At least, some have been so timed.

•

NOBODY KNOWS where that California grape called the Zinfandel originated.

•

MAILMEN in Egypt complain they too often are bitten by camels.

POLLEN never deteriorates.

•

DID YOU KNOW that the renowned Apache Geronimo in his later years was kicked out of the Dutch Reformed Church for gambling?

•

TREES typically can move water from roots to top leaves at a speed of about an inch a second.

•

THE YOUNGER the new father, the more likely the infant will be a boy.

THE ANDES mountain range is longer than the United States is wide.

•

AMONG INDIA'S street vendors are professional ear cleaners. For a fee, any of same will usher you to the side of the walk and swab out your ears with a soft-tipped bamboo stick dipped in sweet oil.

•

SO YOU THOUGHT the longest creature on earth was some sort of whale? No, in 1865 at New England's Cape Ann, a jellyfish washed ashore. It measured 245 feet from tentacle tip to tentacle tip. And no lengthier beast has ever been recorded.

•

THE HELL of the Himalayan faiths is not hot but bitter cold.

•

MUSKRATS smell funny. That's why they're called muskrats.

•

THE SCOTS outside Scotland outnumber the Scots inside Scotland by seven to one.

•

PRICE UPDATE: In Iraq's Baghdad now, a cup of coffee with toast costs $12.

WHAT FIRST made peanuts so much in demand was their portability. They served as field rations for soldiers in the Civil War.

WHEN THAT sort of shrimp called krill gets scared, it jumps out of its shell. The shell floats down. Attackers chase it. The krill scoots away.

ANSWER DEPT.

Q. "WHICH AGE group of which sex proves statistically to be the best drivers?" A. Women from age 16 to 25.

Q. "WHAT WAS the Aztec purpose in making human sacrifices?" A. They believed the sun would weaken if it weren't fed human blood. Or so goes the legend.

•

Q. "HOW MANY different poker hands are possible in a 52-card deck?" A. 2,598,960. If you dealt a hand every second, it would still take you more than a million years to play all the combinations.

•

Q. "SAYS HERE May 1 — May Day — long was known in New York City and Boston as Moving Day. Why?" A. Most leases there used to be dated from May 1 to May 1.

•

Q. "HOW FAR north did Confederate soldiers get during the Civil War?" A. Pretty far. Vermont's St. Albans, to be specific. On Oct. 19, 1864, Southern raiders robbed three banks there of $200,000, then jumped to Canada.

•

Q. "WHERE WAS the world's first high school built?" A. Near Niagara Falls. More specifically, at Lockport, N.Y. In the 1850s.

HISTORIANS but not all others know that Christopher Columbus never did find out what he discovered. Until the day he died, he thought he'd landed on Asia.

•

IF 8500 businesses change ownership nationwide today, call it typical.

•

BEETHOVEN was 5-foot-2.

•

"NIFTY" started out as the unpretentious slang for "magnificent."

•

SUNGLASSES were invented long before any other sort of spectacles.

•

SPIDERS can't chew.

•

NO, THERE'S no such thing as a queendom. It's a kingdom, son, even if a queen's running it.

•

WAS A TIME when the elevated ladies of China — during the Han Dynasty, this — painted shadow rings around their eyes. They all looked like pandas.

GOOD NEWS, MARY... YOU HAVE 136,427 HAIRS, AND YOU'RE NOT EVEN A BLONDE!

RARELY WILL you find anybody with more than 140,000 scalp hairs, but when you do, it will be a blonde, count on that.

THE OLDE ENGLISH ancestors of people named "Prescott" stayed in the priest's cottage.

•

NINETY-FIVE percent of the books published annually make their authors less than $5000 each.

•

FEW READERS of the big serious novels of Herman Wouk are aware that Wouk once wrote comedy for Fred Allen.

•

CIGARETS in Israel run $4 a pack, about.

IF THAT COW and sheep are both typical, the cow eats seven times as much as the sheep.

•

MAYBE 3 PERCENT of all the horses sent to the racetracks earn back the money invested in them.

•

ITEM NO. 4882C in our Love and War Man's file labeled "Three stages of a man's romantic life" reads: "Triweekly, try weekly and try weakly."

•

THE HULA originally was danced only by men.

A FALLING object travels more slowly at the equator than at the North Pole.

•

PURSE SNATCHERS of Italy ride motor scooters. The women of Italy have learned to carry their handbags on the away-from-the-street side of their bodies.

•

THE LAW IN Florida's Daytona Beach says you can't legally fall asleep there in public between 11 p.m. and 6 a.m.

•

AMONG university students over age 35 nationwide, the women outnumber the men by almost two to one.

ANSWER DEPT.

Q. "QUICK, WHAT'S the only country named in honor of a person?" A. Saudi Arabia. Now. Also, once, there was Rhodesia. No more.

•

Q. "IF ALL the farmers stopped producing food today, how long would the world's stockpile of food last?" A. Two months maybe. When the ready supply exceeds more than two months' need, prices drop drastically.

FIVE penguins in covered cages were flown 2200 miles from the Antarctic to an inland place, banded, then released. It took them 11 months to waddle, then swim all the way home.

Q. "WE'RE BORN with 300 bones. But as grown-ups, I read, we have only 206 bones. What happened to those missing 94 bones?" A. Each fused with another to make one bone.

•

Q. "ARE ANY people allergic to just plain water?" A. A few. If their hands stay wet for more than several minutes, they break out in rashes. So they wash then dry quickly.

•

Q. "WHAT CONTINENT has the highest average altitude?" A. Antarctica. Exact average uncertain. Ice.

Q. "WHY DO the Venezuelan Indians smoke their cigars backwards — with the lighted ends in their mouths?" A. So they don't waste the smoke, they say.

•

Q. "IF AN ASTRONAUT on the moon flashed a light at us, how long would it take us to see it? If the sun somehow blinked out for an instant, how long would it take us to see that?" A. Moon, one second. Sun, eight minutes.

•

Q. "WHAT'S THE motto of the French Foreign Legion?" A. "The Legion is our Fatherland." In Latin.

BARNYARD HOGS kill more people every year than sharks do.

•

THERE WAS a time when the moon had moons — lots of them, many 60 miles in diameter. But they fell to moon.

•

YOU WERE aware that an octopus has three hearts, weren't you?

•

EXTANT TODAY is a small cult of vegetarians who ask you not to mow your lawn in the belief it gives pain to the grass.

•

FLIES FLY FASTER in sunlight than in shadow.

•

AM NOW TOLD the world's longest ski run is a four-mile zipalong near Zermatt, Switzerland.

•

TAKES the saguaro cactus 30 years to grow one branch.

•

PENGUINS MATE once a year, and that's it.

IT WAS the fellow on the end of the rope in one of mankind's oldest games — tug o' war — who gave us the television title of "anchorman."

A 3-MONTHS-OLD fetus in the womb already has its lifelong fingerprints.

•

NO INSTRUMENT to measure wind speed has ever survived a top tornado force, so nobody knows how fast the fastest tornado winds blow.

•

AVERAGE admission price to movies in the last 30 years has gone up 525 percent. Postage, though, has gone up 567 percent.

•

METEORITES are never round.

AN ARIES woman tends to keep her good looks longer than others, according to those who take their stargazing seriously.

•

DID YOU REALIZE civilization got oleomargarine before the appendectomy? Oleo patent, 1871. First appendectomy, 1885.

•

ONE DRIVER in four nationwide couldn't start the car on at least one morning last winter.

•

COWS hate spinach.

THE ORIGINAL Russians were Scandinavian traders known as the Rus.

•

ALBANIA IS no bigger than Maryland.

•

SIR FRANCIS DRAKE'S famous three-master "The Golden Hind" was smaller than a modern tugboat.

•

MONACO at the south of France is not all that far south, actually. It's on the same latitude as Portland, Maine.

•

THE SILKWORM eats, eats, eats — it multiplies its body weight 10,000 times in about 26 days.

•

IF IT WAS some kind of arthritis — 300 years ago — it was called gout.

•

THE LAW OF 80-20 works in traffic tickets, too. Twenty percent of the offenders get 80 percent of the tickets, about.

•

"STINKING LAKE" is what Canadian Indians used to call the Pacific Ocean. They didn't think much of it.

MOST coonskin caps were made of skunk.

OPERATORS of auto salvage yards say one of the fastest selling car parts on their lots is any model's left front door.

ANSWER DEPT.

Q. "COMPARE the divorce and separation rates of Catholics and Protestants." A. They're about the same — 13 to 15 percent. Notre Dame scholars found out about that.

Q. "DOES ANY river cut completely through the Rocky Mountains?" A. Only one — Canada's Peace.

•

Q. "ARE THERE any truly wild horses in the world?" A. Only the Przewalski's horses of Mongolia. All others come down from horses once domesticated.

•

Q. "WHAT does 'Singapore' mean?" A. "City of the Lion."

•

Q. "WHICH IS bigger — the United States or Europe?" A. The United States is far bigger, if you mean Europe excluding the Soviet Union.

•

Q. "DOESN'T some state still have a law that specifically prohibits wife-beating after 10 p.m.?" A. Doubt it. Pennsylvania had such a law until the early 1970s, however. It prohibited wife-beating on Sunday, too.

•

Q. "IS ANYBODY alive able to read the oldest written language known?" A. Yea, about 250 people are said to understand Sumerian. It's in Sumerian that you get the earliest account of Noah's flood.

MADAM, if you weigh 144 pounds, you're exactly average among American women, according to the statisticians.

•

ALL THE young men on Pitcairn Island get married by age 19.

•

NOTHING in the record suggests any Viking ever wore a horned helmet. That picturesque caricature evidently was concocted by a Wagnerian costume designer.

•

THE HAND GRIP of the baby one day old is much stronger than the grip of a baby one month old.

•

IF THAT STEEL ship and that wooden ship are the same size, the steel ship is lighter.

•

PRESIDENT Theodore Roosevelt was another of those believers who always carried a rabbit's foot for luck.

•

MEN HICCUP more than women.

WINDIEST STATE in the nation, according to those who profess to know, is Oklahoma.

WILL YOU BUY the claim that all the ice cream eaten by Americans in one year would fill the Grand Canyon?

•

CURIOUSLY, a canoe is just about the safest vehicle afloat — handled by an expert — and just about the most dangerous — handled by an amateur.

•

THE WHITE horse didn't start out white. Turned white as it grew.

•

PAJAMAS originated in India to lounge around in but not to sleep in.

NOT EVERYBODY knows that Cinderella's dog was named Bruno.

•

YOU GET a lot of rain around your place? Consider Yakutat, Alaska — with 132 inches a year.

•

WHEN BATS fly out of a cave, they always turn left.

•

THE MEN outnumber the women in only 66 of the world's 188 countries.

•

RODEO EXPERTS say almost all bull riders are short.

TO MOST of the world it is a curiosity that U.S. television commercials encourage dogs to eat more and people to eat less.

•

CENSUS TAKERS in China's Canton recently noted 20,000 bicyclists crossed one intersection in one hour.

•

KAYAKING is a required subject in Greenland's schools.

•

CLAIM IS it takes about 100,000 genes to build a human being.

•

THERE ARE a lot of muscles in your hand and wrist together, true, but a cat's tail has three times as many.

•

NOT ALL of Stradivari's violins were "great." Their tones vary.

•

THE ITALIANS sell a lot of wine that winds up resold as French and German wine.

•

THAT TUXEDO of the swimming penguin is camouflage. From above, it looks like the dark sea. From below, it looks like the light sky.

SOME STARFISH reproduce by dropping off an arm, which then develops into a whole new starfish.

THE MOTHER tarantula kills 499 of each 500 spiderlings she hatches.

•

MULES AREN'T particularly stubborn.

ANSWER DEPT.

Q. "WHAT'S HUMAN life expectancy in Africa now?" A. 49 years.

Q. "IN ALL of major-league baseball, what's the yearly cost of broken bats?" A. Twenty-six teams each break about 500 bats at $12 a bat — $156,000.

•

Q. "WHO WAS the first governor of Alaska?" A. Wlodzimierz Krzyzanowski. Here's to the proofreader — clink!

•

Q. "IS THERE any of these United States without a wildlife refuge?" A. Only one — West Virginia.

•

Q. "IF A MAN could leap like a cricket in proportion to size, how far could he jump?" A. 120 feet.

•

Q. "WHICH ETHNIC group in this country is the best educated overall?" A. The Russian-Americans.

•

Q. "ANY TRUTH to the claim that frozen vegetables can be more nutritious than fresh vegetables?" A. Some. In winter, especially, if the fresh are shipped up from southern growers. The frozen are packed within hours of picking.

IF THAT fur coat is labeled "chinchillette," you can figure it's rabbit.

•

DIETERS, please note: It is the dark meat, not the white, that has the most fat.

•

AS YOU sleep, a buildup of carbon monoxide slowly replaces the oxygen in your blood stream. If your body didn't have a mechanism to awaken you, the scientists say, oversleep could kill you.

•

"THE LAND of 10,000 Lakes" — Wisconsin — has 12,034 lakes, actually.

•

A DONKEY can swallow five gallons of water in two minutes.

•

POLLSTERS say only three out of 100 wives on payrolls would rather stay home.

•

DESERT veterans learn you can't get that life-saving water out of a barrel cactus just by tapping into it. You've got to beat it to a pulp.

OF SINGLE men 24 years old, one in six will get married in the next 12 months. One out of five single women that age will marry in the same period.

ELEPHANTS like tobacco. No, dummy, they eat it.

•

WHY DO appreciably more women than men wear eyeglasses?

•

BRITISH SAILORS ate limes to ward off scurvy. American sailors ate cranberries to do that.

•

NO, SIR, 200 coconuts a year is not too much to expect from a cultivated coconut tree. Figure it produces for 75 years. That's 15,000 coconuts.

A COCKROACH spends more time cleaning itself than a cat does.

•

THE TERM "Zero Hour" was coined a few wars ago — WW I, to be specific — to designate the moment set to charge from a trench.

•

WHEN SWEDEN banned car horns, the traffic accident rate dropped appreciably.

•

IN NO NATION is a government spy identified in the official paperwork as a spy.

YOU CAN figure about 10 Americans will be treated today for vitamin overdoses.

•

THE BACTERIA in your body outnumber all the people on Earth by 22 to 1. About.

•

IF YOUR eyesight were the best and the conditions just right, you could see a match struck at night 50 miles away.

•

RURAL HOUSEHOLDERS in ancient Greece kept snakes indoors and out to control rats and mice, much the way farmers keep cats today.

•

TAKES SEVERAL weeks for a person to starve to death, but without sleep the human body dies in about 10 days.

•

ONE PACKAGED food out of every four costs you more for the container than for what's inside.

ANSWER DEPT.

Q. "WOULD BUTTER melt in the Red Sea?" A. Yes, and swiftly. At 95 degrees F., it's 7 degrees warmer than butter's melting temperature. Why do you ask?

YOU KNOW about the carnivorous plants that trap insects in their foliage. But were you aware that in Venezuela there are plants that eat insects with their roots?

Q. "HOW LONG is the copyright on a silicon chip good for?" A. 10 years.

•

Q. "IN THE Orient, what country, if any, is mostly Christian?" A. Only the Philippines, predominantly Catholic.

Q. "WHAT ARE the three classifications of stray dogs?" A. 1. Feral — born wild, never domesticated. 2. Lost — escaped from owners. 3. Uncontrolled — allowed by owners to run free.

•

Q. "WHERE'S the world's largest four-faced clock?" A. In Milwaukee, Wis. Its minute hands are 20 feet long.

•

Q. "WHAT'S the fastest-growing country in the world?" A. Kenya. At an annual rate of 4.1 percent. Compounded nightly.

•

Q. "WHO invented popsicles?" A. Frank Epperson. He left a spoon in his lemonade one winter night.

•

Q. "WHAT'S the best hotel in the world now?" A. Can only relay opinions of some world travelers that the Oriental in Thailand's Bangkok deserves consideration for that distinction.

•

Q. "WHAT SORT of dog has skin with accordion pleats in it?" A. The Chinese fighting dog — char-pei. Rare breed, that one.

AN OVERABUNDANCE of extracted human teeth is what we have. Dentists pull 60 million a year.

•

EVEN TO this day, most Europeans regard sweet corn as hog fodder.

•

THOSE WHO run roulette games say most players favor the odd number over the even.

•

USED WIDELY in Japan of late is a 27-cent disposable umbrella.

•

A FUNDAMENTAL document of law, the U.S. Constitution, mentions only one crime. Ask your lawyer friend to name it. Correct. It s treason.

•

CHRONICLERS of historical figures have listed the occupation of Adam as "gardener."

•

GEESE, TOO, gaze into each other's eyes for signs of sex appeal. At least, I presume they do. Male geese have blue eyes, female geese brown eyes.

ANCIENT ART suggests the first cowboys to rope bulls with lassos were Egyptians in the Nile valley.

YOU WANT to start a riot? Under the law, you need at least three people.

•

GROUND LEVEL in California's San Joaquin Valley is 30 feet lower than it was 60 years ago. Pump out the water to irrigate, and the land sinks.

•

IF YOU want to grow a beard, sir, figure on an inch every eight weeks.

•

AN OUNCE of don't-say-it is worth a pound of didn't-mean-it.

THE AVERAGE female breast measurement in West Germany has increased by almost one inch in the last 10 years. Or so report the bra makers. They can't explain this phenomenon.

•

WHAT, YOU can't name the state with the largest number of national parks? Arches. Bryce. Capitol Reef. And Zion. Say Utah.

•

THE KALASH tribespeople of Pakistan sod the roofs of their mountain houses. Their big complaint: The goats eat the shingles.

DO YOU spend 48 minutes a day going back and forth to work? That's another American average now.

•

NORTHERN Wisconsin 15,000 years ago was buried under ice a mile deep.

•

BICYCLE DEATHS nationwide outnumber airplane deaths by four to one.

•

BAD CONCRETE gets weaker with age, but good concrete gets stronger.

•

YOU DON'T bump into many men named Florence anymore. Used to, though. Before Mr. and Mrs. Nightingale named their little girl Florence, it was almost exclusively a man's name.

•

IT WAS the Arabs who invented windmills.

•

YOU CAN'T picket at the U.S. Capitol. Can't wear a campaign button there, either.

•

YOUR BRAIN has at least twice as many nerve cells as that of a gorilla.

QUICK, what animal has its nostrils on the top of its head? Say the whale.

ONLY ABOUT 20 percent of the people can stand up to talk to a large group without feeling the pangs of that thing called "stagefright."

•

HOW LONG can you hold your breath? The sperm whale can hold its for more than an hour.

•

ONE OUT OF 100 atheltic scholarships went to women a decade ago. Now 30 out of 100 do so.

ANSWER DEPT.

Q. "WHO WAS the first man to cross North America north of Mexico?" A. Alexander Mackenzie, the Scottish fur trader. He worked his away across Canada a dozen years before Lewis and Clark got to the Pacific.

•

Q. "SPOCK on 'Star Trek' — what's his family name?" A. Xtmprsqzntwlfb.

•

Q. "WAS THERE ever a British monarch who never set foot in Britain?" A. One only — Queen Berengaria, wife of Richard the Lion-Hearted.

•

Q. "WHICH U.S. state has the highest proportion of citizens of English ancestry?" A. Utah. With 54 percent.

•

Q. "CAN goats climb trees?" A. Some trees. Some goats. In Morocco, the goats like the fruit of the argan tree. They get up as high as 20 feet or so to have at it.

•

Q. "ANY FISH in Great Salt Lake?" A. Not a one.

ANY HOG that lives longer than eight months now is an old-timer. That's the life span of the typical ham-on-the-hoof in commercial pig farms.

•

SOME JAPANESE are buying American farm catfish for sushi.

•

THE ESKIMO, don't forget, never takes his dog inside.

•

IT TOOK 3500 gallons of water to get that steak to your table, sir. Eat an egg, instead. That only takes 120 gallons of water.

•

DEER hate garlic.

•

IN MEXICO, tequila is big, but brandy is bigger.

•

YOU KNOW the deaths related to weather? More are reported in Texas than in any other state.

•

SAYS HERE the energy of one sizable hurricane in one day could power the United States for three years.

THE COUNT of attorneys has nearly doubled in the United States in the last 15 years.

MOST CROWDED city in Europe is Naples.

•

IN ESTONIA, ditchdiggers earn about twice as much as physicians. The best jobs there are those that bring tips from foreigners: bartenders, cab drivers, waiters, doormen.

•

HALF the Americans over age 55 have no natural teeth left.

•

THE DUTCH of New Amsterdam were the first in this country to cook "olykoeks." It translates as "oily cakes." What we're talking about here, Pilgrim, is doughnuts.

IN BULGARIA, a nod means no, a handshake yes.

•

AMONG the fiercest of the ancient Celtic warriors were horse-riding women. One of these, Boudicca, led the pack that burned London to the ground.

•

FIRST PILOT'S license issued in the United States went to Glenn H. Curtiss, the fellow who designed the first airplane to land on a ship.

•

DID I tell you Buckingham Palace was built on the site of an old brothel?

FOUR out of five left-handed children are born to right-handed parents.

•

DID I TELL YOU an artificial pancreas is only about as big as a hockey puck?

•

HOW'D YOU LIKE to be a Siberian welldigger? Some permafrost there runs a mile deep.

•

THAT HARVARD student most likely to drop out is the youth who earlier went to a private prep school.

•

THOSE IN this country who don't like bugs spend a total of $10 million a year on little cockroach traps.

•

"EVERY HERO becomes a bore at last," said Ralph Waldo Emerson. A hero to many in his day was Ralph Waldo.

ANSWER DEPT.

Q. "WHAT'S the difference between the silk moth and any other moth?" A. Most moths emit short silk threads. Silk moths emit long, long threads.

DID YOU know Christopher Columbus stood less than 5-feet-6?

Q. "WHO invented the rubber ball?" A. Nobody knows. What is known is Christopher Columbus took some oddly shaped bouncing balls from Haiti back to Europe, and that was Europe's first glimpse of such.

•

Q. "WHEN was the Johnstown flood?" A. Which one? In that Pennsylvania town, a flood in 1977 killed 80 people. Another, in 1936, killed 30. The worst, in 1889, killed 2200. The most flood-prone city in the country, Johnstown.

Q. "AMERICANS drink more wine on one day of the year than on any other. What day?" A. Thanksgiving.

•

Q. "HOW RARE are the real redheads?" A. One in 40 nationwide is said to be genuinely red-haired.

•

Q. "WAS A TIME, according to the antique experts, when a citizen always painted the family name on the best household bucket. Why?" A. When that bucketful of water was handed up to a volunteer fireman, the householder hoped to get the bucket back.

•

Q. "HOW MANY Republicans have served two full terms as president?" A. Only two, so far. Eisenhower and Grant.

•

Q. "AREN'T the bones of birds hollow?" A. Of birds that fly, yes. But not penguins. Their bones are solid. Ballast.

•

Q. "CONTRARY TO the opinion of this character beside me, I claim landing of an airplane is more dangerous than taking off. Right?" A. Quite right. Twenty-five percent of plane accidents occur on takeoff, 60 percent on landing.

LOWEST natural temperature ever recorded near the South Pole was minus 126.9° F in 1960. Near the North Pole, minus 96° F in 1964.

•

THOSE WHO study "erythrophobes" — people who blush easily — say children don't blush at all for reasons of embarrassment until age 6.

•

THE ICE pack over the North Pole is as big as the lower 48 states.

•

CLAIM IS 20 earthquakes strike daily at one place or another, but only the sensitive seismographs detect them.

•

A RETIREMENT home for horses? Am told there's one such near Methuen, Mass. Dray horses can live out their days there.

•

EVEN IF you're never sick a day in your life, your biological clocks will limit how old you can grow. The normal limit, medicos say, is 118 years.

A LOAF of bread is taxed more than 200 times before it gets to your table.

ONLY ONE person out of four in Montana lives in a city.

•

IF YOU drove you car 500 miles on vacation, your holiday this year was typical of the national average.

•

THE BUTTERFLY'S sense of taste is 1000 times more sensitive than the honeybee's. It could detect a teaspoon of sugar in a bathtub of water.

AVERAGE COST of a new car — without taxes — would be less than $4500

•

YOUR ARM, if normal, makes 27 different movements. The best artificial arm you can get only makes six.

•

JACKALS mate for life.

•

YOUR BONE marrow turns out 17 million red blood cells per second.

CLOCKS in Saudi Arabia are set to solar time. It's noon there each day when the sun is directly overhead.

•

IF YOU HAVE access to well water, take its temperature. That will be the average temperature year-round of the air thereabouts.

•

SORRY, there aren't any hotels in Tibet. No restaurants. No buses. No trains. You can't even go there unless China invites you.

•

ONE NATION contains a third of all the fresh water on this earth — Canada.

•

IF YOU DRIVE your car 10,000 miles a year — and that's average — it gets about the same annual mileage as the average New York City elevator.

•

STATISTICS suggest one out of every 10 American women sometime will be raped.

•

RAPID REPLY: Yes, sir, the Alabama Hills are in California, not Alabama.

TOMATO PLANTS contain more nicotine than tobacco plants, I'm told.

ANSWER DEPT.

Q. "MOST of the sailors with Christopher Columbus were Spaniards, right?" A. Basques. They made up the biggest ethnic group among them all.

•

Q. "WHICH STING is the worst — the wasp's, hornet's, yellow jacket's or honeybee's?" A. Hornet's. It injects more poison into the wound than any of the others.

Q. "DO THE RUSSIANS shoot off fireworks in the Soviet Union?" A. It's done, but only by the official Fireworks Detachment of the Ministry of Internal Affairs.

•

Q. "WHAT PROPORTION of the teenage brides are pregnant when they marry?" A. One in six.

•

Q. "WHY DO the cookbooks always say, 'Soak the beans overnight'?" A. That gets rid of about half the "oligosaccharides" in those beans. They're the complex sugars that cause flatulence.

•

Q. "WHAT'S the best way to serve okra?" A. To somebody else.

•

Q. "QUICK, name the only Islamic country in Europe." A. Albania. With 70 percent Muslims.

•

Q. "A WOMAN with 13 children is quite a rarity anymore, right?" A. Maybe not such a rarity, sir. Research reveals there are about 150,000 mothers of 13 in this country.

IF LAST WEEK was typical on the operating tables of the plastic surgeons, 1420 Americans had the bags cut away from under their eyes.

•

TWENTY-ONE percent of all first babies are conceived before marriage.

•

THE LATE Orson Wells said: "If there hadn't been women, we'd still be squatting in caves, eating raw meat. We made civilization to impress our girlfriends."

•

AVERAGE SKIER spends only two days a year on the slopes.

•

BY AGE 70, to be typical, you're supposed to have eaten 26 acres of grain. If you have not done so, better get with it. Start at the southwest corner.

•

IT'S ACTUALLY against the law in Yukon, Okla., to pull your dentist's tooth.

•

OVERHEARD: "Experience is valuable — it gives you a comb after you're bald."

BELIEVE I forgot to mention that a pig-skinning machine can skin 400 pigs in one hour.

YOUNGEST PERSON ever listed in "Who's Who in America" is Tatum O'Neal.

•

NOW HERE'S a feline expert who claims any cat that can roar can't purr and any cat that can purr can't roar, and I can't disprove that one, either.

•

CALIFORNIA'S mountains get more snow than the North Pole.

FIRST HEIR apparent in the United Kingdom to have a university degree is Prince Charles.

•

LITTLE GIRLS hop more than little boys. The why of this has never been fully explained.

•

SEE IF YOU can find an autograph of Julius Caesar. It'd be worth about $2 million.

SNAILS ARE hermaphrodites. Each is both male and female. When two mate, both lay eggs.

•

"IT WOULDN'T hurt a baby if it never had a bath." So say two British physicians, Drs. Margaret Kerr and Gavin C. Arnell.

•

MELT THE ICE of Antarctica and half the world's population would be forced to move up from flooded coastlines.

•

THE MONA LISA is painted on wood.

•

A QUEEN termite can lay an egg a second while she's at it. Remarkable. That's 86,400 eggs a day. Stop her!

ANSWER DEPT.

Q. "WHAT'S a 'rockoon'?" A. The rocket-boosted balloon that pushes weather instruments 60 miles high.

•

Q. "WHAT makes Mars red?" A. Rust.

WHY IS IT called the French horn? Germans developed it.

Q. "WHAT'S the most common crime committed by women?" A. Shoplifting, by far. That's the charge in seven out of 10 arrests of women, in fact.

•

Q. "IF I DIPPED out a glassful of Great Salt Lake water and let it evaporate, how much salt would be left in the glass?" A. About an inch.

Q. "DIDN'T RUSSIA used to have only five days in its week?" A. For 11 years, yes. From 1929 to 1940, the Soviets used a Revolutionary Calendar — five days in each week, six weeks in each month.

•

Q. "WHAT'S a typical retirement age for a U.S. military officer?" A. Commissioned, 43. Non-commissioned, 39.

•

Q. "DID the great athlete Jim Thorpe have an Indian name?" A. He did. "Bright Path."

•

Q. "WHAT'S the most densely populated city now?" A. Hong Kong. With 5.4 million people. It's only about a third the size of Rhode Island, please note.

•

Q. "DID SHAKESPEARE ever mention pretzels?" A. Never did. They weren't invented until about the time of his death.

•

Q. "WHAT'S the highest altitude in New Orleans?" A. Not counting the levees? Four feet.

OUR TERM "compound," meaning "enclosed settlement," comes from the Malay "kampong," meaning "native village." I guess English is richer than other languages because the early English speakers traveled so much. They pilfered syllables from everybody.

•

THE JOB of the alpine St. Bernard dogs was not to rescue the snowbound but to go by the most direct route to the victim, and thus mark a trail for the rescuing monks.

•

AMONG THE OLD Anglo-Saxons, a husband could divorce his wife on the ground that she was too passionate.

•

CLAIM IS that that freshwater sea under the Sahara desert covers as large an area as France.

•

KING CHARLES XII always buttered his toast with his thumb.

•

THE ARABIC spoken in Yemen has no verb "to smoke." In that tongue, you "drink" your cigarets or whatever.

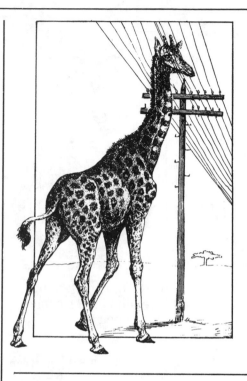

MOST common cause of power outages in Nigeria is the giraffe — which usually knows enough to duck under electric lines but forgets when spooked.

SOME antique car owners in England still celebrate the great leap forward of 1896 — when London repealed the rule that every car on the road be preceded by a man with a red flag.

•

THAT a fruit fly beats its wings 13,000 times a minute is also astonishing, what?

LATEST REPORTS indicate the French trains have now overtaken the Japanese trains as the world's fastest. Japanese at best, 112.3 mph. French at best, 134 mph.

•

ANCIENT MEN painted their mouths red before they went into battle, according to the old Babylonian writings.

THERE ARE as many molecules in a teaspoonful of water as there are teaspoonsful of water in the Atlantic Ocean.

•

THE BONES in a horse outnumber the bones in a man by 216 to 206.

•

SIR, WHEN do you brush your teeth? Just before breakfast is said to be the time of day when that chore does you the least good.

•

THE GREAT Soviet Encyclopedia claims 58 million World War II bombs and artillery shells were found in the Soviet Union and disposed of between 1945 and 1972.

•

TURNS OUT Maryland is not the only state with an official state sport (jousting), after all. Alaska's official state sport is dog-sledding.

PEANUTS make you fat and tobacco makes you cough, and they're the only two crops left completely protected by the U.S. government.

ANSWER DEPT.

Q. "HOW COME so many Navajo Indians limp?" A. A painful arthritic condition — so common among them it's not regarded as a disease — caused by a congenital dislocation of the hip.

Q. "WASN'T TV's Diane Sawyer a Miss America winner?" A. Not that one. She won America's Junior Miss contest in 1963 at the age of 17.

•

Q. "HOW MUCH money do people lose every year in the Atlantic City casinos?" A. Last year — $1.95 billion, however much that is.

Q. "ASK YOUR Chief Prognosticator if break dancing will still be in vogue 20 years from now?" A. He expects it to shuttle in and out much in the manner of tap dancing.

•

Q. "WHO WAS the first licensed pilot to occupy the White House?" A. Dwight Eisenhower.

MAGPIES hold funerals. When one dies, the others ceremoniously fly over, and each in turn swoops to peck once at the dead. Macabre, maybe, but there's a purpose. Bird scholars say the ritual resets the pecking order of the flock.

•

ONE middle-aged American man in every four is called John, William, James, Charles or George.

•

AMONG DOGS, too, the male is more difficult to housebreak.

•

EVEN IF you put together all the amateurs who play softball, tennis and golf, the bowlers would still outnumber them.

•

THOSE WHO band birds now say they've learned that many migratory birds each season go back not only to the same tree they left the previous year, but to the same branch.

•

YOU'RE NOT old enough to remember when "villain" meant "farm hand" and "silly" meant "innocent." And neither am I.

Q. "WHICH IS an 'oculist' — an 'ophthalmologist' or an 'optometrist'?" A. Either.

ITEM NO. 833C in our Love and War Man's file is Leonardo da Vinci's definition of marriage: "Putting one's hands into a bag of snakes in the hope of pulling out an eel."

•

SOUTHEAST ASIANS for centuries stashed pairs of pearls in the belief they'd mate to make more pearls.

•

NAMES OF more than 150 racehorses start with "Dr."

ONLY HISTORICAL figure whose birthday is a legal holiday in all 50 of the United States is George Washington.

•

THE HIGHER the altitude, the lower the cancer rate.

•

A BIG JET plane burns more fuel in taxiing from ramp to runway than a Goodyear-type blimp needs to fly eight hours a day for nearly a week.

THE "COCO" in coconut comes from the Portuguese word for "grimace." To some, the coconut looked like a contorted face, evidently.

•

ORDER broccoli in England and what do you get? Cauliflower.

•

ONE TYPE of cockroach — the brown-branded roach — loves TV. No, it doesn't watch. It eats the insulation.

•

SEATTLE LAW says you can't carry a concealed weapon that's more than six feet long.

•

WHAT the Japanese call "an Americanburger" is a soybean patty laced with chicken strips served on a bun.

•

TRADITIONAL Japanese wash themselves thoroughly before they get into their baths.

ANSWER DEPT.

Q. "HOW MUCH do psychiatrists charge these days?" A. $90 an hour is the nationwide median.

MONKEYS have no feet. Technically, they're classified as "four-handed."

Q. "WHERE'S the most expensive hotel suite in the world?" A. Believe that would have to be the penthouse atop the Grand Hotel on Paradise Island in the Bahamas — at $10,000 per night.

•

Q. "IS ENGLISH the native language of any South American country?" A. Only one — Guyana.

Q. "SAYS HERE newborn babies are 'legally blind.' What's that mean?" A. Vision no better than 20/500.

•

Q. "WHO WERE the lifelong famous lovers who never saw each other naked?" A. Robert and Elizabeth Browning, the poets who left sufficient footnotes to allow that report.

IF TODAY is typical, before it's over more than 8000 Americans will become pregnant without meaning to do so.

•

RUSSIANS don't chew gum.

•

THOSE SCIENTISTS who daily check out particles in the air over Hawaii — there are a few, occasionally — can tell when the farmers in China start to plow.

•

TO BUY a new car in Norway, the buyer needs 80 percent cash.

•

BELGIAN shrimpers used to fish on horseback, trawling their nets through the knee-deep surf. A few still do.

•

MOST ANIMALS mate in daylight. Most birds, too. Will check out reptiles and report back. Stand by.

•

THE CAST-IRON dome of the Capitol in Washington, D.C., heats up with the sun. It's like a sunflower. It moves three, maybe four inches as the sun moves.

SIR, by the time you reach 70, if you're typical, both the tip of your nose and your earlobes will have dropped half an inch.

ADELIE PENGUINS are bulimics — they gorge, regurgitate and gorge again.

•

IF SOMEBODY around your scatter does a ton of laundry a year, that's typical.

•

IF IT'S a sardine, it could be pritnear any little fish that gets caught. There's no one sardine species.

THE ENGLISH of the upper class 100 years ago always served two kinds of food on white napkins: asparagus and ice cream.

•

ROSES GO BACK further than people.

•

DREDGERS over a 14-year period haul more crud out of the Suez Canal than the original diggers dug up to make it.

NOBODY REALLY knows — to this day — whether Jack the Ripper was a man or a woman.

•

EVERY SEVENTH bird worldwide is a finch.

•

IN GREECE half the dentists are women.

•

ONLY FOUR people, and not a one of them a close personal friend, showed up at the Baltimore funeral of poet Edgar Allan Poe.

•

YOU LOSE more hair — if you have any left to lose — in November than in any other month.

•

THE VISION of a honeybee at rest is blurred. The vision of a honeybee on the wing is clear.

•

WHERE'D YOU get the notion that "Lucifer" was another name for the Devil? Nothing in the Bible says that.

•

WHEN YOU SAY "Uncle Ben was oryzivorous," you mean he ate rice, that's all.

WHAT WE now call "light beer" was known as "small beer" in the Middle Ages, and the historical footnotes aver it was the drink of the lower classes.

ANSWER DEPT.

Q. "HOW COME poor country folks in Georgia are called 'crackers'?" A. Some early Georgia settlers were jail breakers from the North, and jail breakers long ago were called "crackers."

•

Q. "THE THREE largest islands in the world are Greenland, New Guinea and Borneo. What's the fourth?" A. Madagascar.

Q. "DID AMERICA'S first sheep come over with Columbus?" A. No, they showed up 48 years after his first trip here.

•

Q. "WHY ARE vultures bald?" A. They push their heads into places where feathers would get messy.

•

Q. "IS IT TRUE the legendary Babe Ruth was a bartender once?" A. More than once. Quite true.

DID YOU spend 1 hour, 47 minutes doing nothing yesterday? That's said to be an average for Americans.

•

A FRENCHMAN who writes a bad check — knowingly or not — is barred by law from use of his checking account for a year.

•

A U.S. SUPREME Court session runs from 10 a.m. to 2:30 p.m.

•

MORE AND MORE lone fathers are bringing up their own children. About a million do so now. That's 65 percent more than in 1970.

•

OYSTERS HAVE 20 times more cholesterol than eggs.

•

CAGED PARROTS outnumber caged canaries now.

•

ONE THING you can say for July — it's the month when the fewest people catch cold.

•

MEN WORE toupees before women wore lipstick.

A 25-POUND turkey has 4000 feathers. Not precisely 4000. But around there.

KOREAN WOMEN don't change their names after marriage, either.

•

AM TOLD it's still true that Parker Brothers has manufactured more money for "Monopoly" than the U.S. Treasury has produced in its entire history.

•

REMEMBER, it takes three feet of sugar cane to make one lump of sugar.

•

OBSERVED Edna St. Vincent Millay: "It's not true that life is one damn thing after another — it's one damn thing over and over."

THE PRICE of prostitution is up in Nevada, correspondents report, with $150 an hour not untypical.

•

CURIOUS, is it not, that our word "matinee" — a show we see in the afternoon — comes from the French word for "morning"?

•

OUR Language Man says a third of all the writing in English is made up of these 25 small words: The, and, a, too, of, I, in, was, that, it, he, you, for, had, is, with, she, has, on, at, have, but, me, my, not.

ONE SURGEON in 10 wants music piped into the operating room.

•

TYPICAL Argentinian eats twice as much meat every year as does the typical U.S. citizen.

•

THAT RARITY known as the native Californian will tell you Santa Monica was a film center before Hollywood. So was Long Beach. Likewise Culver City.

•

NEITHER ancient Greece nor old Rome — those cradles of civilization — had anything like a university.

•

THE SPANISH word for "words" is "palabras," and it was a corruption thereof that gave us our word "palaver."

•

SAWYERS in this country on any given day knock down about 1000 trees for telephone poles.

ANSWER DEPT.

Q. "WHO WAS the first daily newspaper columnist?" A. Eugene Field. Worked for the old Chicago Daily News.

"KNUCKLE" used to mean "knee joint." And falling to one's knees in subservience was the origin of that expression "knuckle under."

Q. "WAS THERE ever a United States of South America?" A. Sort of. Simon Bolivar's Gran Colombia lasted eight years, but was dismembered finally into Venezuela, Colombia and Ecuador.

Q. "IF THE FIRST pilot's license was issued to Glenn Curtiss in 1911, then the Wright brothers' flight in 1903 was illegal, right?" A. Not right. No law covered the matter except the Law of Gravity, and it wasn't illegal — just stupid — to break that one.

•

Q. "WHAT WAS the second sentence uttered by astronaut Neil Armstrong after first setting foot on the moon?" A. "The surface is fine and powdery."

•

Q. "WHY DID the Scottish Parliament in 1457 outlaw the game of golf?" A. Thought it would detract from archery, a sport the Scots thought doubled as their civil defense.

•

Q. "WHAT WORD becomes shorter when you add two letters to it?" A. Short.

•

Q. "WHAT'S the world's largest manufacturer of cameras?" A. Timex. For Polaroid.

•

Q. "THE 180th meridian makes up most of the International Date Line. How many roads cross it?" A. Only one — on Taveuni in the Fiji Islands.

AT LEAST 200 Americans claim they own the pistol that killed Abe Lincoln.

•

IT'S SAID that half of all U.S. women have had hysterectomies by age 65.

•

WHITE PEOPLE have more eye trouble than black people.

•

A SEVENTH of Ireland is bog.

•

OUR CALENDAR still isn't perfect — it errs by one day every 4000 years.

•

IN THE APE language created by Edgar Rice Burroughs, "tar" meant "white" and "zan" meant "skin" — ergo, "Tarzan."

•

NINE OUT OF 10 businesses in this country are family-owned.

•

EACH EYE of a pineapple puts out one pale blue flower that blooms only a day. It's not a single fruit, the pineapple, but a cluster of fruits.

DEER LOVE chewing gum.

MAHATMA GANDHI said: "To the millions who have to go without two meals a day, the only acceptable form in which God dare appear is food."

•

LATEST PRICE on grown gorillas: $85,000 each.

•

ONLY 1.2 percent of India's entire population lives in Bombay, but that group alone pays a third of the country's taxes. It's not fair. I'd move.

•

NEW BOOK on the market: "Sex as a Sublimation for Tennis." What do you make of that?

ARTISTS, not writers, put wings on angels. The Bible has these spiritual creatures flying around, but it doesn't say anything about wings.

•

SONGS of whales rhyme.

•

LOT OF PEOPLE wish they had blue eyes, evidently. It's the most popular color sold to the buyers of colored contact lenses.

•

YOU CAN SQUEEZE about half a gallon of oil out of one shark liver. That's not so much, really. The liver is the only place where a shark stores its fat.

THE FOUR largest Moslem nations in the world are Indonesia, Pakistan, Bangladesh and India. What's the fifth? Say the Soviet Union.

•

RAINDROPS won't form in perfectly unpolluted air. Without rain, no grass. Without grass, no people. We owe a lot to pollution.

•

LONDON to New York City is a three-hour flight by Concorde. By the clock, you get there two hours before you leave.

•

TO GET the weight of your skin, divide your body weight by 16.

•

TO WASH your underwear in your birdbath is specifically outlawed in Duncan, Okla.

•

THE WEATHER, always eastbound, travels faster in the winter than in the summer.

ANSWER DEPT.

Q. "ONE SOUND is common to all the languages in the world. What is it?" A. "A" as in "father."

DID YOU BLOW your nose 256 times last year? That's typical, say the Kleenex makers.

Q. "IS IT NOT true that human sweat glands exude no odor?" A. Not quite true. But you can say the sweat glands that develop at puberty are the only ones that exude an odor.

•

Q. "WHY IS a brindled cat called a 'tabby'?" A. Originally alluded to a mottled brown and yellow silk from the Attabiyah quarter of Baghdad.

Q. "WHERE'D WE get the phrase 'tit for tat'?" A. From the Dutch "dit vor dat" meaning "this for that."

•

Q. "WHAT'S the name of the highest lake in the world?" A. Has no name. But it's in Tibet.

•

Q. "ISN'T the Cape of Good Hope the southernmost tip of Africa?" A. No, sir, Cape Agulhas, 90 miles away, is 32 miles farther south.

•

Q. "WHERE'S the stormiest place on earth?" A. Bay of Bengal, I'd guess. Seven of the 10 most destructive storms ever recorded hit there.

•

Q. "HOW MANY U.S. presidents died broke?" A. At least four. Thomas Jefferson, James Monroe, William Henry Harrison and U.S. Grant. Maybe more.

•

Q. "WHAT'S the epitaph on William Shakespeare's tomb?" A. "Cursed be he that moves my bones."

•

Q. "WHAT ANIMALS in the zoos draw the most people?" A. The big cats.

HERE'S another day in America, so it is, and another 2800 teenagers are getting pregnant.

•

MORE PEOPLE speak Chinese, but people in more places speak English.

•

UP BEFORE the Maryland legislators is a proposal to license birdwatchers. What will happen there if you're caught watching birds without a license?

•

ALASKANS are particularly fond of flowers, evidently. Florists there sell more of same per capita than florists in any other state.

•

WOULD YOU like a llama for a household pet? About 4000 Americans possess one of same.

•

OLD ROMAN socks had toes.

•

FOURTH MOST used language in the United States is sign language.

PEOPLE WHO exercise regularly are better decision makers than people who don't. Or so says a Purdue University professor who has studied the matter.

A BILLION minutes ago Christ walked in Galilee. A billion dollars ago was 10.3 hours ago in Washington, D.C.

•

YOU SAY you didn't know Donald Duck had a middle name? Indeed. Fauntleroy.

•

RESEARCHERS SAY sea lions are smarter than dogs. But not much.

OVER THE ARCTIC, reflections from the sea sometimes distort the light in the sky, so the sun looks square.

•

DID I TELL you a rhino's horn grows three inches a year?

•

OVERHEARD: "There will be prayer in public schools, law or no law, as long as there are final exams."

THE RUSSIAN name for Sunday is "Resurrection."

•

POSTED IN the Banco de Ponce in New York City: "Attention, would-be robbers — this is a Spanish-speaking bank. If you intend to rob us, please be patient for we might need an interpreter. Thank you. The Management."

•

THE TYPICAL cockroach spends more time cleaning itself than does the typical cat.

•

A FRIEND to everybody is nobody's real friend. Who said that?

•

YOU SEE pictures of birds catching fish. You don't see pictures of fish catching birds. Fish do, though. Muskies, pike, European catfish — they lie along the surface and catch the skimming birds.

•

A "DACTYLOGRAM" is a fingerprint.

•

THE BEST routes westward across North America were selected by bison — none of which possessed an engineering degree.

THE CIVIL War was the last in which American generals personally led their troops into battle.

ALLIGATORS grow 8 inches a year.

ANSWER DEPT.

Q. "WHAT'S the average annual temperature worldwide?" A. 58° F.

•

Q. "WHAT animal has the longest horns?" A. The sable of Africa. They grow 5 feet, arcing toward the rear.

Q. "WHY ARE 'cairn' terriers called that?" A. In Scotland, a "cairn" is a rock pile. Earliest of those little hunting dogs were adept at diving into rock piles after foxes and wildcats.

•

Q. "WHERE would I have to go to see the most hummingbirds?" A. Ecuador — the world's hummingbird mecca with 163 species.

•

Q. "WHEN the spitting cobra of Africa spurts its venom into the eyes of a victim from 7 feet away, doesn't it blind that victim?" A. For about a day, it does.

•

Q. "ROBERT Chesebrough at age 22 discovered petroleum jelly and reportedly swallowed a teaspoonful of it every day of his life thereafter, claiming it was the secret of his good health. How long did he live?" A. To 96.

•

Q. "DID YOU say an ant has five noses? Why?" A. Each nose is designated to pick a different odor, that's all I know.

•

Q. "WHO invented felt?" A. A herdsman in Outer Mongolia, as insulation for the circular tent called the "ger."

MONKS in medieval Europe devoutly believed they had to pray at specific times each day to protect their souls. This one fact is said to have had much to do with the development of modern clocks.

•

ADMIRAL Lord Nelson, killed at the Battle of Trafalgar in 1805, was shipped back to London for burial, preserved in a cask of rum.

•

SOUTH AMERICA'S Paraguay uses paper money only, no coins.

•

YOU SAY you thought the hummingbird was the only bird that could fly backwards? So did I. But numerous sightings have been reported of the Abyssinian Blue Goose flying backwards.

•

IT WAS Mae West who said, "I only go for two types of men: domestic and foreign."

•

NO PLACE in Great Britain is more than 65 miles from the sea.

TWELVE THOUSAND miles is not too far to ship ice. Or it wasn't. Before refrigeration, sailing vessels took block ice from Boston to Calcutta.

ARGUMENT continues over the first waterbeds. Shepherds long ago, it's said, slept on goatskins filled with water, so merit that distinction as the originators.

•

YOU SAY it's your birthday? You and about nine million other people worldwide, then.

•

THAT SHOE known as the oxford was so called for no other reason than that students at Oxford University popularized it around 1910.

ACCORDING TO the reports about new products, you now can buy a T-shirt for your cat.

•

MUSIC-MINDED followers of British royalty note with some satisfaction that Prince Charles can play the banjo and Princess Di can tap dance. Imagine it.

•

THOSE AFFLICTED with high blood pressure learn early that "sausage" derived its name from "salsus," the Latin word for salt.

HOW THE PEUL women of Mali keep their earlobes intact I do not know. They carry their valuables in earrings about the size of purses.

•

IF THE MARRIAGE lasts more than 13 years, it is more likely to end by death than by divorce. So say the oddsmakers.

•

HERE'S ANOTHER physical act recognized in every known society: Shrugging of shoulders means "I give up."

•

IN PARIS, the first thing George Hugo did when he bought his new car was take off the windshield wipers. "That way," he said, "I won't get any tickets."

•

THE WOMEN on payrolls in Japan average about half as much income as the men on payrolls there.

ANSWER DEPT.

Q. "WHY IS a $10 bill called a 'sawbuck'?" A. Such bills used to have an 'X' instead of a '10' on them. You know how the legs of a sawhorse, sometimes called a sawbuck, are shaped like X's. That was the original allusion.

MEN WORE wigs of wool. Muggers yanked the wigs forward so their victims couldn't see. This, long ago in England. It's where we got our phrase, "pull the wool over his eyes."

Q. "ISN'T horse racing this country's most popular spectator sport?" A. Was for 30 years. Not anymore. Baseball has taken over as No. 1. Horse racing is now No. 2. No. 3 is car racing. No. 4, football. No. 5, basketball. No. 6, dog racing.

•

Q. "WHO ARE the most highly paid college professors? How about the most lowly paid?" A. Top, deans of medicine, with the median at $100,-000 a year. Bottom, beginning history instructors at $17,000.

Q. "ONE STATE has more vehicles per square mile, more miles of highway per square mile, and more cars per mile of highway than any other state. Name it." A. New Jersey.

•

Q. "DO ASTRONAUTS get airsick?" A. Two out of five do. They've coined a word for it. Astronausea.

•

Q. "WHICH IS the fastest growing state in the nation? And why?" A. Utah. Highest birth rate.

THE BEST waitresses tend to be good-natured and talkative, though somewhat sardonic. The best waiters are inclined to be serious and taciturn. Such was the consensus of a sizable gathering of restaurateurs in Geneva, Switzerland. They couldn't explain the reason for this difference.

•

RALPH NADER owns neither a car nor a TV set.

•

BILL COLLECTORS say the wife is the paymistress in two out of three American homes.

•

GOLF'S legendary Byron Nelson won 18 tour events in 1945, and earned $63,336. The PGA's top money winner, Hal Sutton, won two in 1983 and earned $426,668.

•

AREN'T ANY dry-cleaning shops in the Soviet Union, not a one.

•

NOW SLIGHTLY more than half the pharmacy students are women.

DURING the last 50 years in the Western world, somebody has killed somebody else on an average of every 20 seconds.

FOURTEEN out of every 100 wives are older than their husbands.

•

MEDIAN AGE for all U.S. military personnel is 25.

•

DON'T FORGET, 96 out of every 100 babies are born head first.

•

AMERICAN hotelkeepers say only one guest in five unpacks the suitcases.

THERE ARE albino snakes, too.

•

STILL TRYING to figure out how to make your fortune? Nothing to it. Find something profitable to make out of used disposable diapers. They now account for more than 5 percent of the solid trash in garbage dumps.

•

A FOURTH of Los Angeles's land is for cars.

THERE are six widows for every widower.

•

THAT U.S. STATE with the most Indians — Oklahoma — has no Indian reservations.

•

REMEMBER, that woman is a "philematophobe" if she hates to be kissed. The word is rarely used.

•

SOUTH AFRICA executes at least 50 people a year, sometimes a lot more. In 1978, for instance, that country put to death 132. Of these, one was white.

•

ASK YOUR family mathematician to prove there are more inches in a square mile than seconds in a century.

ANSWER DEPT.

Q. "WHAT proportion of the murders go unsolved now?" A. 28 percent.

•

Q. "WHAT TURNS green when sunburnt?" A. Carrots? Potatoes? Turnips? They do that.

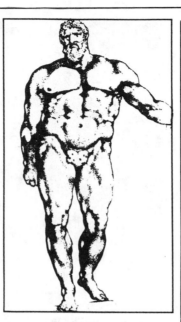

YOU'RE NOT bragging, sir, when you claim you're a mass of muscle. Forty-three percent of you is muscle, in fact, and that's quite a mass, no?

Q. "HOW LONG overall has this country been run by presidents who weren't actually elected to be president?" A. 23 years, 324 days.

Q. "CAN YOU live without sugar?" A. Without manufactured sugar, certainly. For centuries humans have done so. It has been commonly available only for the last 100 years, about.

•

Q. "WHO WAS the last prisoner kept in the infamous Tower of London?" A. That was Rudolf Hess of Germany during World War II.

•

Q. "NAME the only world heavyweight boxing champion to retire without ever having lost a professional fight?" A. Rocky Marciano.

•

Q. "WHERE'S the world's most expensive land?" A. Has to be London. Some goes for $6000 a square foot.

•

Q. "WHAT proportion of rape victims were acquainted with their assailants before the attack?" A. 48 percent, according to one set of police statistics.

•

Q. "WHAT ARE the seven ingredients of that drink known as a 'Zombie'?" A. Rum, rum, rum, rum, rum, rum and rum.

THAT STATE wherein are sold the most padded bras is California.

•

ONLY ONE in five suicides leaves a note.

•

THE HUMAN male is not the only one who sends orchids to the object of his affection, please note. Male bees attract sex partners with orchid fragrance.

•

FAR MORE dogs than cats are obese.

•

DURING World War II, only about 1 percent of all Japanese soldiers in the South Pacific ever surrendered. Many were killed in action, and suicides accounted for many, too.

•

GOURMETS SAY the female lobster tastes much better than the male.

•

A PREPONDERANCE of the servicemen who undergo courts martial are tattooed, studies have shown.

Q. "DOESN'T a woman's hair grow faster than a man's?" A. Appreciably.

EVIDENCE indicates a person tends to dream in sleep more during electrical storms.

•

FIGURE 6.6 percent of all men are left-handed. Only 3.8 percent of all women are left-handed. Why this difference?

•

IN BIRMINGHAM, Ala., lives a man named Ash Wednesday.

•

"DOES HE love me . . . or does he not? . . . He told me once . . . but I forgot." Who first wrote the foregoing? Although the untitled four-liner has been credited to various latter-day wits, it was written, in fact, about 100 years ago, and researchers can't identify the author.

•

THE AVERAGE smoker who quits can be expected to gain only 3.7 pounds.

•

THE 17-YEAR-OLD girl

spends more money on shoes than does the woman in any other age bracket, according to the market researchers.

•

WHY TV's "Dallas" succeeded so spectacularly in West Germany but bombed in Japan is another entertainment mystery.

•

RESEARCHERS explain how they know the sailfish at 70 mph is the fastest of all game fish: When hooked, they take the line out that fast.

•

THE MEDICAL sex change from female to male is said to be simpler than the change from male to female.

•

YES, SIR, sailors aboard ship can feel earthquakes, definitely.

•

AUSTRALIANS are raising square pineapples now.

•

ONE OUT OF every five men over age 50 eventually undergoes a prostate operation.

•

SOMEBODY STEALS a car

SEVEN out of 10 spectacles wearers keep their glasses on almost all the time they're awake.

every five minutes in New York City.

•

CURRENT THEORY is that jealousy is an inherited trait.

ANSWER DEPT.

Q "CAN YOUR ears be stretched permanently out of shape?" A. That they can, say the medicos. Much of the ear is cartilage. It continues to grow throughout your lifetime. Extremely heavy earrings dangled from pierced lobes eventually can give a woman a sort of spaniel look.

•

Q. "IS THE capital of Missouri written St. Louis or Saint Louis?" A. Nice try, young fellow. It's written Jefferson City.

•

Q. "WHERE DOES Megan rank now on that list of the most popular names for girls?" A. It's No. 10. Behind: No. 1, Jennifer. No. 2, Ann. No. 3, Jessica. No. 4, Karen. No. 5, Michelle. No. 6, Katherine. No. 7, Rebecca. No. 8, Deborah. And No. 9, Robin.

•

Q. "ISN'T 'E.T.' dead?" A. The actor, Michael Patrick Bilon, who played the character in major parts of that film is now deceased, yes.

•

Q. "LOUIE, YOU say you like bowling better than golf? Why?" A. Lose fewer balls.

•

Q. "WHAT'S IN that mixed drink called a '57 T-Bird'?" A. A half shot of vodka, a touch of amaretto, a little triple sec and a squirt of lemon juice.

WHY THE young ladies in women's colleges drink more hard liquor than the coeds in universities I do not know, but researchers say that's a fact.

•

IN WICHITA, KANS., it is specifically against the law for a father to brandish a gun in the presence of his daughter's boyfriend.

•

AIRLINE SEATS are designed to fit men who stand between 5-feet-7 and 6 feet and who weigh between 162 and 208 pounds.

•

YOU'LL BLINK your eyes intermittently anyhow, but such is the power of suggestion that you'll blink them a few extra times while reading this paragraph. No?

•

YOU KNOW that cervical collar worn by neck-injury patients? It's said to prevent snoring.

•

THE LADY is typical if her routine calls for her to walk four miles a year around the household beds while making up same.

I AM SORRY MY DEAR, BUT OUR *GRAVEST FEARS* SEEM TO BE CONFIRMED... A *FILTHY* SPECK OF **DUST!**

THE LATE Howard Hughes and numerous others have been depicted as highly fearful of dust. Client asks if there's a name for that irrational dread. There is. Amathophobia.

THIS APPLIES whether the party is a man or a woman: A strongly masculine personality, when looking across the room, will stare directly. A strongly feminine personality will let the glance wander. Such is the report of the hidden-camera researchers.

•

NOBODY KNOWS who invented eyeglasses.

WHY IS IT the young ladies along the Pacific Coast wear out fewer pairs of stockings than do the girls on the Atlantic Seaboard? A hose maker reports that. But without explanation.

•

A GOOD POKER player won't bluff more than once every 15 hands, according to some card-game experts.

CINCINNATI was regarded as the most beautiful city in America by both Winston Churchill and Charles Dickens.

•

THE WINNERS of Miss America contests, with few exceptions, tend to gain weight right after they win the title.

•

NO WONDER the reindeer is such a good swimmer. Each hair on its body is as hollow as waterwings.

•

WHEN Japanese fishermen started using pink nets a few years ago, they boosted their catches by 60 percent, but the why of it is still a mystery to the fisherfolk.

•

AM TOLD a duck's quack never makes an echo.

•

THE STANDARD eight-minute marriage ceremony in Leningrad's Palace of Weddings costs the equivalent of $1.65.

•

YES, it does happen from time to time that a snail kills a garter snake.

A SOCIOLOGIST'S recent studies proved to him that among all U.S. white-collar workers male newspaper photographers were the sloppiest dressers.

ANSWER DEPT.

Q. "WHAT PROPORTION of the sex crimes are committed by married men?" A. About 26 percent of those on record. And 60 percent by single men. And 14 percent by men separated, divorced or widowed.

•

Q. "WHO FIRST invented the actuarial tables upon which insurance companies base their premiums?" A. Same fellow who discovered that renowned comet bearing his name, Edmund Halley.

•

Q. "YOU SAID the original Siamese twins, Chang and Eng, quarrelled all the time. About what? Their matrimonial life? Their occupations?" A. Not those. They married sisters, together fathered 20 children, and made a living by renting themselves out for public appearances. But Chang liked his liquor and Eng was a teetotaler. Never could they reconcile the wet and the dry. That's what frustrated them.

•

Q. "WHAT'S THE average salary now of grade school teachers?" A. $16,879.

•

Q. "WASN'T IT Thackeray who said, 'Heaven will be no heaven to me if I do not meet my wife there'?" A. No, sir, Andrew Jackson said that. Thackeray said, "Remember, it is as easy to marry a rich woman as a poor woman."

TOTAL WORLD population of that species known as the Wyoming toad is thought to be two — one male, one female. Stand by for an update.

•

HOW CAN you call yourself a student of the Bible if you don't know how many people were aboard Noah's Ark? Say eight.

•

CLAIM IS 1000 basic words make up 90 percent of all writing.

•

UNIVERSITY tuitions in Canada, typically, run about half as much as those in the United States.

•

OUR CHIEF Prognosticator says we'll soon see motorized supermarket carts, but he doesn't say why.

•

UNDERSTAND one book publisher is about to put out a volume on deceptive practices of veterinarians. It's called "Animal Quackers."

•

TWO MONTHS' salary, at least, is said to be what the

HISTORY'S most famous elephant, P.T. Barnum's Jumbo of the last century, frequently was medicated with two gallons of whiskey a day. Sounds like some of Barnum's bunk, what? But no, that fact is from keepers' records.

typical boyfriend now spends to buy his girlfriend a diamond ring.

•

OUR LANGUAGE Man says only four words in the English language end in the letters "efy." Can you prove him wrong? Start with "stupefy," "liquefy," "putrefy" and "rarefy."

•

GASOLINE in South Korea costs $3.76; in Saudi Arabia, 13 cents. Those are the price extremes worldwide.

MIAMI UNIVERSITY in Florida gives cash bonuses for top grades, I'm told. That seems strange, does it not?

•

CALIFORNIA LAW says no pet gerbils unless you want to experiment on them in a laboratory. When loose in desert country, they devastate crops.

•

TOYMAKERS WATCH the divorce rate. When it rises, so do toy sales. Four parents and eight grandparents tend to compete, though subtly maybe, for a child's affection, so buy toys.

ANSWER DEPT.

Q. "WHEN DID the legal idea of alimony get started?" A. Little more than a century ago. In 1857, to be exact. The British Matrimonial Causes Act proclaimed a husband's legal responsibility went on after a marriage ended. Before then, a husband could take off or turn his wife out, either way, without paying anything.

•

Q. "IN TEMPERATURE, what's 'absolute zero'?" A. The point at which all molecules stop moving because of the intense cold. In centigrade, it's minus 273 degrees.

A HIPPOLIMNAS MISSIPPUS AND A SIDE OF FRIES!

BUTTERFLIES are cannibals.

Q. "DID YOU ever see an eclipse of a new moon?" A. Won't bite on that one, sir. Any moon that isn't full is eclipsed.

•

Q. "THE WORD 'news' was coined from the points of the compass, right?" A. In effect. More specifically, some early U.S. newspapers ran drawings of the globe in their mastheads, and those drawings carried the N, E, W and S designations, to indicate their reports came from all directions.

Q. "DOESN'T ALASKA have four time zones?" A. Not anymore. In November of 1983 it changed to two, Alaska time and Bering time, one and two hours earlier than Pacific time.

•

Q. "THAT PUBLIC television program called 'Nova' — what's the title mean?" A. "New" in Latin.

•

Q. "WHAT'S the world's safest train?" A. A monorail called the Schwebebahn in Wuppertal, West Germany. It has carried more than 1.3 million passengers since 1901 without a serious accident.

•

Q. "THAT FAMOUS sporting-goods store — L.L. Bean in Freeport, Maine — has stayed open all night every night since 1951, except on the occasions of a fire across the street and two funerals. One was for John F. Kennedy. For whom was the other?" A. L. L. Bean.

•

Q. "IS BOB HOPE — as I've read — a university professor?" A. Not quite. His 40-plus honorary degrees don't qualify him for that. However, he did take on the pleasant chore this spring of teaching four comedy courses at Southern Methodist University.

IT'S ESTIMATED the average person speaks 31,500 words a day. That's only about a third as many words as there are hairs on the scalp of the average red-head. It's about a third as many, too, as the number of words in a typical paperback novel.

•

NEW YORK CITY'S Broadway started out as Bloomingdale Road.

•

STUDENTS, hear this: To rule that you can't pass notes in class is a violation of your constitutional right to free speech. Or so decreed the State Department of Public Instruction in Iowa. Pupils in that state, therefore, can pass such notes at will.

•

SCORPION MILK is worth $2800 a gram now. For vaccine research. But it's hard to get. Not that there aren't plenty of scorpions. There are. But scorpion milkers are scarce.

•

A BRITISH medical journal published this treatment for the common cold in 1841: "Nail a hat on the wall near the foot of your bed, then retire to that bed, and drink spirits until you see two hats."

ALASKA'S Anchorage recorded a snowfall during the winter of 1982-83 exactly half the 142 inches that fell in Arizona's Flagstaff.

WHY ONLY 43 percent of the Americans polled say they'd never eat snails is hard to figure.

•

DO YOU daydream as much as 35 percent of your waking hours? Researchers say most do.

•

TO WAX your car 2.5 times a year is average, too.

•

IN MOST of the native tongues of the West Indies, there is no word for weather, I'm told.

SALE OF hearing aids has gone up by 40 percent since President Reagan started wearing one.

•

IN THE 1830s, a patent medicine sold well under the name of "Dr. Miles' Compound Extract of Tomato." It was ketchup.

•

IT WAS ONLY in the most recent decade that a Rhode Island legislator proposed that a $2 tax be levied in that state on every act of physical romance.

CONSIDER ex-convicts who don't have the experience to resume a special line of work. What sorts of jobs do they apply for, mostly? A study of this matter turned up one occupation in particular that interests most: private security guard.

ANSWER DEPT.

Q. "IS IT TRUE that bagpipe players clean their bagpipes with Scotch whisky?" A. That's the story. They season the bag by pouring Scotch plus a teaspoonful of honey as well as egg whites into the sheepskin air sack to keep it moist.

●

Q. "THE NAME, please, of that Antarctic bird that intentionally defecates on people — isn't it The Dogwalker?" A. No, the skua — but you make a nice point.

●

Q. "WHAT'S 'Twi-Fante'?" A. A language spoken by more than 5 million West Africans.

●

Q. "WHAT'S the leading cause of death now in the military?" A. Drunk driving.

TOOK our Language Man 20 years to learn how to spell "exacerbate" and another 20 to pronounce it. That's just too much. The word isn't worth it.

Q. "DO FORMER professional football players tend to live longer than other people?" A. No, on the contrary. Average age of death among the ex-pros is 58.

●

Q. "MEDICAL statisticians have proved it's not the poor but the rich who are most likely to die of exotic ailments. Why?" A. They travel more.

Q. "DO BATS mate in flight?" A. Only if in a hurry.

●

Q. "WHY WAS the spelling of Ohio's Cleveland changed from the original Cleaveland?" A. None other than the Smithsonian reports that was the work of a headline writer who needed to cram it into a one-column width.

IN THAT matter of color preferences, most men like blues and greens while most women like reds and yellows. Testers learned this while studying the fingerpaintings of hospital patients.

●

ONLY MEN and ants wage war in battle formations.

●

IT'S EVIDENTLY instinctive in elephants to put out fires. When a herd comes across an unattended campfire, at least one charges the blaze to stamp it out.

●

THE MOTHER with three or more children tends to live longer than the mother with an only child. Statistically.

●

HALF THE bounced checks pay for liquor.

●

WAS LONG thought that the man is more adventurous than the woman. Researchers know, however, that more women than men migrate from city to city in search of whatever.

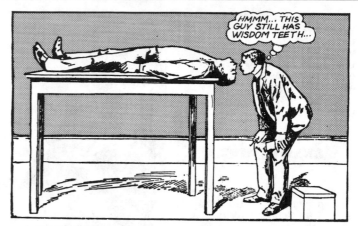

HMMM... THIS GUY STILL HAS WISDOM TEETH...

NEXT PHYSICAL thing the human species will lose because of evolution will be the wisdom teeth. After that, the little toes. Or so contend the anthropologists.

THAT WORD "whingding" started out as standard nomenclature among addicts for a fit induced by drugs.

●

GENIUSES tend to be much shorter or much taller than average.

●

A "TEASEL" is a prickly little flower that grows in Oregon, New York State and France. Textile people use it to raise the nap on wool cloth. To "tease" your hair comes from that.

THAT SWAN will live 50 years, probably.

●

IS HERPES unknown in Finland? A recently arrived Finnish client, who has not researched the matter scientifically, believes such to be the case. He suspects high-temperature saunas can be credited.

●

IF SHE HAD 135 labor pains with her first baby, she was typical in that one matter.

U.S. POSTAL Service employees are entitled by law to an hour and a half for lunch.

•

"KAKISTOCRACY" is the fancy word for "government by the worst people in the society." You don't hear it much, curiously.

•

HOW TO FIND a dropped contact lens: Darken the room. Shine a flashlight over the floor. The lens will reflect a sparkle.

•

THE WORD "autopsy" comes from the Greek "to see for one's self."

ANSWER DEPT.

Q. "WHAT ANIMALS, besides humans and porcupines, mate face to face?" A. Making a list? Add whales and dolphins.

•

Q. "CAN YOU come up with the most common sports injury?" A. Sprained ankle.

•

Q. "WHAT DO the military mean when they speak of combat deaths by 'misadventure'?" A. That's when combatants kill their own men by accident.

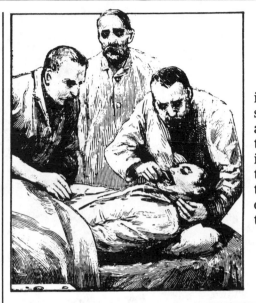

AM ASKED if there's any such a thing as an artificial tongue. There is. It's rare, though. Fewer than 10 Americans are known to wear same.

Q. "MANKIND makes up what proportion of the earth's living things?" A. An estimated 0.00000000000000000000013 percent.

•

Q. "THE SWEDES like red vodka. Where does the red come from?" A. Scarlet peppers.

•

Q. "WHAT'S THE most people ever killed in a tornado?" A. 689. On March 18, 1925. It cut from Missouri to Indiana.

Q. "DIDN'T Roy Rogers once make a gay movie?" A. What's a gay movie? In 1952, he starred in a film called "The Gay Ranchero." But it had nothing to do with sexual preferences.

•

Q. "HOW MANY rivets in a pair of Levi's jeans?" A. Six now. First of same had 501 rivets. Incidentally, the average family is said to own 13 pairs of variously brand-named blue jeans.

THE NUMBER of female eggs necessary to propagate the entire next generation of the human race could be contained within a hen's eggshell.

•

CLAIM IS the niftiest of the piano players can get 200 different sounds out of one piano key, depending on finger stroke and foot pedal.

•

CONSIDER those girls between ages 10 and 14 in Nepal — 13.86 percent of them are married.

•

YOU NEED about 10 hours to walk through the 23-acre maze of New York City's American Museum of Natural History.

•

SICK HORSES don't kick people.

•

SO STEEP are the terraced vineyards on the Italian Riviera, the grape pickers at work dangle in rope slings.

•

SIX MILES an hour is a fairly average speed for a polar bear out for a 100-mile swim.

IN SOUTHEAST Asia, you can buy elephant putty. It's used to camouflage the cracks in the hides of elderly elephants so the sellers of same can get higher prices. Old circus hands here know all about it.

THE BEST of the tennis players don't snap their wrists when they serve. They rotate their forearms. Next week, a golf tip, possibly. Don't miss it.

•

MOZZARELLA cheese used to be made only from buffalo milk.

ONLY A FOURTH of the items in the Library of Congress are books.

•

CANAL DIGGERS of The Netherlands divided the city of Amsterdam into about 90 islands connected by 400 bridges.

IN THE 20 years that bracketed the great California Gold Rush of 1849, about 300,-000 wagon-train travelers died on the trail west. From illness, mostly. Only an estimated 362 were killed by Indians.

•

FORTY-FOUR percent of the babies born out of wedlock are the issue of teenage girls.

•

MATRIMONIAL researchers now say about 19 million grownup Americans — divorced, widowed, never wed — say they'll not get married, either never or never again, whichever.

ANSWER DEPT.

Q. "HOW LONG does it take to climb the stairs to the top of the Empire State Building?" A. About two-and-a-half hours, typically.

•

Q. "YOU SAID moose don't mix. Not ever?" A. Only briefly. The female moose bellows to beckon. Males come running. She selects. Moments later, they all go their separate ways. Solitary critters, moose. They don't even hang around with their own gender.

IF YOU CAN predict a nation's financial future by the number of patents awarded to its inventors — and some scholars say this is a good indicator — West Germany can expect rich rewards. It's the country wherein the most independent inventors are applying for patents.

Q. "WHO WAS the model, if any, for the football player depicted on the Heisman Trophy?" A. Its first winner, Jay Berwanger, University of Chicago, 1935.

Q. "NAME THE first menthol cigaret." A. "Spud." Invented in 1925 by one Lloyd "Spud" Hughes of Mingo Junction, Ohio.

•

Q. "HOW BIG is the Great White shark at birth?" A. Nobody knows. No pregnant Great Whites have ever been caught.

•

Q. "HOW MANY Sundays year around won't there be professional football games on TV now?" A. Seven, if all works out.

•

Q. "CHINA IS rapidly running out of pandas, I read. How rapidly?" A. All I know is there's said to be fewer than 1000 left.

•

Q. "DOES ANY state have an 'official dog'?" A. Only Pennsylvania. The Great Dane.

•

Q. "WHAT'S THE most popular soup in America?" A. Chicken noodle.

•

Q. "WHAT'S the Gutenberg Bible printed on?" A. Thin calfskin treated to take ink. Called vellum.

IF THAT female soldier in the U.S. Army wears earrings when in battle fatigues, she's out of uniform.

•

IN GREAT BRITAIN, the televised dart throwing matches, for some peculiar reason, seem to get a much bigger audience than do the televised fishing tournaments.

•

A THIRD of mankind would rather die than eat bacon for breakfast.

•

MORBID MEMO: A seventh of your life is Mondays.

•

THE DOORBELL of California Angels pitcher Tommy John plays "Take Me Out to the Ball Game."

•

ORANGUTANS rape orangutans.

•

POLL-TAKERS now say about 82 percent of the college women nationwide would chuck their career ambitions altogether for the constant affection of a man.

LIONS HAVE to be extremely sexy to perpetuate their kind. Eighty-five percent of the cubs die. And it takes about 1500 matings to produce one litter.

AM TOLD you can buy land is Australia still for less than a nickel an acre.

•

FOUR INFANTS a day are abandoned in the public places of Brazil.

•

FIFTY-THREE rulers in world history have been known as "The Great." It is also true that 49 of them ruled in cold climates, but I'm not sure that signifies.

CREATIVE nomenclature is pretty popular in the horse breeding game, too. In Nevada's Reno, Kathy Knight named her new filly "Knightmare." Not bad, not bad.

•

A CAMBRIDGE researcher says he has proved a sleepless night dulls your mental edge for not just one but at least two days.

•

AVERAGE WAIST measurement of the American woman is 27 inches. That, according to the dressmakers.

AM ASKED to identify the oldest joke known to western man. In the most ancient of Greek records is this: "How do you want me to cut your hair?" inquired a talkative barber. "In silence," replied King Archelaus. That particular Greek civilization didn't survive, understandably.

•

U.S. HOSPITALS import about 6000 nurses a year from the Philippines.

ANSWER DEPT.

Q. "WASN'T ACTRESS Cloris Leachman a Miss America?" A. A contestant, anyway. She was a Miss Chicago.

•

Q. "SAMUEL Langhorne Clemens called himself Mark Twain. What did his wife, Mrs. Clemens, call him?" A. "Youth."

•

Q. "WHAT'S THE greatest love poem of all time?" A. Debatable. A survey of 1500 literary scholars came up with one answer, however. Their choice for that distinction went to A. E. Housman's "Bredon Hill."

Experienced waitresses will tell you that married men are better tippers than unmarried men, and unmarried women are better tippers than married women.

Q. "HOW COME a police van is called a 'paddy wagon'?" A. Alludes to the Irish policemen of yesteryear, so many of whom were affectionately nicknamed Paddy.

Q. "IN THE lingo of the surfers, what's a 'toad'?" A. A deadly dangerous ocean wave. Toad is an acronym for Take Off And Die.

•

Q. "WHERE'S the world's biggest bowling alley?" A. In Japan. The Tokyo World Lanes Bowling Center — 252 lanes.

•

Q. "WHO WAS the first woman to take birth control pills?" A. Name of that experimental subject is not in the record at hand. Can only tell you that one of the first was Adolf Hitler's ladyfriend Eva Braun.

•

Q. "HOW COME the Mona Lisa has no eyebrows?" A. The women of that time in Florence thought it becoming to shave off their eyebrows. It was a cosmetic fad.

•

Q. ISN'T THE word 'geriatrics' new?" A. As new as anybody who's 32 years old. It was coined in 1951.

•

Q. "IS A U.S. Army soldier out of uniform if he carries an umbrella?" A. He is. She isn't.

AM TOLD you won't cry when you peel onions if you whistle while you work.

•

A GAMEMAKER in Norwich, Conn., markets — yes, it's getting orders — one particular jigsaw puzzle with 52,-000 pieces for $60,000.

•

CHLORACNE is a skin condition caused by exposure to dioxins. A chemical company in its literature says it's "not usually disabling but may be fatal."

•

SOVIET WOMEN generally believe that abortion is safer than the pill, correspondents say.

•

IF YOU SAY you've got an "armful" of wood, you're from New England. If you say you've got an "armload" of wood, you're from someplace else. Probably.

•

THE WORLD'S tropical rain forests are being cut down at the rate of 3000 acres per hour, I'm told.

WHEN YOU lightly compress your tongue between your lips and expel air, you damply deliver what's known in the vernacular as a Bronx cheer. It has a highbrow name, too: "a bilabial fricative."

ONLY ONE out of every 20 young athletes who sign professional baseball contracts ever makes it to the majors.

•

MAINE lobsters 100 years ago cost one cent each. Farmers bought them for fertilizer.

•

HOW DO YOU account for the fact that the words for north, south, east and west are the same in Chinese as in the language of Brazil's Tupi Indians?

NO MARTINI drinker of the old school should fail to recognize the name of Dr. Francisco de la Boe, who was a professor of medicine at the University of Leiden 300 years ago. In his search for a therapeutic compound, he invented gin — clink! — and, indeed, it caught on.

•

RARELY do buildings burn down in La Paz, Bolivia. At 12,000 feet, there's not enough oxygen to feed fast fires.

THE TYPICAL hostelry in Ireland 250 years ago usually kept on hand a pair of dueling pistols for the benefit of combustible travelers who'd failed to bring their own.

•

A HEN has two ovaries. The left makes eggs. The right is on standby. Backup. Never does anything unless the left goes on the blink.

•

SHEEP don't swim.

•

GENERALLY there are two rich men for every rich woman. But more specifically, the rich women are both richer and older than the rich men.

ANSWER DEPT.

Q. "WHY ARE the men on railroad track repair gangs known as 'gandy dancers.'?" A. Inventor of one sort of shovel was a man named Gandy. When a crewman tamps ballast into place along newly laid track, using such a shovel, he bends, steps, hops, contorts in a manner that merits such nomenclature.

THE INVENTOR of the Kodak camera, George Eastman, hated to have his picture taken. Very few photos of him exist.

Q. "WHEN ARE the northbound killer bees due to get to the United States?" A. About 1988 is the latest prognostication in this matter. The Texas town of Brownsville is supposed to be their first stop. Then on to New Mexico, Arizona and California.

Q. "WHAT SORT of critter eventually emerges from a Mexican jumping bean?" A. A bean moth. Eggs are laid in the bean's flower. The pod surrounds them. A larva develops. It eats the bean from inside out, and lines the bean with silk. Periodically, it contorts its body, making the bean wiggle. Finally, it chews a hole in the bean's wall to fly out.

•

Q. "WHAT'S the murder rate in this country now?" A. A killing every 24 minutes.

•

Q. "YOU SAID the widower who remarries waits three years before doing so? How about the widow who remarries?" A. Seven years.

•

Q. "HAS THERE ever been snow on the ground at the same time in every one of the United States?" A. In every one of the 48 contiguous states, there has. And not so long ago, either. On Jan. 31, 1977. First time we know of.

•

Q. "HOW FAST did those oldtimey steamboats on the Mississippi travel?" A. About 8 mph.

IN THE RICH family, the oldest son is most likely to be successful. In the poor family, it's the youngest son who tends to make out best.

●

ONE OUT OF every three young women breaks two or more engagements before she marries. One out of every six young men does likewise. That's the statistical report of the university researchers.

●

THE WORD "second" is of French origin. Before the Anglo-Saxons borrowed it from across the English Channel, they used to say first, other, third, fourth, so on.

●

LOT OF CAR mechanics in the Soviet Union make more money than most doctors there. Incidentally, two out of three Soviet doctors are women.

●

WAS A TIME when not just circus horses but all well-trained riding horses dropped to their knees, like camels, to receive their riders. That was before A.D. 420 when the stirrup was invented.

WHEN ATHLETES say a compatriot has "rabbit ears," they mean he's extremely sensitive to criticism.

DOES NICOTINE inhibit dreams? Must. It's known that nonsmokers dream more.

●

THE BIG-EYED wolf spider of Kauai, Hawaii, has no eyes. And the Lake Tahoe stone fly doesn't fly; it lives and dies more than 200 feet underwater.

●

ANY CELLO player who takes commercial flights to concerts will tell you that the cello needs a full-fare ticket, too.

THOSE BIRDS known as condors, the few left, eat mightily. Typical breakfast can be 150 mice at a cost, for those who feed them in captivity, of about $75.

●

ILLINOIS AVENUE is the square most frequently occupied in that game called Monopoly.

●

AM TOLD the typical wearer of contact lenses spends about $100 a year on maintenance supplies.

NUMEROUS soldiers, wounded by single rifle bullets, have told the medics they heard those bullets coming. If a rifle shot travels faster than sound, asked I, how could they have heard the bullets? A retired first sergeant, Thomas C. Gordon of Red Bluff, Calif., explains: "What the wounded man hears is a miniature sonic boom from the speeding bullet. The sound gets to his brain through his ears more swiftly than does the pain from the more distant wound. Yes, I heard both of mine — leg and chest."

•

YOUR SKIN weighs twice as much as your brain, if typical.

•

A BLINDFOLDED dolphin can find a nickel on the bottom of its tank.

ANSWER DEPT.

Q. "IS THERE really such a creature as a bookworm?" A. There is. Its scientific name: anobium pertinax.

•

Q. "WHAT MAKES a real pearl yellowish?" A. Especially salty water.

THE TYPICAL cigaret smoker takes only about eight drags per cigaret, according to the American Lung Association.

Q. "WHAT CAR company turned out the first station wagon? When?" A. Ford. In 1929. It was a Model A. Sold for $650.

•

Q. "WASN'T the famous lawman Wyatt Earp jailed for horse stealing in California?" A. Jailed, no. Kicked out of the state, yes.

Q. "WHAT'S the ratio of men to women in the retirement age bracket?" A. Over 65, it's 69 men per 100 women. Over 85, it's 48 men to 100 women.

•

Q. "HOW MUCH do the Chinese pay for the gallstones of milk cows now?" A. About $200 a dried ounce. Dealers in Hong Kong buy them, grind them up, and peddle them as one of the ingredients in what they claim are aphrodisiacs. Slaughterhouse operators in South Africa take considerable care to search for them in butchered stock.

•

Q. "A BASEBALL game can't end in a tie, right?" A. In Japan, it can. The Japanese put a time limit on their baseball — three hours, usually. Our Chief Prognosticator thinks the time requirements of television eventually will force such rule changes here, too.

•

Q. "HOW MUCH money does David Hartman get for hosting ABC-TV's 'Good Morning, America' show?" A. $2.1 million a year.

YOUR RESISTANCE and mine to physical ailments usually is at its annual low in March, medical researchs say. More North Americans die in March than during any other month.

•

SIR, do you say "I love you" to your wife every day? The query was not too personal, evidently, for the husbands in a recent nationwide survey. Two out of five said yes, every day.

•

THE OLD English defined a "moment" as a minute and a half.

•

CURRENT COUNT of female bartenders is up 55 percent over 20 years ago.

•

A RABBIT'S ears go limp when it dreams, but I don't know why.

•

GIVE THAT plucked eyebrow 92 days to grow back.

•

THE PLURAL of "piecemeal," bear in mind, is "flockmeal."

"A COURTING MIRROR" is what it was called. Generations ago, a bashful fellow proposed matrimony by looking into said mirror, theoretically leaving his reflection therein, then handing same to his girlfriend. If she looked thereupon, that meant yes. But if she put the mirror face to the tabletop, that signified no. It's how we came by that synonym for no: "to get turned down."

CREDIT THE Antarctic with at least three weather superlatives: the coldest continent on earth, the sunniest and the windiest.

NOT ONLY is a blonde far more likely than a brunette to get a divorce, statistically, but a blonde is more likely to remarry, too.

A HOUSEHOLD dog invariably likes one member of the family better than any other.

●

IF A ZOOMAN refers to 2.1 (two-point-one) tigers or whatever, he means two males, one female.

●

WERE YOU acquainted with your matrimonial mate for at least two years before you married? Such is the case in two out of three marriages.

●

A RESEARCHER for a U.S. National Health Survey counted 4.5 million headache reports to learn that women have more headaches than men by two-to-one.

●

THE MILITARY'S special technique for throwing a hand grenade is such that women appear to be better able than men to do it by the book.

ANSWER DEPT.

Q. "THOSE MOST famous Siamese twins of all time were named Eng and Chang. Which was which?" A. In Thai, Eng means left and Chang means right.

EXERCISE during the day should help you sleep. But exercise at night might keep you awake. Or so say the medicos.

Q. "WHAT WAS the shortest reign of any pope?" A. Two days. Pope Stephen II won the election on March 24, 752, but stepped down even before the cardinals got home.

Q. "DO BARNYARD roosters have to be taught how to crow?" A. No, even roosters born deaf start to crow when they're ready.

●

Q. "HOW MANY corncob pipes can you get out of one corncob?" A. Four. At least, that's the routine in Washington, Mo., where two factories turn out all the commercial corncob pipes still made in the world.

●

Q. "HOW LONG has it been since the State of California had grizzly bears in the wild?" A. Since August of 1922 when Jesse B. Agnew killed the last of same there at Horse Corral Meadow in Fresno County.

●

Q. "WHO HOLDS the record for having the most wives? King Solomon?" A. No, sir, King Solomon only had 700 wives. King Mongst of Siam had 9000 wives and concubines. It was hard to tell which were wives and which were concubines. They got all mixed up.

●

Q. "THE DODO BIRD is extinct. What killed it off?" A. Pigs.

DO BIRTH control pills make some women more amorous? The researchers have been working on this one for a long time, scientifically and otherwise. Professors at Princeton University and the University of Wisconsin queried about 6000 wives. Acts of love, they learned, were about 46 percent more prevalent among the pill users.

•

THE CITY of Liverpool has never been known as Liverpuddle, but the people therein are called Liverpudlians nonetheless.

•

A FOURTH of the soldiers conscripted into the Soviet Union's army don't speak Russian.

•

UNDER LOCAL law of Phoenix, Ariz., garbage is city property. The hungry who forage for same, therefore, can be charged with theft.

•

ONLY THREE words in the English language end in "ceed" — "proceed," "exceed" and "succeed." Such is the claim of a language expert. Can you prove otherwise?

APPEARANCES LIE. Take the gorilla. Among the least criminal of beasts, that one. A vegetarian that doesn't even kill for food. No murder, no rape, no robbery. But what other animal can incite greater fear?

BEAVERS SPEND 50 percent of their time in the water, but they always go in out of the rain.

•

BARTENDERS in Italy never put ice in any drink.

•

IF A TIME CLOCK recorded the deaths of teenagers in liquor-related car wrecks, it would make its mark every 1 hour 43 minutes.

THE BEGINNING of each month once was proclaimed aloud to the throngs by a head priest. Link that to the fact that the word "calendar" came from the Latin "to call out."

•

ANCIENT warriors of the Polynesian island of Tonga were finicky about their women and their boats. Their women they always stole from Samoa, their boats from Fiji, rarely the other way around.

CINCINNATI's lawgivers have to rewrite it, somehow. State health officials there are authorized to poison rats but aren't allowed in the sewers. Sewer district employees are allowed in the sewers but aren't authorized to poison rats.

•

AM TOLD a phone booth costs about $1000 now.

•

THE RIVER SPREE runs through Germany's Berlin. Beer halls and night spots lined its banks, once. A client claims that's where we got the expression "to go out on a spree." Maybe so, maybe so.

ANSWER DEPT.

Q. "I NOTE in print that more physicians in New York State are sued for malpractice than doctors elsewhere. Why do the bunglers gather there?" A. That's not it. New York has more ambulance-chasing lawyers, that's why.

•

Q. "HOW OLD is an unmarried man before he's considered to be 'a confirmed bachelor'?" A. Age 36, according to the statisticians.

WHEN a horse tries to throw its rider, you and I may allow as how it bucks, but the fancier talkers say it executes an "estrapade."

Q. "WOMEN take more time off from work than men, don't they?" A. A little more. They go home sick about twice as frequently but stay home about half as long.

•

Q. "IN ART, most murals are frescoes, right?" A. No, but most frescoes are murals.

Q. "SAYS HERE Teddy Roosevelt was the first U.S. President to drive a car. I thought William McKinley did that?" A. McKinley rode in one. A hearse. His last ride.

•

Q. "WHAT'S the speed limit on West Germany's Autobahn?" A. Isn't any.

THE COUNT of unmarried couples who live together has more than tripled nation-wide in the last 13 years.

•

TOOK William Shakespeare only 14 days to write "The Merry Wives of Windsor," I'm told.

•

WISCONSINITES say there has never been an organized game of lacrosse in La Crosse. And Iowans say davenports have never been made in Davenport.

•

A LITTLE BOY skipped rocks on the Orange River of Hopetown, South Africa, in 1866. One rock he pocketed and took home. It turned out to be the 21.75 carat diamond that four years later started history's greatest diamond rush. But all he knew was it wouldn't skip.

•

AT 16,000 feet of average elevation, Tibet is not a likely candidate for a tidal wave, what? Never can tell, though. Fossils of sea creatures have been found in the rocks there. It was underwater once.

WHEN YOUR granddad was a lad, a man could buy an airplane, of sorts, for $300.

AM TOLD those cosmetic surgeons who do hair transplants now charge about $550 an hour.

•

THAT WORD "khaki" comes from the Hindi "khak," meaning "dust."

•

WHEN WALT DISNEY designed the first Mickey Mouse, he drew the body parts with a series of circles to make the figure easier to animate.

TWO OUT OF FIVE Japanese marriages are arranged by go-betweens.

•

BEES in a typical hive eat 500 pounds of honey a year.

•

SOMETHING ELSE that could keep you busy for a dozen years or so might be to list the ways in which Alaska is unique. For starters, it's both the westernmost and easternmost state in the nation.

OBSERVED one Leonard Lauder: "When a person with experience meets a person with money, the person with experience will get some money, and the person with the money will get some experience."

•

TREE RINGS also record earthquakes.

•

ONLY ONE obese teenager in 28 ever slims down to normal weight.

•

THE CLOSER you get to the equator, the more kinds of evergreens you find.

•

WHY IS the unwanted drinker identified in cocktail lounges as "86"? Am now told nationally accepted uniform police codes use "86" to mean "disturbance in a tavern."

ANSWER DEPT.

Q. "WHAT'S A 'drawing room'? And why?" A. Short for "withdrawing room," that. It was a room, smaller than the dining room, to which the ladies withdrew after dinner, leaving the men to their cigars and brandy. The term is about four centuries old.

BUILDERS of Europe's medieval castles perched the latrines out over the moats.

Q. "DOES ANY sort of whale have a throat large enough to swallow a man?" A. Only one, the sperm.

•

Q. "HOW OFTEN in the United States does some police officer shoot somebody to death?" A. Once a day, about.

•

Q. "WHAT COUNTRY has the most lawyers per capita?" A. Israel.

Q. "HOW DOES President Ronald Reagan sign his name?" A. With any of these, depending: Ronald Wilson Reagan. Ronald Reagan. Ron Reagan. Ronald. Ronnie. Dutch.

•

Q. "A GOOD typist can do 80 words per minute. How fast could the old-time telegraph operators tap out their messages?" A. Maybe 25 words per minute.

IF A MOTHER'S first-born is a boy, she is less likely to want a large family than if her first child is a girl. Or so claim the researchers. And if her first two children are boys, they say, her desire for a third child is far less than if the first two are girls.

●

OF THE 18 most common men's names, the least liked are Albert, Henry, Frank and Harry. So reports a Los Angeles surveytaker.

●

HOW OLD were you when you first got married? Average age of first-marriage brides and grooms changes from decade to decade. Now, it's 22.3 years for the brides, 24.8 years for the grooms.

●

THE GLOVEMAKERS say men's hands have been getting a little smaller over recent generations while women's hands have been getting a little bigger, but they can't explain the why of it.

●

OPEN QUESTION: "Davy Jones's locker" is sailor talk for "the bottom of the sea." But who was the original Davy Jones, if such a person existed?

IF YOU live to be 70, you'll have devoted 13 years just to talking. Such is the contention of a Vassar scholar.

EVERY SPORT knows the name Spalding. But not all know that Albert Goodwill Spalding, before he became a sporting goods magnate, was the nation's top baseball pitcher of the 1870s.

●

THOSE INTO falconry say the best bird for that sport is not the falcon but the red-tailed hawk.

●

GENTLEMEN, place your bets. Which is the world's largest parade? Pay that man who said, "Memphis' Cotton Carnival."

WORD MECHANICS still debate whether Harry Truman's middle initial "S" should have a period after it. Let the argument end. Chiseled onto President Truman's tombstone in Independence, Mo., is the name as he specified: "Harry S. Truman."

●

THE BUNK shortage aboard U.S. Navy nuclear subs is such that some sailors sleep in torpedo tubes, I'm told.

●

THE JAPANESE spend more money on prescription drugs than any other nationals.

AMONG shoplifters who get caught, the women outnumber the men by almost seven to one.

•

HALF the people who drown are alone at the time.

•

NO WORD mechanic looking for the exact set of syllables should overlook "tyromancer," which means "one who tells fortunes while watching cheese coagulate."

•

"STRESS" is common to firefighters and police officers. You knew that. But a University of Nebraska expert on stress — Dr. Robert Eliot — says the professional most likely to suffer from stress is the farmer.

•

YES, the teenage girls who smoke now outnumber the teenage boys who smoke.

ANSWER DEPT.

Q. "WHAT proportion of the dogs nationwide are purebreeds?" A. One out of three is the offspring of parents of the same breed, though not necessarily registered.

NOW, LISTEN CLOSELY...

A RIFLE BULLET travels faster than sound, no? Then how do you account for the fact that many soldiers, wounded during World War II by single rifle bullets, later told medical researchers they "heard it (the bullet) coming."

Q. "HOW MANY of the gynecologists are women?" A. One out of seven.

Q. "ISN'T IT a crime in the Soviet Union to spread venereal disease?" A. That it is. In fact, it's even a crime to get it. Penalties vary. Understand the severest are imposed in the Georgia region. Two years in prison is a typical sentence for the ordinary patient. Five years is not uncommon for those convicted of infecting minors or more than two other people.

•

Q. "WHAT ARE the odds that a couple married 40 years will get divorced?" A. One in 1000, about.

•

Q. "REMEMBER when that group of fashion models in Washington, D.C., filed a claim to the Internal Revenue Service for a depreciation allowance? How did that case come out?" A. The IRS ruled officially that age does not diminish the beauty of American women.

•

Q. "WHAT'S THAT tribe of people who get sick every time they try to walk on dry land?" A. The Bajaus? They live on boats, rocking on the water from birth to death, in the Malays. A stroll on shore makes them dizzy.

NOTHING SUBTLE about the male gerbil in love. To inform the object of his affection that he's interested in romance, he rapidly pounds the ground — thump! thump! thump! — with both hind feet.

•

THE U.S. divorce rate has doubled in the last dozen years, nearly tripled in the last two decades.

•

THREE out of five new supermarket items fail to sell.

•

SOVIET ARMY soldiers get no time off at all during the first year, then five days' furlough during the second year.

•

NO, DEAF people don't get seasick.

•

IF YOU don't think you're a slave to habit, sir, reverse the contents of your right and left front pockets, then see how you do the rest of the day — in making change, in unlocking doors.

IT HAS been noted that some women get so hung up on birth-control pills that they take them in every conceivable situation.

"TAKE ME out to the ball game," opens the chorus of a most familiar song. What most people don't know is it's about a young lady named Katie Casey who compulsively spends all her money on baseball tickets, peanuts and popcorn.

•

ONE thoroughbred racehorse in ten earns its keep on the tracks. What's its keep? About $15,000 a year.

•

THE MOVIE makers typically shoot two pages of script a day.

CREDIT old Anonymous, too, with the observation: "Modesty is the art of drawing attention to whatever it is you're being humble about."

•

A MAGNIFYING mirror reshapes itself slightly with changes in barometric pressure. So theoretically, sir, you could learn to tell something about the morning's weather by looking at your own reflection while you shave.

•

SPURT SPEED of a rat is only about 5 mph.

PROFESSIONAL butter-makers aren't all that numerous, not anymore. Fewer than 1000 people nationwide are so classified now.

•

SAYS HERE most people don't get any new freckles after age 20. Could that be right?

•

CLEOPATRA knew her poisons worked. She tested them on slaves.

•

FEMALE canaries don't sing.

•

THE TENDENCY to develop a double chin is inherited.

•

THE BANK tellers in this country outnumber the clergy by 480,000 to 296,000.

•

THAT RATTLESNAKE, if typical, will grow three rattles a year.

•

THE UNITED STATES' greatest naval victory — Midway — occurred only six months after its greatest naval defeat — Pearl Harbor.

SCIENTISTS in China report they can predict weather with about 80 percent accuracy by monitoring the croaking of frogs.

ANSWER DEPT.

Q. "WASN'T THERE a time when some people actually sold children to traveling circuses?" A. That happened. Maybe not frequently, but often enough to prompt Georgia legislators to enact a state law to penalize anyone who might "sell a minor under age 12 . . . to rope or wire walk, beg, be a gymnast, contortionist, circus rider, acrobat or clown."

•

Q. "HOW LONG does a flash of lightning last?" A. Three-thousandths of a second, about.

•

Q. "WHO COINED the term 'soap opera'?" A. That individual's name is not in the record at hand, regret to say. Can tell you the company that indirectly paid for the inspiration, however. Proctor & Gamble.

•

Q. "WHAT'S A 'seersucker' suit?" A. A suit of light fabric — linen, cotton, rayon, whatever — usually striped and slightly puckered. Why it's called that I do not know. You'd think seersucker would be something you'd put on corn flakes. It comes from the Hindi for "milk and sugar."

•

Q. "CATGUT comes from sheep, right?" A. And horses.

•

Q. "HOW LONG will the food last, typically, aboard a U.S. nuclear sub?" A. About 90 days.

HALF THE homeowners in Arkansas live in houses valued at less than $31,000, and half live in houses valued at more. Half the homeowners in Hawaii live in houses valued at less than $118,000, and half live in houses valued at more. That's it, the low and the high nationwide in this matter of median house values.

●

IN THE VITTLES department, if it's crisp, kids tend to like it. If it's mushy, they don't. That's a generality which has proven out to one summer camp cook over 30 years.

●

WHATEVER day of the week any year begins on — Monday, Tuesday, Wednesday, so on — that year will have 53 of those days entire.

●

TOP SPEED of the human sneeze is about 200 miles an hour.

●

MR. GEORGE BURNS at age 87 has an opinion on sex, too: "Do it behind locked doors. If what you're doing can be done in the open, you might as well be pitching horseshoes."

THE UNHAPPY truth is that bees spend most of their time doing nothing.

WAS A TIME there in France when it was dangerous to say anything pleasant about violets. At least, in public. Napoleon had liked them so much he'd made them the flower of the empire. After he was ousted following Waterloo, to speak well of violets was tantamount to praise of Napoleon. And that was bad. Very bad.

●

TO THAT LIST of innovations given to the world by California, add the salad bar.

●

ALBANIANS nod the head to say "no" and shake the head to say "yes."

LIGHTNING when viewed through the mists over Niagara Falls oftentimes appears bright red.

●

FLEAS HAVE FLEAS. Fleas' fleas have fleas, too. So do fleas' fleas' fleas.

●

A WYOMING couple some years ago named their son "Winter" and their two daughters "Spring" and "Summer." Sounds right. Winter seems masculine, Spring and Summer feminine. Whether they ever had a fourth child is not in the record at hand. If so, hope it was a girl. Autumn would make a dandy name for a girl.

THOMAS EDISON in his later years preferred to read in Braille.

•

IT WAS NOT a federal felony to assassinate a U.S. president until after John F. Kennedy was murdered.

•

MAYBE YOU can make something out of the fact that "idiot" comes from the Greek for "those who do not vote."

•

HOW WOULD you go about proving the claim that wet sand weighs less than a like volume of dry sand?

•

MAJOR-LEAGUE baseball teams in Japan are not identifed with their cities, but with their corporations.

ANSWER DEPT.

Q. "WHO INVENTED the gyroscope?" A. A doctor named Jean Bernard Leon Foucault. But he wasn't much of a doctor, might mention. He couldn't stand the sight of blood. So he took up physics.

HARVARD originally ranked its students by their social position, not by their scholarship. For example, John Adams, one of the best of the scholars in his 1755 class of 24 students, was rated only 14th.

Q. "AMERICANS spend most of their time in three places: their homes, their job sites, and — where's the third?" A. Shopping malls.

Q. "IN WHICH of the world's metropolises live the most black people?" A. No. 1 is New York City, with about 1.7 million. No. 2, Zaire's Kinshasa in Africa, with about 1.6 million. Surprising, isn't it, how little we know about places elsewhere? Few Americans have ever heard of Kinshasa. Take China. There are dozens of million-plus cities there, but most of us can't name more than a couple.

•

Q. "HOW DOES a magician stop his pulse at will?" A. A tightly knotted handkerchief in the armpit will do it. The magician can exert pressure against it or relax, almost imperceptibly, and the wrist pulse will stop and start accordingly.

•

Q. "MANY PEOPLE believe the moon affects their behavior. I don't get it. How do they rationalize that?" A. The moon affects the tides. Land-living critters emerged from the seas. Genetic memory persists, and jillions of years after the original influence, it influences still. Or so goes one of the notions.

•

Q. "HOW MANY jobs can a U.S. president fill by appointment?" A. About 3000.

AVIATION pioneers worked feverishly, and by Sept. 8, 1910, finally, there were enough airplanes for a collision. Over Austria's Wiener-Neustadt, two craft, eagerly piloted by brothers named Warchalovski, smashed into each other. If this account of the world's first airplane crash sounds to you like the story of mankind, you're too pessimistic. Cheer up.

•

MORE MEN than women come away from class reunions with that "Where did I go wrong?" feeling.

•

A MAGAZINE for cat fanciers reports that half the cats that sleep in houses more specifically sleep in beds with their owners.

•

THAT WATER grass known as wild rice is not rice at all.

•

"QUICK as a wink" is listed repeatedly in the various trivia collections as one-twentieth of a second. But how can that be? I can't wink 20 times in a second. Can you?

FISH don't drink.

THE 1929 winner of the Kentucky Derby was a horse named Clyde Van Dusen trained by a man named Clyde Van Dusen.

•

THREE TIMES as many men as women commit suicide over wrecked love affairs.

•

JUST IN your lifetime, sir, the continents of Europe and North America will have drifted farther apart by about your height.

•

FIRST FOOD to go into international trade, I'm told, was pickled herring.

NO LITTLE LEAGUE baseball pitcher should be allowed to throw a curve until his elbow is strong enough to handle the torque. So contended Hall of Fame pitcher Robin Roberts.

•

ANY SATURDAY night of a December, January or February — that's when to expect the most burglaries.

•

IN DENMARK, you can buy banana-flavored toothpaste.

•

CROCODILES have no tear glands.

U.S. LAW COURTS spend more than half their time handling cases involving cars.

•

YOU CAN GET homemade lasagna now at the Jianguo Hotel in Beijing, I'm told.

•

IF YOU WORK for the Campbell Soup Company, you don't smoke on the job during business hours. That has been the policy for more than a century.

•

AT QUAKER weddings, all the guests sign the marriage certificate.

•

IF THAT DOG is a spaniel — any one of the 10 kinds — its name, at least, came from Spain.

•

PLASTIC SURGEONS in Manila use a new surgical tool with which they can create instant dimples.

ANSWER DEPT.

Q. "WHAT'S the smallest incorporated town with a post office in the United States?" A. Lost Springs, Wyo. Population, 6.

IF YOU DIDN'T ever break, cut, file or bite your fingernails, each would be six feet long by the time you reached age 50.

Q. "ASK YOUR Love and War Man if he knows which day of the week was named in honor of the Scandinavian goddess of marriage?" A. Friday for Freya, he says. He also knows that Tuesday was named after Tiw, the Norse god of war.

Q. "DID PRINCE Philip of England propose marriage to Queen Elizabeth II? Or vice versa?" A. That's a royal secret. But the Englanders who know more than we — and care more — think she took the initiative.

•

Q. "IS THERE any tissue in the human body that has no blood supply of its own?" A. One. Cartilage.

•

Q. "ISN'T CHICAGO Mayor Harold Washington engaged to be married? To whom? For how long?" A. He is. To Mary Ella Smith. Has been for the last 20 years, reporters there say.

•

Q. "WHAT ARE the odds a running back in the National Football League will undergo knee surgery?" A. Fifty-fifty.

•

Q. "IN GOLF lingo, what's a 'Red Grange'?" A. A score of 77. That was the number on Red Grange's football jersey.

•

Q. "DO ANY people eat bats?" A. Many do. In some South Pacific island restaurants, you can buy a bat dinner — bon appetit — for about $25.

A SECRET TUNNEL links Buckingham Palace to London's subway system. An escape route, that, in case of a national emergency.

•

WHAT an Australian means by "gum nut" is what you and I mean by "the real McCoy."

•

THAT AUTOMOBILE most sought by car thieves is the Chevrolet Corvette. Its theft rate is 17 times higher than average.

•

ONE kindergarten teacher in 100 is a man.

•

DID YOU KNOW Napoleon had a morbid fear of the number 13? And that he never started any project on a Friday?

•

THE MAN WHO created the Graham cracker — Sylvester Graham — was a highly vocal health buff. He preached far and wide that people could prevent headaches by limiting their sexual activity to no more than 12 occasions a year.

IT'S NOT ENOUGH to say the citizen with silver locks has bubbles in the hair. Tell it all: After the hair follicles stopped making pigment, they let hundreds of tiny air bubbles into the hair shafts, and these reflect light, giving the hair a silvery look.

NOBODY over age 60 can drive a car legally in Singapore. And nobody under 25 can rent a car legally in France.

•

THREE MOST popular names for newborn baby girls in New York City today are: 1. Nicole. 2. Danielle. And 3. Tiffany.

MEN OFTEN forget their change at the cashier's counter in cafes. But women never do. So says a cashier of lengthy experience.

•

MR. AVERAGE MAN 60 years ago smoked 269 cigars a year. Now he smokes 50 cigars each year.

THE HAITIAN seamstress who sews up major league baseballs does so with a needle in each hand. At 10 cents a ball, she can stitch together maybe 36 balls a day.

●

IN JANE FONDA'S "Workout Book" is a chapter on "Advanced Buttocks."

●

ITEM NO. 922C in our Love and War Man's file is a medical statistic from New York City's Hospital Emergency Rooms: Three of the 1557 people who sought treatment therein during 1982 for human bites said the wounds had been inflicted in affectionate passion.

COMING onto the market now: sliced peanut butter. Packed like cheese slices. If sliced peanut butter comes, can sliced jelly be far behind?

ANSWER DEPT.

Q. "HOW DOES Prince Charles of England sign his correspondence?" A. "Charles." Nothing more. Both personal and official.

●

Q. " DIDN'T Julius Caesar marry off his entire army once?" A. That was Alexander the Great. On an evening to remember in 324 B.C. in Susa, Persia — to unite two empires — he mass-married 10,000 of his Macedonian soldiers to that many Persian women. If it were to happen today, you'd see it on late-night cable.

●

Q. "WHERE'D WE get the word 'ghetto'?" A. From the Venetian word "geto," meaning foundry. There was a foundry on an island in Venice. So the island itself was referred to as "the geto." In 1516, Jews were restricted to that island.

●

Q. "NAME the female mammal with the richest milk?" A. The elephant seal — 54 percent butterfat.

Q. "WHAT national capital is heated entirely by water from hot springs?" A. Iceland's Reykjavik.

●

Q. "DID ANY one voice ever do the Tarzan yells?" A. Yes, after the early experiments wherein hogcallers harmonized with baritones to get that effect, the studio found a film cutter who could handle the job alone. He was the father-in-law of one of those Tarzans, Buster Crabbe. His name — Tom Held.

THE SORT of car you drive influences your chances of being ticketed for speeding. Or so the researchers aver. They say they've documented at least one statistic: The speeder's automobile most likely to be stopped is the red Corvette.

•

IF YOU DON'T want to admit hemorrhoids, say you've got varicose veins. Same thing. Only the whereabouts makes the difference.

•

IN NORTH DAKOTA, some businessmen want to drop the "North" and just call the state "Dakota." They think the "North" name now sounds too much like the winter wind. What will South Dakota do, then? Change "South" to "Sunny"?

•

ARCTIC SMOG in the spring is thicker than Los Angeles smog.

•

SHY ISAAC NEWTON, the gravity man, served in the British Parliament. Only once therein did he speak for the record. It was to ask that a window be opened.

McDONALD'S has more employees than U.S. Steel.

WISCONSIN restaurants are required by legislation to serve free cheese with their meals. Don't know whether they all do it, but that's the law.

•

MORE THAN 3700 public libraries in the United States and Canada lend Polaroid cameras.

•

ALMOST TWO out of five people worldwide now live in cities.

•

A TYPICAL jockey in Thoroughbred racing saddles a horse more than 1000 times a year.

IS IT NOT appropriate that more than half the books between soft covers are sexy romance novels?

•

DID I tell you that 43 percent of all the pregnant women in the United States draw paychecks?

•

A 50-YEAR-OLD termite is not unheard of.

•

ON HIS Model T, Henry Ford made about $2 a car. He built 15,007,033 of them from 1907 to 1927. If my battery is still good, that's $30,014,066.

HOW CAN 50,000 men disappear without a trace? History records that such happened. King Cambyses of Persia in 525 B.C. led that number of fighters into the Egyptian desert to attack Amun on the Libyan border. Up boiled a sandstorm of hurricane proportions. Students of antiquity think the desert thereabouts now contains in its depths the mummified bodies of all those soldiers, drowned in sand.

•

WHAT I DON'T LIKE about African lions is the first thing they eat after they kill their prey is the intestines.

•

CURIOUS LITTLE critters, moles. The turns in their tunnels are almost all 90 degrees.

•

ONE OUT OF every three marriages in this country 200 years ago was of the shotgun variety. Or so the historians estimate. In the previous century, only one out of 10 was a must marriage. Likewise, in the subsequent century. Today, that statistic is back up again — to maybe one out of four. Theorists explain it simply: Whenever the society seems to be coming apart, premarital sex increases considerably.

VEGETARIANS know that the oldest living animal — the giant turtle — eats no meat.

AREN'T ANY flower girls at weddings in England. Never have been.

•

SOME DOGS embarrass easily. Many newly clipped poodles, for instance, tend to hide behind the furniture until their wool grows back out. Don't blame them.

ANSWER DEPT.

Q. " DO MERMAIDS have souls?" A. Not unless they marry mortals, according to the mythologists.

Q." DID YOU SAY the basenji has no bark?" A. No, I said the palm tree has no bark. That African pup known as the basenji has a bark it rarely uses.

•

Q. "DIDN'T PRESIDENT Ronald Reagan once do a song-and-dance comedy routine in Las Vegas?" A. For two weeks in 1954, yes. At the Last Frontier Hotel there. Wasn't what he did best. It didn't go over.

•

Q. "QUICK, NAME the only professional golfer ever to shoot a tournament score lower than his age?" A. Sam Snead.

•

Q. "IF RICE PAPER isn't manufactured from rice, why is it called that?" A. Because nobody remembers fatsia papyrifers, the Taiwanese plant from which it is made, probably.

•

Q. "WHO OWNS the meteorite that falls on my land?" A. You do.

•

Q. "WHICH SLOTH came first, the deadly sin or that South American tree beast?" A. The animal was named after the sin. It sleeps 18 hours a day.

EVERY SPECIES has its "do's" and "don'ts." Take the red-sided garter snake. It won't mate in its den. Only in the bushes.

●

AN OLD Minnesota law prohibits hanging men's and women's underwear on the same clothesline.

●

IF YOU have a normal head of hair, 85 percent of it is growing while 15 percent is not at any given time.

●

SEVENTY PERCENT of the population nationwide lives on 1 percent of the land.

●

THE LAW in Atlantic City, N.J., decrees that slot machines there must pay players 83 percent of the take. The slots reportedly are set up to kick out that much in winnings over 8000 revolutions, which normally amount to about a day and a half of play.

●

THE AMERICAN Bowling Congress specifically authorizes a tourney manager to cancel the contest immediately in case of war.

Q. "IN HOW many U.S. cities do more people get to work on mass transit than in cars?" A. One only — New York City.

YOU'LL SPEND 25 hours a year making beds, about, even if you only make one bed a day.

●

THE ORIGINAL Pharaoh of old Egypt was a palace not a person.

●

AMERICAN Indians in general have larger brains than American Caucasians.

●

YES, THERE is such a beast as a crocogator.

IF NO more than a fifth of the sky is cloudy, the weather reporter can call it clear, technically.

●

LITERAL translation of "Sinai" is "bag of sand." Of "Damascus," "sackful of blood."

●

TO BE fairly accurate, you can translate "a coon's age" to mean a dozen years.

●

THE THREAD in one silk worm's cocoon may unwind to the length of 10 football fields.

IT'S THE custom among numerous families in Switzerland to plant an apple tree when a baby boy is born, a pear tree when a baby girl is born.

●

YOU CAN run faster outdoors than indoors, remember.

●

FIREMEN ARE trained to stay to the right when climbing stairs. So? Escapees should stay on the right when descending stairs. To avoid tangling with the firemen.

●

AM TOLD a triple-play in baseball is rarer than a hole-in-one in golf.

●

BEFORE hair turns gray, it darkens with age.

●

MOST MEN have thicker blood than most women.

ANSWER DEPT.

Q "CAN YOU get a toothache from a heart attack?" A. Happens. Claim is the pain in 18 out of every 100 cardiac cases is referred to the jaw or teeth. In most cases, though, it's felt in the shoulders, arms and neck.

DID I TELL you a lightning bolt is five times hotter than the surface of the sun?

Q. "DO MEN and women compete together in any of the Olympic contests?" A. In rifle shooting, at least.

●

Q. "ISN'T A U.S. passport valid in every country on earth?" A. Except for Libya, that's right.

Q. "WAS ANYBODY ever executed for war crimes in the Civil War?" A. One man only. A Major Wirtz, who'd been in command of the notorious Confederate prison at Andersonville, Ga., where 13,000 prisoners died, mostly of utter neglect.

●

Q. "WHAT ARE the scientists trying to develop in their experiments with DNA?" A. Designer genes.

●

Q. "HOW MANY head of cattle does President Ronald Reagan run on his California ranch?" A. Three. Did I mention he doesn't own an automobile? A Jeep and a tractor, yes, but no Sunday-go-to-meeting type car.

●

Q. "WHAT'S THE penalty for drunken driving in Norway?" A. First offense, 21 days in jail plus a year's loss of the driving license.

●

Q. "WHERE'S 'Bharat'?" A. That's the official name of India.

●

Q. "WHAT SORT of pill is the one called an oddball?" A. Sounds as though you mean "nod ball," which is quaintese for sleeping pill.

A THIRD OF the convicts in U.S. prisons say they were drunk at the time of the crime.

•

A MOSQUITO has muscles, too. But they tighten up when the temperature drops below 60 degrees F. So they can't generate the 300 wingbeats a second needed to keep the little rascals in the air.

•

THERE IS no record that any native of Tatary — any Tartar — ever invented a sauce.

•

NINETEEN out of every 20 people who diet to lose weight give up shortly, it's now said.

•

PERHAPS I forgot to warn you that the smoking of opium can make you constipated.

•

CHICAGO IS closer to Moscow than to Rio de Janeiro.

•

TO BE A "journal," precisely, it has to be a "daily account." So to be a "journalist," precisely, you have to write every day.

A PUP can't remember anything for more than 30 seconds. Vets say this explains why you have to get to the little rascal promptly after it strikes, if you want to housebreak it properly.

DID YOU visit the doctor 2.6 times last year? That's the national average.

•

HALF THE population of Honduras is under age 15.

•

ADD TO the redundancy list: "old adage."

•

AMONG YOGURT eaters hereabouts, strawberry is the No. 1 flavor now. Plain is No. 2. Raspberry, No. 3.

ALMOST but not quite seven out of every 100 passengers on USA-owned airlines fly first class.

•

WHAT'S called a TV "talk show" in the United States is known in Great Britain as a "chat show."

•

IN 1981, a wild coyote killed a 3-year-old girl in Glendale, Calif. It was the first documented case in the United States of a coyote killing a human being.

WHAT DID you get for a high school graduation present? Brooke Shields gave herself a $2 million apartment in New York City.

•

TRUE, reading can be work. But this is where you learn that the Sun King of France, Louis XIV, had a stomach three times bigger than a normal man's. You wouldn't want to have missed that, certainly.

•

BEFORE people on the downside of a moodswing said they had the "blues," they said they had the "blue devils." But what they said to characterize a depression before that, I don't know.

•

SIR, do you possess that thing called "animal magnetism"? It's what women look for, I'm told, when checking out men. At least, it's what's looked for by members of a women's group called Manwatchers, Inc. This San Diego outfit supposedly takes note of "watchable" men. Physical grace and personality count for much in a fellow, they say, but animal magnetism, that's No. 1. If you don't have it, how do you fake it? Bark? Bellow? Jump up on a tree limb?

THE HATBAND came before the hat, note.

RAPID REPLY: No, my dear, "Euthanasia" is not an organization of oriental teenagers.

•

SAID philosopher Tom Weller: "It is better to remain childless than to father an orphan."

ANSWER DEPT.

Q. "WHAT does the A and W stand for in A & W Root Beer?" A. Allen and Wright.

Q. "WHO first delivered that conversational gambit, 'Tennis anyone' "? A. A Broadway stage character played by none other than Humphrey Bogart.

•

Q. "HOW come some cigars are called 'stogies' "? A. Drivers of the old Conestoga wagons once affected a preference for long, coarse, slender cigars then on the market in Pennsylvania. These were first called Conestogas, then stogies.

•

Q. "LOUIE, you're so dumb you think Omaha, Spokane and Johnstown are names of horses!" A. Won't bite on that one, my friend. Spokane won the Kentucky Derby in 1889, Omaha in 1935, Johnstown in 1939. Incidentally, you left out Seattle Slew, 1977.

•

Q. "IS IT true that carbonation rushes alcohol into the bloodstream?" A. Quite true. Effervescence speeds the essence.

•

Q. "WHAT'S 'yoga' mean, literally?" A. "Yoked with God."

•

Q. "WHO was the first U.S. president to ride on a train?" A. Andrew Jackson.

IF TODAY turns out typically, 2740 children in the United States will run away from home.

•

COLORADO'S mountains outnumber Switzerland's mountains six to one.

•

TO POP the dent out of that ping pong ball, toss it into boiling water for a moment.

•

THE PEOPLE who fly in and out of Chicago's O'Hare each year exceed in number the population of Spain.

•

IF THE FAMOUS "Midsummer Night's Dream" didn't occur on August 5, Mr. Shakespeare got it wrong. That is the perennial date of midsummer.

•

THE FIRST Colt six-shooter was a five-shooter, actually.

•

OUT OF San Francisco comes a note from a client. It begins: "We've just acquired a large octopus we'd like to dress for show. What sort of stockings . . . ?"

UNLESS THE COURTS of Algeria have changed the pattern recently, a fine levied in said courts can be paid off in beer.

TAKES THAT housefly about 60 days to become a great grandmother.

•

MORE PEOPLE dig for gold in the Klondike today than did so at the height of the 1898 gold rush there.

•

IN CALORIE content, beer and ginger ale come out just about even.

•

YOU'VE READ that Swedish settlers in Delaware built the first log cabins in this country. But did you know they brought their logs with them?

WHALES HAVE no vocal cords.

•

MEMO TO Michael Jackson: "Beat it" was one of the three most popular slang phrases of 1912, according to Life magazine's library. The other two were "It's a cinch" and "What do you know about that?"

•

"NOTHING THAT flies lives on the island of Corregidor." So claims a client. Can you refute that? No birds, no butterflies, no mosquitoes, says he.

IT'S STILL true that more apprehended shoplifters are age 13 than any other age.

•

TWO-THIRDS of the burn patients blame hot liquids.

•

YOUR BLOOD pressure, if typical, is lower in the morning than in the evening, bear in mind.

ANSWER DEPT.

Q. "WHAT WAS the first thing ever cooked by microwave?" A. A chocolate bar. In 1945, Percy L. Spencer put down such a bar beside a radar vacuum tube in Raytheon's lab at Waltham, Mass. In moments, the bar was melted. And Spencer yelled, "Eureka!" or something like that. Second thing cooked — Spencer sent out for same — was popcorn. Third thing — Egad! It works! — was a raw egg.

•

Q. "WHAT'S the average age now when juveniles have their first sexual experience?" A. Boys, 15.7 years. Girls, 16.2 years. That, according to a recent study by Johns Hopkins University researchers.

WHEN TWO roosters fight, eventually one, the loser, will hide its head. In a hole or a pail or a box. If it can find any-place to hide its head. If it can't, the fight goes on until death.

Q. "DID the American Indians have chickens?" A. Not until the Spaniards showed up.

•

Q. "DO THE ASTRONAUTS ever suffer from motion sickness?" A. That they do. At least, almost 50 percent of them do. Few, if any, did so in the cramped space of the early modules. But as the modules got bigger, with room to move around, air sickness hit many.

Q. "ARE THERE any cars in the world's smallest country?" A. About 2000 cars, yes. It's Nauru, a South Pacific island shaped like a hat. Eight square miles. Population, 5000, about.

•

Q. "HOW MUCH money did Willie Nelson make for his song 'The Family Bible'?" A. $50. He sold the rights early. It made a lot of money for the promoters, though.

THE "PEEPING TOM" laws of most states assume the peeper is male, never female, and they prescribe punishments for men, but not for women. In Mississippi, for instance, a man convicted of peeping can get five years, but a woman can't even be charged with that one.

•

WAS NONE other than Kris Kristofferson who said, "All the interesting women are over 30."

•

A MAN on pulchritude patrol wants a woman five to 10 years younger than himself. A woman in the search wants a man her own age. Or so contend the surveytakers who interviewed a sizable sampling of singles. Our Love and War man mistrusts the finding. In romance, says he, the intriguing exceptions outnumber the affairs predictible.

•

BEES can't fly in the rain.

•

THE MAYAN Indians of Southern Mexico — who believe Jesus Christ is the God of the Sun — also believe The Big Church in the Sky is closed on Wednesdays and Sundays.

ARE THERE any tuba players with false teeth? Doubt it.

ENGLAND'S Prince Charles is big on Vitamin C. Takes masses of same daily.

•

THOSE OF Irish extraction in the United States outnumber those of Irish extraction in Ireland by about 12 to one.

•

OBSERVED Somerset Maugham, morosely: "Dying is a very dull dreary affair and my advice to you is to have nothing to do with it." The record of this remark is stashed in our voluminous file labeled "The Negative Nature of Man."

TWIN BROTHERS Hiram and Lowell Beam live in Nashville, Tenn. Clearly, their folks knew they'd be called "Hi Beam" and "Lo Beam," and wanted it that way.

•

YOU'RE SEVEN times more likely to be struck by lightning than win a grand prize in a state lottery, according to the statisticians.

•

FIX THAT: Some nuclear sub crewmen sleep in the torpedo rooms, true, but not in the torpedo tubes, as has been widely reported.

NEED A hobby? Why aren't you out there looking for caves? Spelunkers know of at least 12,000 caves in the United States, but think there are another 50,000 yet to be found.

•

ON THE MARKET now, I'm told, are fortune bagels.

•

HUNGARY for years exported more hippopotamuses than did any other nation.

•

IF YOU DON'T like dogs, move to Iceland. They're outlawed there.

•

IT'S NOW harder to get into a veterinary school than a medical college.

TWO out of three living critters can fly.

ANSWER DEPT.

Q. "SETTLE a bet. The word 'mandarin' isn't Chinese but Portuguese, right?" A. Not quite right, not quite wrong. Comes from the Hindi "mantri" for "counselor." Portuguese colonists in Macao learned the word in Malaysia and labeled Chinese officials with it.

Q. "HOW MUCH of Australia is desert?" A. About half

•

Q. "WASN'T IT critic George Jean Nathan who said, 'She went through the gamut of emotions — from A to B'?" A. No, Dorothy Parker said something like that. Nathan said, "He writes his plays for the ages — the ages between 5 and 12."

Q. "WHAT NATURAL phenomena — floods, fires, earthquakes — kill the most people?" A. Heat waves.

•

Q. "WHAT WAS the '52-20 Club'?" A. Sardonic nomenclature that out-of-work GIs gave to their ilk after World War II. They were authorized $20 a week for 52 weeks while looking for new beginnings.

AN INFANT in a diaper commercial can earn up to $7000 in residuals over a six-month run on television.

•

AM TOLD the longest stretch of river without a bridge is the lower 1100 miles of the Yukon.

•

IT IS NOT enough to say Prince Philip of England was born in his parents' home on the Greek island of Corfu. Say also that he was born there on the dining-room table.

•

HOW CAN YOU recuperate, if you've never cuperated? Or reconnoiter, if you've never connoitered? Or recline, if you've never clined? Or rejoice, if you've never joiced? Or revolt, if you've never volted? Our Language Man continues to reflect on these matters, even though he's never flected on them.

•

NOSE OIL also prevents chapped lips, I'm told. You may have to use the tip of your finger to apply it.

DID I SAY a fish doesn't drink? Fix that! A freshwater fish doesn't drink. A saltwater fish drinks, though. Like a fish.

IN GROUPS, if they're frogs, they're a "colony," but if they're toads, they're a "knot."

•

IF YOU CAN'T find at least 200 other words in the word "transportation," you're just not trying.

•

THE LAST words of capital criminal James W. Rodgers, when asked what he wanted for his final request as he faced a firing squad in 1960: "A bullet-proof vest."

NUMEROUS British daily newspapers publish a "Nude of the Day" — a photograph of an attractive young woman, usually.

•

IN WEST Germany, television commercials can be shown only between 6 p.m. and 8 p.m. No more than 20 minutes of them, overall.

•

IN CONCRETE, Texas, all the buildings are made of wood and all the streets are asphalt.

MORE and more younger people are moving into Colorado, Utah and Idaho. More and more older people are retiring in Florida, Pennsylvania and New Jersey.

•

IT'S POSSIBLE for a married person in China now to receive a life sentence in prison if convicted of engaging in an extramarital affair.

•

UNIVERSITY professors taught 15 hours a week, average, in 1945. Now they teach five hours a week, average.

•

CONSIDER office romances. In companies that object to same. If one of the pair gets fired, odds are two to one it will be the woman.

•

BLAME WEEKEND binges for the fact that Monday is the day of the week with the greatest suicide count.

•

DID YOU KNOW that children can be taught to read before they can be taught to talk? Neither did I. But researchers now say that.

...., BUT DEAR ...., I'M FROM PISMO BEACH!

DO THE people in Los Angeles tend to have bad breath? If so, why? And if not, why do they lead the nation in the purchase of breath fresheners?

ANSWER DEPT.

Q. "MOST PARENTS around here tell researchers they'd rather have boy babies than girl babies. Isn't this true of all societies?" A. All but five, research reveals. Girl babies traditionally have been preferred by the Mudugomor of New Guinea, the Tiwi of North Australia, the Garo of Assam, the Iscobakebu of Peru and the Tolowa Indians of California. Not familiar with them? Me either.

•

Q. "HOW MANY of the published novelists in this country actually make a living from their writing?" A. Maybe 700 of the 35,000.

•

Q. "WHAT'S 'rappini'?" A. Soul food. Turnip greens plucked young. Boil them with small onions and stew meat.

•

Q. "PRESIDENT Reagan at a recent meeting stuck his thumbs in his ears and wiggled his outstretched fingers at the audience. We did that as kids. But I can't remember why. . . ?" A. Gesture of derision, that's all. Originally, it was to mimic the ears of a jackass, but that goes even further back.

•

Q. "IS THE MULE an endangered species?" A. No, sir, if all the mules died out, you'd still get more mules. Just so long as you didn't kill off all the male donkeys and female horses.

IF YOU CAN count six radios in or around your household — remember the cars — your radio inventory is just average.

•

CONNECTICUT LAW endows all beavers there with the legal right to build dams.

•

YOU WON'T hear the official national anthem of Australia at the Olympic Games. There isn't any.

•

WHEN A Hebrew-speaking Israelite wants to use a cussword, he has to borrow one from Arabic. Hebrew lacks sufficient cusswords to meet the normal needs of modern man.

•

WHEN YOU PLAY chess in Poland, your bishop is not a bishop but a "messenger." In Germany, it's a "runner." In Italy, an "ensign." In Russia, an "elephant." In France, a "jester."

•

IN CHINA, there's a breed of cat with long droopy ears. Sort of spaniel-like. They look weird.

•

WALRUSES get sunburned, too.

WHAT'S YOUR definition of "a lady"? An American writer named Lillian Day had an opinion on this. Said she: A lady is one who never shows her underwear by accident.

NOBODY HAS ever proved that a boa constrictor actually can squeeze a man to death. No authenticated cases. So reports a snake expert.

•

THE CULTURE of the Australian aborigine recognizes no sort of Supreme Being.

•

OUT OF EVERY 20 young men, one will notice before his 21st birthday that his hairline is receding.

•

HALF THE WORLD'S birds never fly more than 40 mph.

IN OLD Anglo-Saxon, the word "mare" was the term for an evil spirit believed sometimes to sit on a sleeper's chest. It's half the origin of that word "nightmare."

•

TO THAT widely known fact that the brain itself can't feel pain, please add: It can't feel heat or touch, either.

•

THE EGYPTIANS used pitch to embalm. The word "mummy," in fact, comes from the Arabic "mumiya," meaning pitch.

TAKES ONLY about 14 seconds for a chicken-plucking machine to strip that bird naked.

•

IN A FIGHT between an anteater and a dog, bet on the anteater.

•

WHY appendicitis crops up more frequently in men than in women has not yet been explained.

•

DIET IS NOT just an obsession of the heavy. It's sort of the "in" thing. Sixty out of every 100 high school girls tell pollsters they'd like to diet off a few pounds, but in fact the medical records show only 17 out of every 100 are overweight.

•

IN THE UNITED STATES there are newspapers called the Sun and newspapers called the Star, but not a single one is called the Moon. Why not?

•

AFRICA'S Nile River, stretched straight across North America, would reach from Oregon to Virginia.

SKUNKS make better house mousers than cats, I'm told.

ANSWER DEPT.

Q. "IN WHICH European countries now are the most unattached women?" A. Austria, Poland and East Germany, it's said.

•

Q. "MICE COME out at night. So they can see in the dark, right?" A. Not right, research reveals. They whisker their way around their familiar places.

Q. "HOW MANY of the Big League baseball players in any given season are pitchers?" A. About 260 of the 650.

•

Q. "HAVEN'T most people lost all their teeth by age 60?" A. Not most but almost most. About 45 percent.

•

Q. "WHERE'S the town called 'Joe Batt's Arm'?" A. In Newfoundland. There's a town up there, too, called "Nick's Nose Cove." And still another is called "Ha Ha."

•

Q. "WHAT were George Washington's dying words?" A. "I die hard, but I'm not afraid to go."

•

Q. "HOW MANY door-step babies survive?" A. Motherless foundlings? Sixty percent live a year or longer.

•

Q. "IF THE Panama canal is neither the deepest nor the longest, what's unique about it?" A. It's the only one that connects two oceans.

OUR CHIEF Prognosticator says you'll be able next year to buy bubble gum in toothpaste-like tubes.

•

SELF-MADE millionaires rarely play golf.

•

FIFTY PERCENT of the liquor is drunk by 6 percent of the people who drink.

•

TWO OF history's most renowned lovers — Cleopatra and Don Juan — both are said to have been downright fat.

•

NOW YOU can buy chocolate spaghetti.

•

WHERE'D WE get the word "seeded" to rate tennis players? That's what I asked. A client says: "It's a corruption of 'conceded.' Seeded players were 'conceded' their place in the early tournaments without the need to qualify in the preliminaries."

•

ANOTHER definition of a yacht: a hole in the water into which you throw money.

Q. "YOU ONCE said the toothbrush was invented by a British convict. How did he do it?" A. Bored holes in a bone and shoved bristles into them, that's all. William Addis was the fellow. Before his bright idea, people cleaned their teeth, if at all, with rags.

EXACTLY 100 years ago, the American railroads chose to recognize four standard time zones. Earlier, the railroads used 58 different clock settings. All the trains were on time in those days, on somebody's time.

THE CANARY wasn't yellow until man started to mess around with the poor bird's love life.

•

IF YOU put a couple of bay leaves in your flour, you won't get weevils in it, I'm told.

BUMBLEBEES, too, warm up before takeoff.

•

BABYLONIAN law as far back as 200 B.C. required former husbands to pay alimony.

•

YOUNG mountains grow, and Mount Everest, being a young mountain, is said to be growing a little taller every year. I've been told, though, that erosion off the top cancels out some of that growth.

•

THAT ANIMAL most often envisioned by a sick drinker in delirium tremens is a gray dog, according to a treatment center.

•

More than half of the cars in this country are parked indoors every night.

ANSWER DEPT.

Q. "WASN'T American writer James Fenimore Cooper kicked out of Yale for using gunpowder to blow open a dormitory door?" A. No, for that he was just put on probation. He was expelled for roping a donkey into a professor's chair.

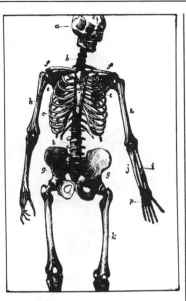

ANOTHER thing doctors learn is that the typical man is 3.84 times as tall as his thigh bone is long.

Q. "WHICH STATE has the most toll roads now?" A. Oklahoma — with 487 miles of same.

•

Q. "WHO WROTE George Washington's Farewell Address?" A. Alexander Hamilton, it's said.

Q. "DON'T YOU have to be dead for at least 10 years before your picture can be put on a U.S. postage stamp?" A. Unless you're a U.S. president, that's true. Former presidents can be depicted thereon in the year after death.

•

Q. "ISN'T THE United States the country with the highest suicide rate now?" A. No, sir, it's No. 20 on that roster. No. 1 is Romania; No. 2, Hungary, and No. 3, East Germany.

•

Q. "WHEN RIDING double on a motorcycle, where should I hang on — to the seat or to the driver?" A. To the driver, say the experts. That way you'll read the driver's body English constantly to keep the best balance.

•

Q. "HOW COME nobody ever gets a headache and a toothache at the same time?" A. It happens. But pain doesn't accumulate. So you only feel one or the other, whichever hurts most.

•

Q. "HOW MUCH is the tuition at Ringling Brothers Barnum & Bailey Clown College in Venice, Fla.?" A. No tuition. But students have to pay for their room and board.

TO THAT list of renowned personages who died while active in bed, please add Attila the Hun.

•

THE IQs of stutterers on the average are 14 points higher than the national average.

•

YES, A LAWYER legally can charge you also for the time it takes said lawyer to draw up your bill.

•

TO BECOME a dentist hereabouts now reportedly takes $50,000 for schooling and $100,000 to set up practice.

•

SUICIDE RATE among psychiatrists nationwide is six times that of the general population.

•

IN LEEDS, England, lives a lady named Ann Chovy.

•

AM TOLD the security-conscious clothiers have just come up with a bulletproof evening gown.

Q. "On May 19, 1885, one Robert E. Odlum jumped off the Brooklyn Bridge. Wasn't he the first suicide there?" A. First to jump, yes, but he wasn't a suicide. He was a swimming instructor. It was an exhibition dive. But it killed him.

THREE OUT OF 100 American householders hang family pictures in their bathrooms.

•

THE DARKER your business suit on the job, sir, the more authoritative you'll appear. Or so say the clothing specialists. Interesting, if true. President Franklin D. Roosevelt liked off-white suits.

THE LAW of Malaysia stipulates a mandatory death sentence for anyone convicted of possessing a gun, a bullet or dynamite.

•

TOYOTA MOTORS has erected a shrine in Japan to all those who've died in the company's motor vehicles.

NOBODY KNOWS what fireflies eat. In captivity, they all starve to death.

•

ALMOST but not quite 10 percent of all Americans never marry.

•

AMONG professional jai-alai players, there are no left-handers. By rule. The reversed spin that lefties put on the ball is too dangerous for right-handers unused to it.

•

UNDER MUSLIM law, a man cannot take orders from a woman.

•

IN ONE out of every five court trials in New York, it takes longer to pick the jury than to try the case.

•

LIBERIA prints no currency of its own. Uses old U.S. dollars, instead. They're shipped in from New York City every so often.

ANSWER DEPT.

Q. "DO barnacles swim?" A. Baby barnacles do. About six inches an hour.

SOME MEDICAL researchers contend that nitrous oxide, the laughing gas commonly used as an anesthetic by dentists, appears to be an aphrodisiac, at least for the female. Whether it also serves as a sexual stimulant for the male is not yet proved, they say.

Q. "HOW OLD do the oldest sturgeon get?" A. Age 120 is the max, according to Science Digest experts.

Q. "HAS THE EARTH been hit in this century by anything from outer space that was big enough to destroy a whole city?" A. Twice, it has. In 1908 and in 1947. By curious luck, both huge chunks of whatever landed in isolated areas of Siberia, hurting nobody.

•

Q. "DID NOAH have dinosaurs on the Ark?" A. Not according to the time-takers who say the dinosaurs died off 76 million years before the Flood.

•

Q. "WHERE IS Santa Claus a woman?" A. Maybe you mean Italy. The gift-giving Christmas figure there is an old lady called "La Befana."

•

Q. "WHAT'S a 'portmanteau' word?" A. A word made from two other words. Like "brunch" from breakfast and lunch. Or "smog" from smoke and fog. Or, at least, that's what "Alice in Wonderland" writer Lewis Carroll called such words.

•

Q. "HOW LONG do elephants sleep nightly? How about gorillas?" A. Gorillas, 14 hours, typically. Elephants, two hours.

ANOTHER difference between men and women in general is what they dread about the future. Women tend to be afraid of growing old. Men are more inclined to be afraid of not growing old, as it were, of death itself. Women fear the trip. Men fear the destination. Or so some scholarly researchers contend.

•

AM TOLD schoolkids now mix chewing tobacco into their bubblegum. That's bad. They can't make it bubble, and they can't hit a spittoon at three feet.

•

A BANK legally can honor the written-out amount on a check even if the amount in figures is not the same.

•

IN THE evolutionary chain, the chimpanzee is about as close to Man as any other animal? Did I tell you chimpanzees are promiscuous?

•

SURELY you can find your own hideaway island, if you look? Within the jurisdiction of the United States are more than 26,000 islands at least 10 acres in size.

THE SIGN "Beware of Dog" was a status symbol in ancient Rome. Actually, it read: "Cave Canem." That the householder had a watchdog signified that he had possessions worth guarding.

MOST BALDING men when they buy hairpieces are accompanied by their wives.

•

THE LETTER "C" started out as a drawing of a camel's neck.

•

A DAY OR SO after you take vitamin B1, your skin will repel mosquitoes, I'm told.

•

BLONDES outnumber redheads nationwide, but not by much. Blondes, 8 percent. Redheads, 7 percent.

IT'S NOT the zipper that's called the fly. It's the fold of cloth over the zipper. So says our Language Man, who studies everything.

•

COURTROOM judges in Canada can't vote in elections.

•

ONE APARTMENT building in Washington, D.C., houses more psychiatrists and clinical psychologists than live in the entire state of Wyoming. That building, incidentally, is known as the Freud Hilton.

DON'T FORGET, it takes three pounds of grapes to make one pound of raisins.

•

RAILROADS account for 50 percent of all passenger miles in Japan, 1 percent in the United States.

•

YOU'RE AWARE, aren't you, that no water from the Gulf of Mexico flows in the so-called Gulf Stream?

•

IN THAILAND'S Bangkok, any couple caught kissing in a movie theater can be fined $25.

•

AM TOLD the best felt is made from Angora fur.

•

TO BE as quick as a wink, it has to happen, precisely, in three-tenths of a second.

•

STATISTICIANS estimate that 1,885,000 people in the United States went to motels last night.

ANSWER DEPT.

Q. "DOES the Bible mention twins?" A. Twice. Esau and Jacob. Perez and Zerah. In Genesis.

IT TAKES 0.54 seconds to crack an egg. U.S. Agriculture Department researchers found out that in a $45,000 project to learn how long it takes to cook breakfast.

Q. "ARE THERE any people on earth who still don't know how to make fire?" A. A few. On the Andaman Islands, natives never let their fires burn out. Some pygmies along the Congo buy fire from the neighboring Bantu tribes. Believe the Tasadays in the Philippines have learned the old fire trick in the last few years.

Q. "IN THE GAME of bridge, a yarborough is a hand with no card higher than a nine. What are the chances of drawing such a hand?" A. One in 1827.

•

Q. "HAVE THERE ever been any societies without the institution of marriage?" A. No, sir, not a one. That's also true of the common cold.

•

Q. "HOW DID William Shakespeare spell his name?" A. Nobody knows. On one page of his will, he spelled it "Shakspere." On another page, "Shakspeare."

•

Q. "I KNOW 'boonies,' short for 'boondocks,' was brought back by the U.S. Marines from the Philippines, where the Tag name was 'bundok,' meaning mountain. But where did we get 'toolies,' which likewise means out in the sticks?" A. "Tules," rewrites our Language Man. From the Spanish for certain bulrushes that grow down along the border.

•

Q. "IF YOU THINK back 1000 years, what was the largest city in what's now the United States?" A. Cahokia. An Indian settlement in southern Illinois. With about 30,000 people.

ON THE MARKET now is a $10.95 book called "Nuclear War Survival Skills." It has a money-back guarantee.

•

MEDICAL inventors have come up with a hearing aid that fits into a partial dental plate. It channels sound vibrations to the inner ear through remaining real teeth. "How dare you shut your mouth when I'm talking to you!" It could become popular.

•

THE SURFACE area within one of your lungs is 20 times greater than the surface area of your skin.

•

IT'S ESTIMATED that American legislators have passed 35 million laws designed to enforce the Ten Commandments.

•

STANDARD distance of a mule race reportedly is 350 yards. A fast mule can make it in 20 seconds. Have you ever seen such a race? Neither have I. For that matter, I've never even seen a fast mule. Know such there be, though.

BEANS, decreed St. Jerome, are sexually stimulating. He forbade nuns to partake of same. To say St. Jerome didn't know beans is a bit too flip, I know, but it's a fact.

NO OTHER primate but man lacks pigment in the palms.

•

GET IT RIGHT: The James Bond character has been played by not just three but four actors: Sean Connery, Roger Moore, George Lazenby and the late David Niven.

•

THERE'S NO real evidence that cedar chests protect woolens from moths.

BEAR IN MIND, these weren't trite when Teddy Roosevelt coined them: "Clean as a hound's tooth," "the lunatic fringe," "pussyfooting," "mollycoddle" and "rubber-stamp Congress."

•

IN THE EARLY days of the atomic bomb development at Alamagordo, N.M., you had to be illiterate to get a janitor job there. At least, unable to read English. If you could decipher the wastepaper, you weren't welcome.

NO TWO ZEBRAS are striped alike. If you don't want to talk about zebras, you can say the same about tigers.

•

ALL KERRY blue terriers are born black.

•

A BULLFROG closes its eyes when it jumps.

•

DINGOES don't bark.

•

IT WAS THE FRENCH who first dreamed up that thing called compulsory military training.

•

CATERPILLARS eat only at night.

•

THERE ARE STILL a few people around who as children never played that game called Monopoly. It turns age 50 this year.

THERE'S no record of any tribe of humans wherein the women were taller than the men.

ANSWER DEPT.

Q. "DISCOUNTING oceans and other natural barriers, how long would it take a relay racing team of Pony Express-style riders to go around the world on horseback?" A. About 30 days.

Q. "DO KANGAROOS live in trees?" A. Some do. Their first step out sometimes is a 50-foot drop.

•

Q. "WHAT DID Francis Scott Key, who wrote the words to 'The Star-Spangled Banner,' do for a living?" A. Practiced law. And practiced. And practiced. And wound up as district attorney in Washington, D.C.

Q. " 'TIN LIZZIE' was the nickname for Henry Ford's Model-T. What was the 'Flying Teapot'?" A. A boiler-engine car called the Stanley Steamer. Old-timers will tell you it could be pressured up to extraordinary speeds for the time.

•

Q. "NAME the actor most often nominated for Academy Awards." A. Spencer Tracy. With eight.

WHAT'S "Recreational Science"? Whatever, Purdue has a professor of same. And he says three mini-vacations rest, relax and refresh you more than does one long vacation.

•

TAKES 31 days to make a golf ball.

•

IF YOU ASK the government statisticians, a household consists of 2.7 persons.

•

IF IT'S a stocking without a foot, call it a "hushion."

•

SEVENTY-NINE percent of the divorced fathers in the United States don't support their children, according to Congressional Report.

•

A "GARBO" in Australia is a man who picks up garbage. And a mail carrier there is a "postie."

•

ENGLAND a century or so ago reintroduced flogging as the prescribed punishment for robbery. And the rate of robbery promptly went up — way up. What do you make of that?

EGGS STAY fresher longer when stored in hens.

PERFUME SALES soar during an economic depression. During a war, too.

•

MORE PEOPLE are studying English in China now than are speaking English in the United States, I'm told.

•

WHAT DO YOU want on your grave, sir? Bert Gudgeon, the barkeep of a public house in Hertfordshire, England, got what he wanted: a beer mug cemented most decoratively onto his tombstone.

CAREERS OF most opera singers last only about 25 years. Age thickens the vocal cords, dries the tissues. There are exceptions, though. Tenor Jan Peerce sang well after age 70.

•

THERE WAS one newspaper for every 35,000 Americans in 1900. Now there is one newspaper for every 130,000.

•

THE POPULATION of the earth will increase more in the next 20 years than it did in the last million years.

WHAT WOULD you give for 5000 acres of Kentucky's greenest land? For exactly such, George Washington swapped his race horse "Magnolia."

•

IF YOU, too, have a family scholar who appears to be abnormally preoccupied with knowledge, you can identify that worthy as an "epistemophiliac."

•

AT CLOSE range, a skunk's scent squirted in the eyes can permanently blind. Did I tell you two skunks in a fight never spray each other? How the species arrived at this natural treaty never to use its super-weapon, I don't know.

•

THE WOMAN who has been married five years has been married one year longer than half the wives in the country.

•

"COTTON CANDY" in France is called "Papa's Beard."

ANSWER DEPT.

Q. "WHAT WAS this country's first organized sport?" A. Horse racing. In 1664.

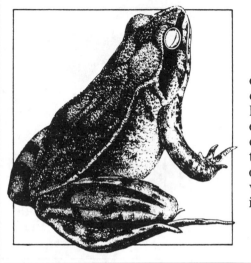

A DUCK can't walk without bobbing its head. A donkey can't bray without raising its tail. A frog can't swallow without closing its eyes.

Q. "HOW DOES the male snail recognize the female?" A. Doesn't have to. Each is both. After they mix and match, both lay eggs. Then both take off, leaving the offspring.

•

Q. "I KNOW golf was banned in Scotland once, but can you back up my bet that it was against the law onetime in this country to manufacture golf balls?" A. Certainly can. At least, against federal decree. During World War II, the stuff in golf balls was needed for war materials.

Q. "WHAT'S THE most common drink in China now?" A. Soup.

•

Q. "SAYS HERE 'J' is the fourth least used letter of the alphabet. What are the three used even less?" A. Q, X and Z.

•

Q. "HOW COME there are no designations for male and female beavers, like buck and doe or bull and cow or boar and sow?" A. None but the beavers know which is which.

LEONARDO DA VINCI was not only an astonishing brain. He was good-looking. Compatriots wrote he was "the most beautiful man who ever lived."

•

THERE IS no record to indicate any Pilgrim ever wore a black hat with a conical crown and a hatband with a silver buckle.

•

VIRGINIA law says a dog can be put to death for "criminal barking."

•

IF YOU'RE age 65, you were born the same year the American Society of Refrigerating Engineers stated publicly that household refrigerators would never become widely used.

•

PRAIRIE dogs kiss.

•

WERE YOU aware that the world's largest toymaker is General Mills?

•

EACH SALT MINE was deposited there by a sea.

WHO NAMED the athletic squads of New York University? Whoever, that school's teams are called the "violets."

WHEN Adolf Hitler ran Germany, it was a serious offense to name a horse what had always been a common name for horses there, Adolf.

•

AMONG telephone operators in the United States, the women still outnumber the men by 100 to 6.

•

EXACTLY WHAT a hedgehog tastes like I cannot say, but the British must think it tastes good. They're buying "hedgehog flavored" potato chips now.

YOU NEVER get too old for an allowance. Not if you're a princess, at any rate. The allowance for Margaret of England runs about $2000 a week. A mere bagatelle, my dear! You'd get twice that much. If we had it.

•

SOME COURTS have decreed that "Men at Work" is no longer an acceptable sign around construction projects. At least, not if any women are on the job. In such instances, the sign painters have been ordered to reword their art to "People at Work" or some such.

AT HAND is a letter addressed to my name from a geneology researcher who claims to have traced my family tree. He certainly knows how to get your attention. It begins: "Your Majesty."

•

AM TOLD we're rapidly running out of Puerto Rican parrots. Only 28 left worldwide. And ten are in cages. What are we going to do about this?

•

THE SHOULDER holster was invented by none other than the Wild West outlaw John Wesley Hardin, I'm told.

•

EMPEROR Hirohito wears a Mickey Mouse watch.

•

SO MANY babies failed to survive more than two years in the days of William Shakespeare that the statistical average lifespan for awhile there was about six years.

•

HALF THE female married lawyers are married to lawyers.

•

WORLD'S OLDEST surname is said to be Katz.

A CHICKEN-EATING weasel in Western Europe used to be called a pullet cat. That gave us "polecat."

ANSWER DEPT.

Q. "DON'T all dogs have fleas?" A. No, not all. The Inca Hairless has no fleas. That little black Peruvian pup doesn't have any place for fleas to hide. Another sort down there — but of a lighter color — has no fleas, either. It's the Peruvian Inca Orchid Moonflower dog. It's kept indoors so it won't get sunburned.

•

Q. "THE PULL of gravity differs from place to place around the United States. This makes you weigh more in some places, less in others. Where do you weigh the most? Where the least?" A. Most, Minot, N.D. Least, Key West, Fla.

•

Q. "SOME STAGE hypnotists can't work in a private office the way they can perform before a large audience. Why not?" A. Only about one person in ten responds to strong hypnotic suggestion. A hypnotist needs a fairly large pool of possible subjects to find the most susceptible. Or so I'm told.

•

Q. "WHY IS that sensitive nerve in your arm called the 'funny bone'?" A. Because it's close to the upper arm bone known as the "humerus," probably.

•

Q. "WHAT CAUSES the astronauts to grow about two inches in height while weightless in space?" A. The spinal column's constant absorption of fluid without gravity to press it out.

WOMEN more often than men dream of being pursued indoors in brightly colored places amid animated conversation, sleep researchers say. Men more often than women dream of appearing naked in public, they say.

•

SAY YOU'RE standing by a railroad track on which is rolling a freight train one mile long. If it traveled as fast as the space shuttle in orbit — 18,000 miles an hour — the entire train would sail past you in a fifth of a second.

•

UNDER Hawaiian law, if that automobile has more than 500 miles, it can't be sold as a new car.

•

IN DENMARK, a woman can "walk like a prostitute" and be arrested because of it. Prostitution is not illegal there, but street soliciting is. After a policeman collared one suspect, he told the judge, no, she didn't say anything to anybody, but her walk made it obvious. The judge accepted that. Then other judges did likewise repeatedly in other cases. The precedent now seems set.

CLINK! — to that Arkansas exterminator who practices his own personal charity. Lives in a small town. Every December he stops by the homes of a score of elderly citizens, sprays their houses for roaches, whatever, then chats for awhile before saying "Merry Christmas" and moving on.

IN A LETTER from Prior, Okla., comes a graduation photo of a young lady named Wynter Wheat. Pretty. They won't forget her face, either.

•

BUMPER Sticker on a plumber's truck: "You Have to Pay the Piper."

•

DID I say "offsides"? Must have been the Frank Gifford influence. The correct word for that football infraction is "offside."

SOME racetrack characters who think they know the ponies won't bet on a horse that hasn't raced in three weeks. Others won't bet on a horse that just arrived from another track.

•

QUERIES from Small Clients: Why can't you peel a mushroom? Did George Washington really gain 14 pounds at Valley Forge? Does a worm roll over when it dies? What's in that drink called a Horse's Neck? Why are all the musical Muppets left-handed?

ALL LITERARY types know well the name of the poet Edna St. Vincent Millay. Not all know, however, that the St. Vincent part was not an old family surname, but rather the name of the hospital in which she was born, St. Vincent's in Rockford, Me. Her mother liked it there.

•

HONG KONG still has a debtors' prison. It's jammed.

•

COST WATCHERS say it will take 17 percent more money this summer than it took last winter to move your house or office goods from one place to another.

•

A TYPICAL Tokyo restaurant seats only about 14 people.

•

U.S. ARMY parachute experts say: If the wind is blowing up to 15 mph, don't jump.

•

PERCIVAL Proctor Baxter was governor of Maine from 1921 to 1925. The one thing more than any other that's remembered about him is that when his Irish Setter died, he ordered all the state's flags flown at half staff.

IF YOU'RE not a jogger, you may not hear what the joggers say: Namely, that jogging is not just a physical fitness routine to tone up muscles and strengthen lungs, but that it's a powerful therapy to relieve depression, anger and anxiety.

ANSWER DEPT.

Q. "HOW MANY rules does your Love and War man have on file about behavior for office parties?" A. One: "Don't go."

•

Q. " YOU KNOW Mike Warren who plays Bobby Hill on 'Hill Street Blues'? Where'd he play basketball?" A. UCLA. As captain of those 1967-68 teams that won the national championships, he studied Advanced Nice Guy under John Wooden.

Q. "AREN'T ROCK stars the highest paid people in the world?" A. Among such, at any rate. Take those four in that group called the Pink Floyd, for example. Each earns more than $5.8 million a year.

•

Q. "IS PRESIDENT Ronald Reagan a collector?" A. Of antique firearms, yes.

•

Q. "WHAT'S THE biggest sort of cat?" A. The Siberian tiger. Grown males average 10 feet 4 inches.

BELIEVE one of the most extraordinary laws of all time was written into the books of the Massachusetts Bay Colony in the 1640s. It decreed that juveniles over age 16 who cursed or physically abused their parents could be put to death.

•

THE NO. 1 ailment that prompts visits to doctors is the sore throat. Back pain is No. 2.

•

MILITARY medical records of servicemen trained in swamp country indicate mosquitoes, given a choice, prefer fat people.

•

THE ENTIRE Library of Congress, microfilmed with today's best techniques, could be stored in six four-drawer filing cabinets.

•

SEVEN out of ten safes can be cracked by experts in 20 minutes. So say some specialists in this line of work.

NOTHING lowbrow about collecting baseball cards, young fellow. The Metropolitan Museum of Art in New York has 200,000.

THAT WOMEN who work for paychecks don't watch as much television as do other women may be obvious, but women who work for paychecks don't watch as much television as do men who work for paychecks, either.

•

ESKIMOS eat almost no salt. They have the lowest incidence of high blood pressure. The Japanese eat the most salt. They have the highest incidence of high blood pressure.

YOU SAY you want to get rid of the possums in your attic? Sprinkle mothballs around up there.

•

IN MAJOR-LEAGUE baseball, players who try to steal bases get away with it 66.3 percent of the time.

•

HERE'S TO Joseph Swann — clink! — who invented the lightbulb. True, Thomas Edison gets the credit, but he merely improved Swann's creation, that's all.

SIX YEARS is about the average longevity of a fashion model's career.

•

IF YOU KNOW anybody born on the fourth day of the month, you might mention to said worthy that the ancient Greeks firmly believed citizens so born were destined to strenuous lives of extremely hard work.

•

THERE WAS a time when the correct English judged a gentleman in part by how smoothly he folded his umbrella, known cutely as his "brolly." This comes to mind because a client asks whether the first umbrellas were made for rain or for sunshine. Credit the sun of old Egypt for that. The word "umbrella," in fact, comes from the Italian for "little shadow."

MANY a modern man walks so little he's flabby, and many an elder blames the automobile for that. It was for precisely the same reason that Thomas Jefferson condemned the horse and carriage. People just don't walk enough anymore, said he.

ANSWER DEPT.

Q. "DON'T electricians in England use ferrets to pull wire through conduits?" A. Been done. Not every British electrician keeps a ferret on standby for this novel technique, however. Telephone crews in West Germany have used dachshunds to pull cable through narrow passages, too, likewise rarely.

Q. "HOW MANY crowns does Queen Elizabeth have?" A. Eight. But they're not hers. They're the property of the British government. When she needs one, she tells the Lord Chamberlain in St. James' Palace. He relays the request to a Regent Street firm, which sends a man in a taxi to the Tower of London for it. He drops it off at Buckingham Palace. Crown for the Queen! Sign here.

Q. "RIDDLE me this, Louie. Three actors have played James Bond. Sean Connery and Roger Moore. But who's the third?" A. George Lazenby, an Australian. In "Her Majesty's Secret Service."

•

Q. "HAS THERE ever been a month without a full moon?" A. Only one of record. February of 1866.

STATISTICAL footnotes of yesteryear suggest that Americans two centuries ago drank twice as much liquor per capita annually as they drink today. I don't believe it. Nobody could drink twice as much as they drink today.

•

SOLDIERS IN the army of the Netherlands have their own union. They get overtime pay for KP duty.

•

IN ONE of England's most remarkable trials, a woman named Mary Hamilton was convicted on Oct. 7, 1746, of marrying with her own sex to the extent of having 14 wives.

•

MISTER, if you can't flip out a deck of 52 playing cards in 37 seconds, don't call yourself a dealer. That's what the time-and-motion boys figure as average.

•

BEER CAN promote gout, I'm told.

•

COMEDIAN George Burns is booked to play the London Palladium in 1996. He'll be 100.

IN THE ENGLAND of Shakespeare's time, a young woman implied her virginity by wearing low-cut costumes that exposed much of her bosom but covered her arms to her wrists.

DON'T ASK ME where they got it, but the old Romans are said to have had a powdered form of aspirin. Likewise, early American Indians.

•

CROWS live 80 years.

•

CLAIM IS three-fourths of the 200 million goldfish grown on purpose in this country are fed on purpose to other fish.

EVIDENTLY, when we make a peanut butter-and-jelly sandwich, we like to think we personally created something. Must be. The packers put peanut butter and jelly into the same jar, and the product flopped.

•

THE STATISTICIANS who deal in averages will tell you North American grizzly bears kill half a person a year.

HOW DO YOU account for the fact that Utah uses three times more Jello than any other state? Do many Mormons crave sugar? That's one theory. Lot of people who don't use alcohol crave sugar, it's said.

•

YOU'VE SEEN "Deer Crossing," "Cattle Crossing," maybe even "Duck Crossing" road signs, but have you ever seen a "Granny Crossing" sign? One such exists near a seasoned citizens housing project in Deerfield, Ill.

•

TO TAKE a bite out of somebody else's hamburger is against the law in Oklahoma, please note.

ANSWER DEPT.

Q. "WHAT'S THIS country's biggest capital city?" A. Arizona's Phoenix. With 790,000 residents. You want to know the smallest? Vermont's Montpelier. With 8241.

•

Q. "WHAT'S the most consecutive losses suffered by any college football team?" A. 50. Macalester College of St. Paul, Minn., managed that between 1974 and 1979. Some record.

TO BE LEGAL in Connecticut, a pickle, when dropped 12 inches, has to bounce. This calls for explanation, doesn't it? The soggy, limp pickle is no good, pickle lovers said. Only crisp, firm pickles can pass the test.

Q. "WHAT MAKES China's Yellow River yellow?" A. Loess, a yellowish topsoil blown off the deserts.

Q. "DID YOU say a hen's egg cooks at 107 degrees F.?" A. On the contrary. I said it's fortunate the egg doesn't. That's a hen's body temperature.

•

Q. "DID Abraham Lincoln wear glasses?" A. He did. One photograph proves that. Otherwise, of the 118 photos of him, 39 are without beard, 79 with beard.

•

Q. "ISN'T a referee in a professional game prohibited from helping an injured player?" A. Amounts to that. Sports laws are such that careful referees, unless they're doctors, don't even touch hurt players.

•

Q. "YOU SAID chickens die in stampedes. They're not heavy enough to trample each other to death. So what kills them?" A. Suffocation.

•

Q. "HOW LONG have we had roadside billboards?" A. Ever since the Civil War.

•

Q. "IDAHO has the most millionaires per capita, right? How have most of Idaho's millionaires made their money?" A. Sale of farmland.

ROMANS HUNG their kerchiefs from their belts; the English hung theirs from their sleeves. It was the "hang" of those kerchiefs that gave us the pronunciation of "handkerchief." But some opinionated scribe long ago changed the spelling of the word on the theory it should be so named because it's used in the "hand."

•

YOUNG WOMEN in India's Karan tribe are given special lessons in the art of weeping. But they're not taught much else. And tribal tradition permits them to cry only on their wedding days.

•

VENEZUELA requires its licensed drivers to undergo psychological examinations. To weed out aggressive characters.

•

HORSEMEAT can sell for $1000 a pound — if it's a special thoroughbred race horse.

•

PINK PIGEONS are stupid. So stupid they can't find food in the wild, lack the craft to build nests, don't even know where to lay their eggs. No wonder there are only 50 of them left worldwide.

NOWHERE but in the United States has the chewing gum habit caught on to any notable degree.

THREE BEERS a day is the allotment for U.S. Marines in Lebanon, correspondents say.

•

ASK YOUR minister if he'd consider a transfer to American Samoa. Church attendance is compulsory there.

•

THE NATIONAL suicide clock ticks off such a death every 26 minutes.

•

MURDERERS on the average are about seven years, six months younger than their victims.

STRONGEST expletive in the Bible is said to be: "The Devil take you!"

•

A WORLD-CLASS figure skater typically has trained six hours a day for 10 years under the tutelage of an expert coach.

•

MEDIAN AGE of cars on the road now is 6.2 years.

•

AM NOW told there's a national organization called the "Association of Physicians Who Do Not Own Mercedes-Benzes."

THE MOST popular toy in China for the last 20 years has been a battery-powered "Mother Hen" that lays eggs while pushing a baby stroller.

•

CHARLES DODGSON, aka Lewis Carroll, the author of "Alice in Wonderland," was an expert photographer. In his particular case, it's a sad curiosity, though, that almost all of the pictures he took were of little girls without any clothes on.

•

THE WIDELY SEEN silhouette of the late Alfred Hitchcock may support this fact, don't know: He insisted on having richly garnished potatoes with every dinner.

•

ALASKA'S wild rabbits — snowshoe hares, actually — love plywood, I'm told. The glue therein, clearly. When they're at peak population, you can bait a rabbit trap with plywood.

•

NOT EVERY minister's son wastes his life, please note. Isaac Taylor of London, England, was a minister's son, and he invented the beer-keg spigot.

THE POLICE Department in Rochester, N.Y., sends flowers to victims of violent crime there.

ANSWER DEPT.

Q. "HOW MUCH money does the author get on the average for a published novel?" A. Typically, $4000.

•

Q. 'WHAT did Sean Connery do before he became an actor?" A. Polished coffins in a woodshop. His medical discharge from the Royal Navy qualified him for money to learn a trade. That was it. Wood polishing.

Q. "WHAT'S a 'Popemobile'?" A. That vehicular glass cage in which Pope John Paul II rides during motorcades.

•

Q. "THOMAS EDISON lost much of his hearing at an early age. But I just read he and his wife attended stage plays. How did he hear the actors?" A. His wife fingertipped key lines of dialogue in Morse code on his knee. Didn't I tell you he taught her the Morse code? Then tapped out his marriage proposal in her hand? She tapped back her acceptance.

THE SUMMER of 1936 was so hot in Brownstown, Ind., that corn actually popped on the stalk, according to the local paper.

•

AMONG DIVORCEES who remarry, the average time between weddings is 4½ years.

•

SIR FRANCIS DRAKE is said to have been one of the few masters who treated his ships' crews so well he never had to use shanghaied prisoners as seamen. Volunteers were ever at the ready. He had the pick of the English sailors. Some historians credit his kindly concern as one reason for his success on the high seas.

•

DID I TELL YOU that you have enough lime in your body to whitewash a doghouse?

•

IF YOU WANT to be a broadcaster, don't forget the "Mackinac" in Mackinac Island is pronounced "Mackinaw," "Cairo" in Illinois sounds like the syrup, and the "lived" in short-lived rhymes with "dived."

WHEN HE lifts his glass to drink, he looks into the glass. When she lifts her glass to drink, she looks over the rim. Usually, usually. That's another difference between the male and the female.

SCARLET pimpernel is a weed.

•

THREE DAYS after a woman changes the color of her hair, she thinks it's her own. The eventual sight of dark roots surprises her. So says a tinter by trade. Sounds about right. A parallel claim is that soon after a man grows a mustache, he can't remember how he looked without it.

ONE IN EVERY 25 homeowners is running a month behind with the mortgage payment.

•

ON THE BORDER between Syria and Lebanon are three small villages, the only places left in the world — at this writing — where the Aramaic dialect spoken by Jesus Christ is still in daily use.

MUSICOLOGISTS will tell you the Vienna statue to Franz Peter Schubert cost more money than all Schubert had earned from his music during his lifetime.

•

FREUD'S true first name was not "Sigmund" but "Sigismund."

•

IF A GIRAFFE'S blood pressure weren't about three-and-a-half times higher than a human being's, it would faint.

•

"HELL'S CANYON" originally was "Heller's Canyon" — in memory of an early Idaho miner.

•

IF THE BOAT motor's propeller turns clockwise, it's said to be "right-handed."

ANSWER DEPT.

Q. "WHY DOES the $2 bill repeatedly fail acceptance? Superstition?" A. Don't believe that's it. Most cash registers don't have enough bins to handle the extra denomination. It's easier for cashiers to hand back two $1 bills than to dig under the trays for one $2 bill.

DON'T TELL them you're getting a face-lift. Be highbrow. Say you're undergoing a "rhytidectomy."

Q. "HOW DID tennis come to be scored by 15, 30, 40, deuce, ad?" A. Early in France, the most common silver piece was worth 60 sous, with each of its four parts worth 15 sous. Tennis was played for stakes. So points were worth 15, 30, 45 sous. Eventually, after the coin denominations no longer signified, the 45 was abbreviated to 40 merely because it was easier to say.

Q. "HAS ANY man elected to the U.S. presidency had a criminal record?" A. Not unless you want to count Andrew Jackson's duelling.

•

Q. "ONE MORE time, Louie, list those five essentials to happiness." A. Health, freedom, financial security, congenial work and reciprocated love. You doing all right?

•

Q. "WASN'T IT the English knights who introduced helmets into warfare?" A. No, sir, credit the Ethiopians with that first. They wore the skulls of horses as helmets.

•

Q. "IN ENGLAND, what's the difference between a 'barrister' and a 'solicitor'?" A. The barrister argues the case in court. The solicitor helps the barrister prepare the case.

•

Q. "CAN YOU verify that the great golfer Bobby Jones never won a penny playing golf?" A. His titles came through amateur tournaments without purses, true, but I wouldn't bet on the widespread claim he never won any money out there, would you?

IT'S NOT a "catastrophe" unless it takes five or more lives, according to the Metropolitan Life Insurance Company. It's not a "catastrophe" unless it costs more than $5 million, says the American Insurance Association.

•

STATISTICALLY, that professional lady still identified by some as the "housewife" is nine times more likely to attempt suicide than is the woman in any other occupation, except prostitution.

•

AGE 24 years 6 months among men must be a special time of life. Surveys of more than 18,000 husbands indicate they think that's the ideal age for a fellow to get married.

•

THE CELEBRITY whose star appears on the Hollywood Walk of Fame has to pony up about $3000 for it.

•

A BASEBALL game I'd particularly like to see is the one scheduled in Fairbanks, Alaska, for June 30. Starts at 11 p.m. No artificial lights.

GENETICISTS say it's now possible to produce a milk cow as big as an elephant.

SOUTH AFRICA hangs about seven felons a week.

•

OUR CHIEF Prognosticator thinks each individual someday will have a personal telephone number no matter how many other people live in the same residence. The phone's ring will let you know whom it's for.

•

AIR FORCE airplanes outnumber Air Force generals now by only 24 to one. In 1945, it was 244 to one.

WHEN BERLIN was under horrendous attack toward the end of World War II, two civilian enterprises there went on operating without letup: the weather bureau and 17 breweries.

•

THAT ATHLETE most likely to come from the largest family is the wrestler.

•

TO TEST your mail scale, if any, put five quarters on it. Should register a little less than an ounce.

REMEMBER, young fellow, to whistle at a girl is against the law in Abilene, Texas.

•

HAIR GROWS faster in the morning than at any other time of day.

•

BEFORE retirement, you put in about 10,000 days on the job, if typical. How many have you got left?

•

THE LATE Mel Blanc, the voice of the cartoon characters, drifted in and out of coma after a car accident. During that time, he said, he could talk as Bugs Bunny before he could talk again as Blanc.

•

WHAT'S a "road"? A body of water? Yes, sir. First meaning in the big book at hand says it's where ships ride at anchor.

•

FROGS DON'T drink water. They absorb it.

•

POLICE statisticians say only one rapist in every 600 reported rape cases is caught and convicted.

•

IT IS the children between 7 and 12 who are by far the most responsive to hypnotism.

IT IS a matter of historical record that Christopher Columbus had freckles.

ANSWER DEPT.

Q. "WHERE CAN you see all six New England states at once?" A. From atop Mount Monadnock in southern New Hampshire.

•

Q. "A CARIBBEAN seamstress says she invariably puts 216 stitches in each item she makes. What does she make?" A. Baseballs.

Q. "DID Benjamin Franklin patent any of his inventions?" A. No, sir, and that's noteworthy. Both he and Thomas Jefferson, another highly inventive fellow, helped formulate the U.S. Constitution, which provides patent protection. Neither, though, took out patents on any of their own creations.

•

Q. "WHERE'D WE get the phrase '. . .in cold blood'?" A. From legal lingo of old. Meant premeditated. So brought harsher punishment than the "hot blood" crimes of passion.

•

Q. "AGING WOMEN seem to wrinkle around the mouth more than men do. Why?" A. Years of shaving thickens the skin around a man's mouth, thus to make it more resistant to wrinkling. Or so theorize the medicos.

•

Q. "YOU SAY the pelican breathes through its mouth? Why?" A. No nostrils.

•

Q. "NAME THE ONLY one of our United States with a round border?" A. Delaware. Its northern border was drawn on a map with a compass. An arc with a 12-mile radius from the spire of a courthouse in New Castle.

WOMEN CONTINUE to take over the jobs traditionally held by men. Typesetters used to be men, mostly. Now they're mostly women. You can say the same for bookbinders, insurance adjusters and bartenders, I've heard. Not so yet with letter carriers. The mailmen still outnumber the mailwomen by seven to one. But stand by.

•

WILL YOU BUY the claim that the average person takes about 18,000 steps a day?

•

AMONG professional athletes in the United States, the men outnumber the women by 53,000 to 13,000.

•

AT LAST COUNT, 1013 buildings in the United States were posted with signs reading: "George Washington Slept Here."

•

WAS IN 1961 that a painting by the French artist Henri Matisse hung upside down for 47 days in the New York Museum of Modern Art before somebody caught it.

HOW DOES an "electrical male chastity belt" work? Shrug. Anyhow, a fellow named Michael McCormick patented such a device in 1896.

ANOTHER autoantonym — one word with opposite meanings — is "stem." As in: Stem the flow, meaning stop. Or: Stem from . . ., meaning start.

•

THREE out of every 100 U.S. residents are illegal aliens, I'm told.

•

AMONG the tastiest dishes known to gourmets is tripe. Wish I'd never been told what it is. Same goes for escargot, might add.

SOME LOCAL laws are most mysterious, but not this one: In Waterloo, Neb., it's illegal for a barber to eat onions between 7 a.m. and 7 p.m.

•

THE MALE hairdressers in the United States outnumber the female barbers by 68,000 to 14,500.

•

SOME but not all medical researchers think there's a connection between coffee drinking and nighttime leg cramps. Shrug.

OUR LANGUAGE MAN says "That's Chinese to me" is the Russian equivalent of our phrase "It's Greek to me."

•

A SMALL hurricane releases energy equivalent to the explosions of six atomic bombs per second.

•

TWICE AS MANY men today — 7.5 million — live alone by choice as did so 15 years ago.

•

THAT WORD "crummy" to mean something undesirable has been around for about 400 years.

MOST common symptom of depression, it's said, is fatigue.

ANSWER DEPT.

Q. "WHO WAS the man who jumped from a burning airplane at 18,000 feet without a parachute and lived to tell about it?" A. Royal Air Force Gunnery Sergeant Nicholas Alkemade. In 1944. He figured it would be quicker than death by fire. But he hit pine tree branches, then springy undergrowth, then deep snow. He was unhurt.

•

Q. "WHAT'S the proper nickname for a man called 'Aristotle'?" A. Ari served for Onassis, Telly for Savalas.

Q. "WHEN WAS the last time the bow and arrow was the primary weapon of a major battle force?" A. In the late 1500s when Spanish archers of the Armada attacked 10,000 English soldiers with guns. That did it. In world-class combat, the bow and arrow was all done.

•

Q. "HOW COME we never hear about George Fibbleton, the fellow who in 1833 invented the first shaving machine?" A. Because it didn't work. Historical footnotes indicate George wound up with numerous small scars on his face.

Q. "HAS THERE ever been a postage stamp to honor the police profession?" A. Not a U.S. stamp. Other countries have put out cop commemoratives, though.

•

Q. "WHEN DID the U.S. Department of Agriculture stop teaching farmers how to grow opium?" A. Sometime before 1942 when Congress outlawed that poppy.

•

Q. "ISN'T cocaine a narcotic?" A. Not in the lingo of the pharmacologists. It's a central nervous system stimulant.

ST. VALENTINE'S Day during the reign of the good Queen Anne of England was celebrated with a love lottery. An adult version of the Post Office kissing game, I gather. Men put numbers in a bowl, women likewise. The numbers were compared, and in disregard of prior matrimonial commitment, each man spent the day with the woman whose number matched his own. In the woods, mostly.

•

IF YOUR PARENTS were divorced, odds run three out of four you'll be divorced, too. Such are the sad statistics.

•

THE TYPICAL $1 box of popcorn at the local movie theater contains about 5 cents worth of kernels.

•

"B" IS THE grade-point average of the typical teenage video-game player, researchers say.

•

IF THAT leather jacket of yours has a wrinkle in it that can't be ironed out, it probably was made from either the neck or belly hide of the beast.

SORRY ABOUT THIS... BUT YOUR BIRTHDAY IS TOMORROW!

IN MAJOR-LEAGUE baseball, add 50 points to the player's batting average if he gets to the plate on his birthday. Research shows that's how the hitters outperform their own records on that special occasion.

IN FOOTBALL, 55 percent of the NFL players are black. In basketball, 80 percent of the NBA players are black.

•

FOR THE FIRST moment or so, a goldfish can accelerate as swiftly as a race car.

•

AMONG show business people, comedians have the lowest divorce rate, research reveals.

FOUR AND TWENTY blackbirds baked in a pie would serve about six, I'm told.

•

DURING THE Alaskan Gold Rush of 1897, salt sold up north for its exact weight in gold.

•

CAN YOU explain why ocean levels north of the equator drop eight inches every spring? Neither can I.

THE POTATO you eat is not the plant's root but its stem.

•

THE FEMALE of all mammal species usually lives longer than the male.

•

CLAIM IS that seabird known as the cormorant can swim as fast as it can fly.

•

AM NOW told the Nile catfish swims upside down most of its life to feed on algae from the undersides of water plants.

•

IN DOG-SHOW literature, if it's listed as "dog," it's a male.

•

NOT ONE layman in 1000 answers correctly when you ask, "What's the largest organ of the human body?" Go on, ask. You'll see. The right reply: "The skin."

•

KNOW YOUR merry-go-round horses: The "jumpers" move up and down. The "flyers" tilt upward as the carousel picks up speed. The "gallopers" remain immobile on the turning track.

EVERY U.S. president has worn eyeglasses.

ANSWER DEPT.

Q. "WHEN WRAPPING something in aluminum foil, which side of the foil should face out, the shiny side or the dull side?" A. Doesn't matter. At all. The manufacturing process makes one side shiny and the other dull, but for no purpose.

•

Q. "HOW LONG does it take your body to replenish a pint of donated blood?" A. The fluid, 24 hours. The red corpuscles, eight weeks.

Q. "WHAT ARE 'five guarantees of life' supposedly granted by China to all its people?" A. Food, clothing, medical care, housing and burial expenses.

•

Q. "WHAT'S the 'lie' of a hockey stick?" A. The angle between the handle and the blade.

•

Q. "HOW OFTEN is Eve mentioned in the Bible?" A. Four times. Those who crave celebrity status might remember that. Getting there first beats paid publicity.

•

Q. "WHAT'S a 'digitorium'?" A. A silent machine for piano practice.

•

Q. "IN WHAT sort of horse races are the horses entered even before they're born?" A. Futurity.

•

Q. "IS IT possible to cross a sheep with a goat?" A. In test-tube experiments, it is. Scientists at the Institute of Animal Physiology in Cambridge, England, have done it. The embryo is implanted in surrogate sheep and goat mothers. They call their hybrid a "geep."

ABE LINCOLN slept in a nightshirt. Warren Harding wore nothing. On the shoulders of Dwight D. Eisenhower's pajamas were five pretty little stars.

•

CHINESE requires no punctuation.

•

FISH, TOO, use body language. Flip a fin, arch the back, change color. They talk to one another that way.

•

NINETY-TWO percent of the baseball players who sign professional contracts never appear in major-league games.

•

MARKET VALUE of the work done by the average American housewife is now up to $774.77 a week, according to the latest calculations.

•

MAY BABIES weigh more, have higher IQs, enjoy better health, and live longer. Generally, generally. Why is that?

•

TAKES 125 chiggers lined up in a row to make an inch.

DID I tell you sheep love chocolate? I did? It's still true.

ONLY the male robin sings.

•

THAT 14 feet of earthworms eaten daily by the typical robin represents only about 40 percent of said bird's diet.

•

REPORT IS President Ronald Reagan has increased his chest measurement one and three-quarters inches since he started regular workouts.

GASOLINE NEVER freezes solid. Gets thick, gummy, waxy. But not solid.

•

IN THE DAYS of Queen Elizabeth I of England, the wedding ring was worn on the thumb of the right hand.

•

WHEN New Jersey wanted to fill the job of state executioner, 50 applicants turned up.

UNIQUE fingerprints show up on the fingers of the fetus at about three months.

•

IT WAS 50 years ago that Public Enemy No. 1 John Dillinger said of the infamous Bonnie and Clyde: "They're giving bank robbery a bad name."

•

YOU CAN PLAY poker in Nevada casinos, but not in Atlantic City casinos.

•

TEENAGE SUICIDE in this country has gone up 300 percent in the last 25 years.

ANSWER DEPT.

Q. "YOU SAID one out of five unmarried women has seriously considered the notion of having a baby and bringing it up by herself without benefit of a matrimonial partner. How many of the unmarried men have seriously considered doing this?" A. One out of four.

•

Q. "HOW LONG does it take to train a lady wrestler?" A. At least six months. More like a year. Hardest thing she has to overcome is said to be her natural fear of falling.

MORE long-distance phone calls are made on Mother's Day than at any other time of the year.

Q. "WHAT'S THAT New York City outfit that calls itself 'G.O.A.L.'?" A. Gay Officers Action League. It's a 51-member group of gays in the city's criminal justice system. Thirty-one are police officers.

•

Q. "WHERE'S 'New Holland'?" A. That's an old name for Australia.

Q. "IN RUNNING, what's a 'dip finish'?" A. That's when a runner thrusts both arms behind the body and leans ahead, forcing the shoulders and chest forward, just before hitting the tape. Claim is the runner can pick up an extra quick foot of distance.

•

Q. "WHY DO so many American Indians live on reservation land even though they don't have to?" A. It's tax free.

•

Q. "CAN FEMALE birds choose the sex of their chicks?" A. New research indicates that. Skeptical? Me, too.

•

Q. "DO THE COPS have a right to examine my telephone call records?" A. They can get the right. More than 20,000 phone bills are subpoenaed every year.

•

Q. "WHAT'S the longest street in Chicago?" A. Western Avenue — 24½ miles.

•

Q. "HOW MUCH of Sweden's population came to America during the great exodus from there in the 19th century?" A. About a third, finally.

IN VENICE about 400 years ago, the call girls outnumbered the married women by 12 to one. No, they weren't known as call girls, certainly. They were listed as "courtesans," all 11,600 of them, in a directory on file today in the Library of St. Mark.

•

HERE'S TO the University of Minnesota — clink! — which fielded the first female cheerleaders. In 1918, that was. Twenty years earlier, that same school fielded the first male cheerleader, but who cares?

•

MANY a turkey stares at the sky open-mouthed during a rain storm. And pritnear drowns.

•

ABOUT THE CLAIM that man is the only animal with a chin. Am now told an elephant also has a chin, but you have to skin it to see same. I haven't done that, not ever, so didn't know.

•

EXPECT NEXT: designer hearing aids that look like jewelry.

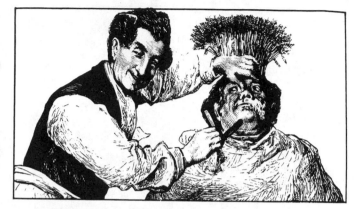

MEN'S HAIRCUTS in North Dakota traditionally have cost about as much as a bushel of wheat.

SAN FRANCISCO'S Barbary Coast was an extremely dangerous place between 1860 and 1880. The record lists 7300 murders there — an average of one a night — in that score of years.

•

UNDERGARMENT makers say more women than ever before are buying the larger sizes of bras.

•

DID I MENTION you have 40 miles of tubes in your kidneys? It's nothing, really. You've got 60,000 miles of blood vessels.

THAT EXPRESSION "low man on the totem pole" is misleading. The whereabouts of the figures on totem poles has never signified status.

•

NO, IT'S not unusual for a baby robin to eat 14 feet of earthworms a day.

•

CROP-DUSTER pilots in the Soviet Union spray coal dust over fields in the early spring. It absorbs the sunshine's heat, so melts the snow a bit more speedily.

THE BIGGEST encyclopedia in the set is always the one labeled "S."

•

AVERAGE TIP of diners nationwide now is 14.5 percent of the check, researchers report.

•

YOU CAN'T legally drive a red car in Minneapolis. That's the law there.

•

TWO OUT OF three people who buy running shoes don't run in them.

•

THE STATE of Wyoming was named in honor of Wyoming Valley, Pa.

•

EVERYBODY knew artist Norman Rockwell wouldn't make it when he dropped out of school in the 10th grade.

•

HOW MANY pig latin words come to mind that are also regular words? Start with "ashtray."

ANSWER DEPT.

Q. "QUICK, name the only animal with retractable horns." A. The snail.

IF A lifeguard in Georgia follows the letter of the law, said savior will not show up at the beach unless dressed in a bright red bathing suit and a neck harness attached to a 200-foot rope.

Q. "ISN'T ACTOR Judd Hirsch a physicist?" A. He holds a B.S. in physics, all right. From City College of New York. Class of '60. Don't believe he'd call himself a physicist, though.

•

Q. "WHAT TWO famous actors won Oscars not for their acting but for their directing?" A. Robert Redford for "Ordinary People" and Warren Beatty for "Reds."

Q. "THE WORD 'falsehood' did not come from the fact that knights of old wore 'false hoods' to conceal their identity, sir. 'Hood' is merely a suffix to show condition, as in childhood and motherhood." A. You've demolished another bright idea with the hard facts. Hope you're satisfied.

•

Q. "WHAT KIND of car did the president of the palindrome society buy?" A. A Toyota.

MEDICOS think one out of every 12 people never catch colds.

•

NOBODY CAN fold a piece of paper in half 10 times.

•

THE METHOD of numbering houses with even numbers on one side of the street and odd ones on the other got started in Philadelphia.

•

A THOUSAND years before Christ, the Olmec civilization along Mexico's Gulf Coast used penicillin.

•

BULLFROGS croak with their mouths closed.

•

STARFISH have no brains. None.

•

CAN YOU disprove the claim that the word "horseradish" started out as "harsh radish"?

•

A RELATIVELY recent law of Boston specifically permits musicians to serenade in the streets there anytime.

STRAIGHTEN UP, GRANDPA

AFTER AGE 40, sir, you can expect to start getting shorter. By about a quarter of an inch every decade.

YOU CAN USE a phrase all your life without ever stopping to think what it really means. Take "to lose your temper." If steel loses its temper, it breaks rather than bends, no?

•

MY DEAR, if you go to the dress rack labeled Size 16, you're one of many ladies who do likewise. How many? Approximately 30 million.

THOMAS JARMAN, reputed in law to have been the greatest legal expert on the last will and testament, died without leaving a will.

•

THE GERMAN poet Heinrich Heine bequeathed his entire estate to his widow on the condition she remarry — "so at least one other man will regret my death."

AM TOLD honeybees run about 5000 to the pound.

•

THE YOUNGSTER who runs away from home once is not so unusual. Nor is the youngster who runs away from home habitually. But the youngster who runs away from home twice and only twice is a rarity.

ANSWER DEPT.

Q. "WHEN YOU blow soap bubbles, they rise. Why?" A. Because your breath in them is warmer than the surrounding air.

•

Q. "WHAT'S the smallest kind of cow?" A. The pigmy buffalo of Southeast Asia. Three feet high at the shoulders.

•

Q. "WHAT PROPORTION of the convicted murderers in U.S. prisons are on death rows?" A. At last report, 1163 out of about 34,000.

•

Q. "CAN an elephant jump?" A. No. Walk, shuffle, canter, gallop and lope, yes. But not jump.

MOST OF the farmers I knew as a kid smoked either cigarets or pipes. But today's statistics show that, among the major professionals, the farmer is the least likely to smoke.

———————

Q. "WHAT'S A 'Bimmer'?" A. A BMW car. Owners of same seem to like that pet name.

Q. "IS RADAR always accurate?" A. Nothing electronic in the hands of amateurs is always accurate. I say this as one who word-processed the curious claim that the late Josef Stalin, the Georgian, came from the Ukraine. This computer should have known better than that. No, not always accurate. The record shows that police radar in Madison, Wis., recently clocked a parked car at 56 mph.

•

Q. "HOW MANY 14-year-old widows are there in the United States?" A. About 300, probably. That would be a typical count for any given year.

•

Q. "HOW FAR do you have to drive the average diesel automobile before you start getting back in fuel savings the extra cost of the car?" A. About 100,-000 miles. That, according to the American Automobile Association.

•

Q. "WHERE'D we get the phrase 'rule of thumb'?" A. Two explanations are offered: 1. The distance from the thumbnail's tip to the first knuckle was once used as the original inch measure. 2. British law long ago stipulated a man couldn't beat his wife with any rod thicker than his thumb.

WHEN ASKED which they'd prefer, a boy or a girl, most expectant parents say a boy, if they're willing to state any preference. Yet adoption agency records clearly indicate the majority of childless applicants seek baby girls. Curious.

•

THE MAN WHO did the most for milk, it's now thought, was Louis Pasteur, but he wasn't thinking along those lines at the time. In fact, he once said, "Wine is the most healthful and most hygienic of all beverages."

•

WHY THE South Carolinians get more dental cavities than people elsewhere I do not know.

•

IN SPACE ORBIT, the shuttle's manipulator arm can lift 32.5 tons. On earth, it can't even lift itself. A whole different game, that space engineering.

•

CONSCRIPTS in the Soviet army have to sew strips of white cloth inside their uniform collars, so inspecting officers can tell therefrom whether said soldiers washed their necks.

CHRISTOPHER Columbus signed his name Colombo, Colomo, Colom and Colon, but never Columbus.

"A STUDENT who changes the course of history," noted Franklin P. Adams, "is probably taking an exam."

•

IF THE TYPICAL work week were cut by five hours, another nine million jobs would open up. Or so say the theorists.

GROCERY shopping used to be a once-a-week chore for most. Not anymore. Supermarket trips now average two and a half per week.

•

MOST STUDENTS accepted at U.S. medical schools have a college grade point average of 3.3 — equivalent to a B plus.

IN THE EARLIEST days of radio, "soap operas" were called "washboard weepers," please note.

•

EXTREMELY TALL people say their cost of living runs about 50 percent higher than average.

•

MAN IN ILLINOIS has put together a robot that vacuums carpets. Does good work. But the man has to take all the furniture out of the room first. It has made carpet vacuuming an extremely difficult job.

•

NOBODY makes steel nails in this country anymore. They're all imported.

•

A LIVING, breathing 8-pound horse? You bet. Fantasy, a foot-tall filly, merited that description when born recently at the Hobby Horse Farm in Bedford County, Va. World's smallest horse.

•

SOME LONDON parking meters require the equivalent of about $1.32 an hour.

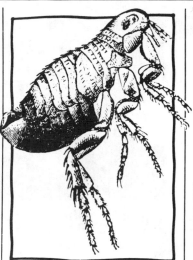

THERE'S a sort of Transylvanian phenomenon about the life cycle of the flea. Its first blood meal brings it to sexual maturity.

ANSWER DEPT.

Q. "IN WHAT battle were the most American casualties?" A. Antietam, during the Civil War. The slaughter was astounding. Near Sharpsburg, Md., on Sept. 17, 1862, soldiers in 12 hours brought down 22,-719 men.

Q. "HOW BIG is the biggest diamond?" A. It's 616 carats. Named most imaginatively as "The 616." De Beers has it on display in South Africa's Kimberley. That city is also the site of the world's biggest man-made hole in the ground — 1.5 kilometers in diameter and 400 meters deep. Named, most imaginatively, "The Big Hole."

•

Q. "WHO WAS the first person known to have died of radiation exposure?" A. None other than Madame Marie Curie herself.

•

Q. "WHY IS that liquor known as 'gin' so called?" A. Comes from the French "genievre," for juniper.

•

Q. "HOW MANY former U.S. presidents wound up in debt and died broke?" A. At least three — Thomas Jefferson, James Madison and James Monroe.

•

Q. "CAN the weathermakers actually create a thunderstorm?" A. Sort of. By seeding adjacent clouds, they can encourage mergers into one big cloud, which can have the potential for a powerful storm.

I AM SURPRISED to learn that a man on a bicycle converts energy into motion 10 times more efficiently than a seagull on the wing.

•

MANY an ancient Egyptian mummy has false teeth.

•

THE MAN who invented the tubeless tire, Frank Herzegh, got $1 for it.

•

TWENTY-THREE percent of the grownup Americans don't drink any sort of liquor at all.

•

WHERE WERE you when the Beatles first became popular? Not cutting hair for a living, I hope. Claim is 200,000 barbers lost their jobs when those musical lads hit the scene.

•

AT DUKE UNIVERSITY, a series of tests some time back suggested that the drinking of liquor tends to lessen the statistical probability that dice shooters will toss their desired points. Can you buy that?

EXPERTS in the game of poker say your opponents can't judge whether it's your policy to bluff or not if you don't bluff more than 6 percent of the time.

CERTAINLY you know you can make a right-handed rubber glove out of a left-handed rubber glove just by turning it inside out.

•

THE DOUBLE-YOLKED egg is always laid within six weeks after the hen first starts to lay eggs.

•

IT'S KNOWN that elephants can detect water beneath the ground, but it's not known exactly how they do it.

CHINA HAS no Russian tearooms. The Soviet Union has no Chinese restaurants.

•

THE STRICTEST parents are the least educated, surveys indicate.

•

AMONG houseflies, too, the female is stronger than the male.

•

WILD DUCKS get the flu, too.

WHAT YOU might expect has been proved: Good bowlers are almost invariably good horseshoe pitchers — and vice versa.

•

WAS NONE OTHER than Alexander the Great who initiated the custom among men in the Western world of shaving off their whiskers. Alexander didn't have much of a beard. Looked better without any.

•

AM TOLD a weekly newspaper in England is sponsoring a photography contest for "the best action photograph of a snail."

•

OUR Language Man knows what "brand new" means, but he doesn't know why the word "brand" was stuck in there to make a synonym for "new." Do you know why?

ANSWER DEPT.

Q. "DO IDENTICAL twins have identical fingerprints?" A. Almost but not quite. Experts can tell the difference.

•

Q. "HOW MUCH of the U.S. Army is stationed overseas now?" A. 43 percent.

Q. "DIDN'T women once wear lightning rods in their hats?" A. They did. And trailed ground wires from their skirts. In Europe, this was, mostly Benjamin Franklin started this fad in 1753 when he published instructions in "Poor Richard Improved."

Q. "WHAT PART of the whale was once used to make clock springs?" A. Same part that was used to make corset stays. The balleen plates in the mouths of some whales through which they strained their food.

•

Q. "WHAT color M&M's candy sells best?" A. Brown.

Q. "IF I ACCEPT the Turin shroud as real, what am I supposed to believe to have been the height of Jesus Christ?" A. 5 feet 10 inches.

•

Q. "WHERE'D WE get the word 'cliffhanger'?" A. From the old movie serials called "The Perils of Pauline." That heroine repeatedly was filmed dangling by her fingernails.

THE MORE money a young man earns, the more eager he is to get married. The opposite is true of the typical young woman, however.

•

LIQUOR is said to figure in three out of five teenage deaths.

•

IN THAT matter of losing weight, the sun reduces by four million tons a second.

•

IN ENGLAND are 150 nanny colleges. Quite a profession, that one. A nanny there first has to graduate from a two-year course at a nanny college and then be certified by the National Nursery Examination Board.

•

YOU KNOW that sort of walking stick that converts into a folding stool? None other than Thomas Jefferson invented the first of same.

•

IF ALL the Holiday Inns worldwide had been built on the equator with equal distances between them, they'd be 14 miles apart.

*TAKE IT EASY, ED... A **LOT** OF GUYS TRIP ON THEIR **OWN FEET**!*

CHANCES ARE your left foot is just a little bigger than your right.

IF YOU want your picture in the paper, go to China. When President Richard M. Nixon did so, photographers snapped 110,000 shots of him in eight days.

•

CURRENTLY, twenty percent of the wearers of dental braces are grownups.

•

IN ANCIENT Greece, a woman counted her age from the day she married, I'm told.

THE U.S. Bureau of Engraving and Printing spins out $1447 a second.

•

SOME SEA scientists contend porpoises first immobilize the fish they find to eat by emitting high-frequency sounds.

•

DID OUR Language Man mention that the word "wise-acre" comes from the Middle Dutch "wijsseggher" meaning soothsayer?

SAUDI ARABIA'S Sheikh Yamani has a waterbed on his jet plane.

•

DOG SHOWS in England get prime time on national TV.

•

ONLY ONE in five airline pilots smokes.

•

CHINESE rice fritters smothered in honey — that was Marco Polo's favorite dish, according to the written record.

•

THREE out of four optometrists wear eyeglasses.

•

IT'S SAID bees are most inclined to sting people on exceedingly windy days.

ANSWER DEPT.

Q. "HOW DO the chances for divorce today compare with the odds 50 years ago?" A. They run six times greater now, about. In every age bracket.

•

Q. "WHY DO we refer to a burial place for strangers as a 'potter's field'?" A. Check out St. Matthew 27:7. That original potter's field was bought with

NOW for sale by the General Services Administration: abandoned U.S. Coast Guard lighthouses.

the pieces of silver that Judas flung down before he hanged himself.

•

Q. "WHAT DOES a 'gigger' do?" A. Catches frogs.

•

Q. "IS THERE such a bird as a 'two-way homing pigeon'?" A. Know of nonesuch. The U.S. Army during World War II reportedly developed a pigeon that would deliver a message to an assigned destination, then fly back home again. But I should think we would've heard about it since if it ever really happened.

•

Q. "WHY DO some orchard operators whitewash their tree trunks? To repel insects?" A. Not primarily, I'm told. The idea was started by one theorist who thought the white color would reflect the winter sun, which tended to crack the bark of the trees.

•

Q. "WHAT'S THE biggest species of crab?" A. In size, the Japanese Giant with an 11-foot leg span. In weight, the Tasmanian at 30 pounds or so. Incidentally, do you know the one thing all crab species have in common? They're edible, every one.

•

Q. "DOES WHEAT have blossoms?" A. For 15 minutes a season, yes.

•

Q. "WHAT'S the distance of a 'hand' in measuring the height of a horse?" A. Four inches.

THAT MAGAZINE most likely to be stolen from a public library is "Sports Illustrated," research reveals.

•

EIGHTEEN PERCENT of American grownups, it's reported, complain that their feet hurt. The rest prefer not to complain, evidently.

•

NUDE MODELS who pose in figure classes at two of Scotland's art colleges are on strike. They want a pay raise from $3.75 to $4.50 an hour and a minimum studio temperature of 70 degrees F.

•

GET IT DOWN for the record: Among cookies, chocolate chip is No. 1. By far.

•

IF THE OUTDOOR temperature isn't 40 degrees F. and rising, don't lay brick. Mortar freezes.

•

CLAIM IS that most of the victims in terrorist bombings in the United States have been the bombers themselves. Mishandled the explosives.

THERE ARE said to be a lot of places in the Sahara where you can dig down through the sand, hit underground streams, and therein catch freshwater fish. Shrug.

WHO'S "affluent"? Economists say you are, if your household takes in more than $923 a week.

•

IF THAT HORSE is over 34 inches tall, it's no miniature.

•

THERE WAS a time, an ancient time, when first prize in an Olympic game event was not a gold medal but a stalk of celery.

THAT DREAM you dream when you sleep ordinarily lasts about 20 minutes.

•

LOOKING FOR a new line of work? The "Directory of Occupational Titles" has at least 20,000 suggestions for you.

•

MOUNTAIN CLIMBING is less dangerous than construction work, according to the insurance actuaries.

THE BRITISH refer to "newspaper clippings" as "newspaper cuttings."

•

THE WHITE HOUSE has on its staff five calligraphers — those artists whose penmanship shows up on documents, scrolls, invitations.

•

ENGINEERS and business executives — those are what college freshmen most often say they want to be. What they least often say they want to be are school superintendents and school principals.

•

AM ADVISED at least one North Dakota hospital includes in its itemized bill an extra $1.50 if the nurse combs the newborn baby's hair.

•

DID I TELL you U.S. doctors now put artificial joints into 100,000 hips every year?

•

IF THAT scotch whisky has the traditional amber cast, the distillers colored it with caramel. Natural scotch is quite pale. Makers generations ago, though, decided it should look like French cognac, so took to the tint.

> IT'S CALLED 'EXTRA-SWEET BREATH OF MANY ROSES'

Q. "WHO SAID, 'The best way for a woman to smell is not at all'?" A. Montaigne. No friend of the perfume makers, he.

ANSWER DEPT.

Q. "HOW COME tornadoes hardly ever hit big cities?" A. Theorists think the metropolises generate heat that fends off the twisters.

•

Q. "HOW MANY times has the White House been painted?" A. Can only tell you that Bureau of Standards tests in 1982 revealed at least 32 coats of paint on it. The record shows it's usually painted every four years — before each inauguration.

•

Q. "HOW frequently did the United States turn out a new airplane at peak production during World War II?" A. Every six minutes.

•

Q. "WHAT'S a 'Diamond Dick'?" A. You must be talking about the oldtimers' term for a baseball umpire.

•

Q. "WHO SAID, 'The pen is mightier than the sword'?" A. Lord Lytton, otherwise known as Edward Bulwer-Lytton. So much of what is said is meant to justify the sayer, isn't it? If Lord Lytton had been a swordsman instead of a writer, he might have put it down a little differently.

•

Q. "IN HOLLYWOOD lingo, what's a 'St. Bernard'?" A. An extremely bad film. A dog of distinction, as it were.

•

Q. "WHAT'S the FBI pay its starting special agents now?" A. $27,883 a year.

THE CHECKER-UPPERS say three out of five employees sneak their personal mail through their company postage meters.

●

JOHN LENNON wrote in bed.

●

IN OLD Anglo-Saxon, "ang" meant pain, and "naegl" meant nail. That's where we got the word "hangnail."

●

IF YOUR OLD Aunt Min refuses to believe that kids like video rock, you can assume she suffers from "octophobia" — fear of opening one's eyes.

●

THE GREAT French mathematician Blaise Pascal was really trying to create the impossible — a perpetual motion machine — when he invented the game of roulette.

●

IN THE CURRENCY of Israel is a magnetic filament that spells out the central bank's name in code when put through a magnetic reader. Tough to counterfeit, that one.

PEOPLE WHO go to church regularly aren't as fussy about their food as people who don't. Studies seem to prove this, but they don't explain why.

ENGLAND'S Birmingham has more miles of canals than Venice.

●

THE LAW of Siena, Italy, doesn't prohibit prostitution. It just prohibits any woman there named Mary from engaging in that profession.

●

CRICKETS HEAR through their knees.

IN 17 PERCENT of those criminal cases identified as murder, the killer is member of the same family as the killed.

●

HALF THE MEN over 40 weigh too much, medical researchers say.

●

IF THE SPIDERWEB glistens with dew, expect sunshine that day.

TWO motion pictures a day — that's how many the Hollywood film companies turned out on the average during 1939.

•

A BROOK trout is not a trout but a char.

•

YOUNG FELLOW, if you want to marry a 13-year-old girl, go to New Hampshire. That's the only state where it's legal.

•

A COMBINED 8 percent of the U.S. population owns more of value than does a combined 92 percent.

•

WHALES CAN'T roll their eyes.

•

DOESN'T TAKE much oil spilled at sea to create an enormous slick. Three barrelsful will blanket two square miles.

ANSWER DEPT.

Q. "WHERE IS it against the law for a woman to propose marriage to a man?" A. Whitesville, Del. Under an old statute, such a lady can be charged with disorderly conduct.

Q. "Everybody knows the whereabouts of New Zealand. But where's Old Zealand?" A. Somebody messed around with the spelling. Original reference was to Zeeland, now The Netherlands.

Q. "WHAT U.S. magazine publishes the most fiction?" A. The New Yorker.

•

Q. "WHAT SORT of bird migrates the farthest?" A. The Arctic tern, probably. Over 18,-000 miles between the Arctic and Antarctica. It's about as far as you can go without turning around.

Q. "CAN bacteria grow on the moon?" A. Survive there, anyhow. For awhile. Bacteria left there by Surveyor III were found alive three years later.

•

Q. "HAS ANY American president ever written a book about another American president?" A. One only. Herbert Hoover wrote "The Ordeal of Woodrow Wilson."

ALL DOCTORS know something not known to all others: Between 50 and 75 percent of the visits to physicians' offices are prompted by conditions that will go away naturally without medication.

•

IN GREECE, you can go to jail for abandoning your dog.

•

IF THAT Oriental rug is under 50 years of age, it's considered "new," I'm told. Remarkable, what? It has to be at least 100 years old to be classified as an antique.

•

AM TOLD you can't emigrate to New Zealand, the land of golf courses, just to retire. The country won't permit it.

•

ONE IN EVERY five mixed drinks contains vodka.

•

"RELEVELER" ties "redivider" for the longest one-word palindrome.

•

RATIO OF WOMEN to men in the Soviet Union now runs 114 to 100.

THE OLD cavalrymen always carried spares, too. Two extra horseshoes in their saddlebags. One for the front, one for the hind.

NOW THE MEDICOS say the tendency to shed dandruff is an inherited thing. It's not a contagion. You can't get it by using somebody else's comb.

•

IN THE LARGEST office building in the world, the Pentagon, you can walk from any suite to any other suite in six minutes or less.

•

DID I SAY Nevada casino dealers make about $600 a week? "No way!" write several of same. "We get about $225 a week, total!"

YOU WOULDN'T want to miss this country western comment: "If today was a fish, I'd throw it back."

•

CLAIM IS there are more publishers in Santa Barbara, Calif., and more writers in Washington, D.C., than anywhere else in the world.

•

ONE OUT OF every 1000 people in the Atlantic provinces of Canada is a victim of multiple sclerosis. Why that particular region should be such a high-risk area for the disease is unknown.

AFTER YOU PRESS the castor oil out of the castor plant's seeds, what you have left contains ricin, a poison 100 times more deadly than cobra venom.

•

AROUND SUBIC BAY in the Philippines, the U.S. military men outnumber the licensed ladies of the night by 20,000 to 8000. But the unlicensed tend to make up the difference, I'm told.

•

THE MALE sea catfish won't eat until his young hatch. Good thing. He carries the fertilized eggs in his mouth.

•

REAL COWBOYS don't wear short-sleeved shirts.

•

IF TYPICAL, you have about 110 hairs in every square inch of skin on the back of your hand.

•

THE TENDENCY to get dark circles under your eyes — if that you do — is another inherited trait.

IF YOU HAVE what's known in the vernacular as a hooked nose, maybe you were born a few centuries too late. In old Rome, that was thought to be a sign of leadership.

ANSWER DEPT.

Q. "HOW LONG has the National Geographic been using that yellow cover?" A. Since 1910. Long before the researchers proved yellow the most visible of colors.

Q. "IS A SHOT of whiskey really good medicine for snake bite?" A. On the contrary. Liquor dilates the capillaries, so the venom gets into the bloodstream more swiftly. Or so say the medicos.

•

Q. "HOW MUCH do the game officials earn when they work the Rose Bowl?" A. $400 each.

•

Q. "DOES ANYBODY ever get fired from the U.S. Postal Service?" A. Not often. In 1983, less than 0.0039 percent of the outfit's employees got the sack.

•

Q. "I'M TOLD baseball players years ago sometimes reached second base, then stole first? Why?" A. Germany Schaefer of the old Pittsburgh Pirates did that. To shake up the pitcher, he said. It worked.

•

Q. "WHY ARE bubbles round?" A. Because the air in them presses outward equally overall.

•

Q. "IN WHAT musical key do most car horns honk?" A. If it's an American-made car, probably the key of F.

227

FACT THAT the Otis Elevator Company keeps its Washington, D.C., office in a one-story building is of no significance whatsoever.

•

THE SWISS turn their cheeses twice a week, I said. Client asks why. To get the holes as uniform as possible.

•

OUR Chief Prognosticator says the nation in the foreseeable future will continue to need at least 10 times as many janitors as computer programmers.

•

APPROXIMATELY 32,000 U.S. residents are over age 100. About 24,000 are women.

•

WOULD TAKE 48,000 hummingbirds to outweigh an ostrich.

•

PEOPLE wore mantles. They draped them to dry from shelves over fireplaces. After awhile, the mantles became known as cloaks and the shelves became known as mantles.

PLEASE, HONEY? JUST ONE?

IT'S IN the Pennsylvania town of Cold Springs where the law says no liquor can be sold to a man without his wife's permission.

IN ONLY ONE society worldwide are the people known to be entirely free of cancer — the Hunzas of northwest Kashmir.

•

THERE ARE those who think the octopus is as smart as any cat. Doubt that. It's certainly smarter than any fish, however.

AM NOW told farmers flood their rice paddies because flooding kills the weeds but not the rice.

•

CLAIM IS a good plastic surgeon can make a living now in a town of 50,000.

•

IF YOUR bed was manufactured in this country, it's supposed to last 20 years.

THE WAY a man handles his pogonotomy has much to do with how he looks, too, of course. Of course? Pogonotomy is another word for shaving.

•

YOU DON'T find many investments like the Sir Francis Drake expedition anymore. He sailed back into port with so much stolen Spanish treasure that he could repay his backers their investment 47 times over.

•

THE U.S. population can't replace itself without immigration unless each woman has an average of 2.1 children.

•

MAJOR-LEAGUE baseball umpires get 60 baseballs ready to start a game.

•

TWO-THIRDS of the world's lawyers practice their profession in the United States.

ANSWER DEPT.

Q. "WHO WERE the first people in the world to wear wristwatches?" A. The highest-ranking naval officers in the Germany of 1880. Girard Perregaux of France crafted them.

IF KING EDWARD VII of England hadn't been a bit too fat, those men who now wear vests might not leave the bottom button undone. He's the heavyweight who started that small custom of dress.

Q. "WHAT DO you call a group of turtles?" A. A bale.

Q. "YOU SAY it's dangerous to dry out a damp newspaper in the microwave oven?" A. Yes, but it's not dangerous to freeze-dry it.

•

Q. "IN WHICH inning of a major-league baseball game do the fastball pitchers usually reach their peak velocity?" A. Fourth.

•

Q. "WHY IS 'pig iron' called that?" A. Because it used to be poured from the blast furnace into a wide ditch and therefrom into small adjoining troughs. The ditch and troughs reminded onlookers of a sow with suckling pigs.

•

Q. "SCHOOL TEACHERS in general live longer than corporate employees, according to the insurance statisticians. Why?" A. Longer vacations, maybe. That's still under study.

•

Q. "WHY DOES the New Zealander refer to an Englishman as a 'pom'?" A. It's an acronym for "Poor Old Mother," which I hasten to add is short for Poor Old Mother England.

NEARLY A MILLION teenagers nationwide will get married this year, and nearly 500,000 of those eventually will divorce.

●

ATOMS IN a row, remember, measure 200 million to the inch.

●

THE PUPIL of the horse's eye is horizontal. It sees well sideways. The pupil of the cat's eye is vertical. It sees well up and down. The pupil of the whale's eye is kidney-shaped. Shrug.

●

A NEW supertanker isn't launched. Its drydock is flooded. It floats out.

●

ABOUT HALF the stolen cars are never recovered.

●

IF IT'S a small sauce pan used to melt butter, you can call it a "pipkin."

●

THAT WIND deflector mounted over the cabs of some truck tractors is called a "varashield."

YOU CAN DRAW an ounce of gold into a wire 50 miles long. Or somebody can.

REMEMBER, if your dog's tail is smooth, it's known as a "stern."

●

THE U.S. military awards only one neck decoration — the Medal of Honor.

●

INSECTS HAVE "ears," so to speak. Hearing organs of one sort or another. But no insect has them in its head.

●

WHICH OF your legs is the longer? There's a good chance one of them is. Or more precisely, two out of five people have legs of unequal length.

NO JUGGLER has ever juggled more than seven Indian clubs at one time.

●

NOT ONLY can you float in the Red Sea, but you can float on your side.

●

HERE'S TO the kangaroo rat — clink! — who can live a lifetime without ever taking a drink.

●

THE TRAVELING businesswoman on the average is 38 years old. The traveling businessman on the average is 44 years old.

THE BLACK market for U.S. passports is pretty lively in Italy, evidently. U.S. consulates there replace more lost passports than do U.S. consulates elsewhere.

•

BAR BETS are won and lost, too, on this question: What car was named after a football coach? Winner is the bright citizen who says the 1928 Studebaker "Rockne Six." It bombed.

•

TWO out of five newcomers to the United States are Asian.

•

TV'S "DYNASTY" spends about $15,000 a week on clothes for the cast.

ANSWER DEPT.

Q. "HAS ANY golfer ever hit two consecutive holes in one?" A. At least one golfer, if the record is correct. On Sept. 2, 1964, at the Del Valle Country Club course in Saugus, Calif., Norman L. Manley reported that feat on the seventh and eighth tees. Can you imagine how Mr. Manley felt as he tried to tell them about it back in the clubhouse? And how they looked at him?

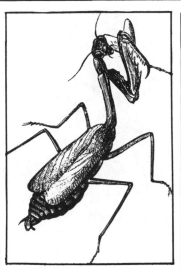

TALK ABOUT finicky. If it's not alive, the praying mantis won't eat it.

Q. "WHERE'D WE get the 'jack' in 'jackknife'?" A. Probably from the name of the maker of the first folding knife, a 17th century Belgian identified as Jacques de Liege — Jack of Liege.

•

Q. "DO WHALES hold their breath when they mate?" A. The underwater male, yes, but not the surfaced female.

Q. "HOW MANY boys are members of the Camp Fire Girls?" A. Name was changed in 1979 to just plain "Camp Fire" in consideration of those boys. They make up about 15 percent of the membership now.

•

Q. "IN PRO FOOTBALL, can kickers tie back the toe of the shoe to get more foot into the ball?" A. In the Canadian league, yes. But not in the NFL or USFL.

•

Q. "WHAT DOES it mean to moor your boat 'Mediterranean style'?" A. That's where the stern is tied to the pier while the bow is held by anchor.

•

Q. "DO ANY car manufacturers require their employees to buy the same makes of cars they put together?" A. Know of none such. But some assembly plants give the closest spaces in the parking lots to drivers of company-made cars. There's leverage in that.

•

Q. "IN WHICH of the lower 48 states is the largest wilderness area?" A. New York, am surprised to learn. It's the six million acres in Adirondack Park.

IN THE MALABAR region of India, a wife can get rid of an unwanted husband simply by leaving his shoes outside the door.

•

MEDICAL CHECKUPS in nudist colonies show a much lower incidence of high blood pressure than is found in the general public.

•

MORE LAWYERS practice in Chicago than in all of England.

•

IF YOU WANT that bar of soap to last longer, unwrap it and let it dry before you use it, maybe in a drawer to perfume up your linens or whatever.

•

HAVE YOU EVER been to a gnathologist? You have, if you've ever had a gold crown on a tooth. That's another name for the dentist who crafts such work.

•

DID I MENTION that it's the parents of the groom who pay for the wedding in Thailand?

THERE WERE camels in North America before there were camels anywhere else.

IT'S ALWAYS exactly the opposite time in Denver and Bombay, meaning they're numerically the same but one's a.m. when the other is p.m.

•

AVERAGE SALARY of professional basketball players now is $301,000. Average career lasts four years.

•

IF A MAN puts his arms around a woman in Macon, Ga., he better be able to prove he has a legal reason for doing so. What constitutes "a legal reason" I don't know, but the law so stipulates.

NEVER refrigerate garlic.

•

THE TONGUE of a grown blue whale weighs more than most elephants.

•

TITLE OF one song now popular in China translates: "How I Love to Carry Fertilizer Up the Mountainside for the Commune."

•

"AN ELECTED official is one who gets 51 percent of the votes cast by 40 percent of the 60 percent of voters who registered," notes one Dan Bennett.

FIGURE your umbrella will last two-and-a-half years? That's said to be typical.

•

HORSE RACERS report half a million dollars is an average price now for a promising Thoroughbred yearling.

•

YOU FIGURE the value of an Oriental rug by the number of knots per square inch.

•

CABLE TV is into 41 percent of the U.S. homes now, I'm told.

•

IN THE reformatory at Caserta, Italy, as guards watched a movie, five youthful prisoners escaped. The movie was about guards who watched a movie while youthful prisoners escaped.

•

A LOT of piranha are vegetarians, you know.

•

SEVEN out of 10 people in this country can't remember life without television.

A BABY'S FACE looks like a baby's face because it's so much smaller, relative to head size, than a grownup's face. The baby's face is an eighth of its head; the grownup's, a half.

CREATIVE JUDGES can give a little class to the law courts. Take that burglary case in Kennewick, Wash. The defendant was sentenced to pay the victim's theft insurance premiums for three years.

ANSWER DEPT.

Q. "ASK YOUR Love and War Man what is the typical frequency of physical romance among married couples between the ages of 35 and 44." A. His statistical file indicates 98 times a year is average.

•

Q. "WHO WAS the first woman to serve as a network news correspondent?" A. Pauline Frederick. ABC. 1948.

•

Q. "WHAT CAN be done to a diamond to enhance its brilliance, if anything?" A. Am told it can be zapped with gamma rays to do that very thing.

•

Q. "PROSTITUTION is legal in Nevada, but there aren't any houses in Las Vegas. Why not?" A. The law bans the profession there only in counties of more than 250,000 population.

•

Q. "WHAT makes a comet's tail?" A. The comet is ice and dust. As it swings closer to the sun, the ice vaporizes, releasing dusty gas over millions of miles.

IF ALEXANDER HAMILTON had had his way, the name of this country would be "The United State of America." Singular.

•

UNDER THE LAW of Maine, buildings made of round logs are tax-exempt.

•

ODDSMAKERS calculate everything; e.g., chances are one in 19 you've got red hair.

•

LARGEST OF the land animals, the elephant, is also the fastest in its mating activity, typically a 30-second beast.

•

IN NEVADA'S Virginia City of the 1870s, the saloons outnumbered the churches by 110 to six.

•

MILITARY marching bandsmen take 120 steps a minute. A woman, if typical, takes 116 steps a minute. A man, usually, 110.

•

IN VERMONT, remember, it's illegal to paint your horse.

THERE IS NOW an oral contraceptive for fleas. Don't know how it works. You put it on your dog, I guess.

AN EAGLE'S feathers weigh twice as much as its bones, don't forget.

•

SOVIET KGB spies have their own jargon, too. A "wet affair," for instance, is their term for a clandestine killing.

•

SOME OF the streets of Paris are so narrow that the city's fire department first sends out men on motorcycles with extinguishers on their backs to do what they can until the boys with the heavy equipment can get their gear in place.

A LOCAL ordinance in Lang, Kans., prohibits anyone there from driving a mule down the main street in August unless said driver wears a straw hat. Can you explain the why of that one?

•

ABOUT 40 percent of the money pulled in by TV evangelists comes from the retired citizenry.

•

HOW LONG do you keep a new automobile, if such you ever get? Typically, the new-car buyer now holds onto same for 5.1 years before the trade-in.

YOUR OLD English teacher would be ashamed of you if you couldn't pick out the three grammatical errors in this two-word sentence: "Them's them."

•

AVERAGE American woman has almost but not quite six pairs of shoes. Statistically, it's 5.6 pairs. Singer Dionne Warwick isn't average. She admits to possession of 300 pairs. It's a start. Actress Lynda Carter reportedly owns 800 pairs of shoes.

ANSWER DEPT.

Q. "HOW MUCH money do the Broadway actors make, typically?" A. Stars, at least $12,500 a week. Supporting players, at least $610 a week.

•

Q. "WHAT'S cinnamon?" A. Tree bark.

•

Q. "WHAT KIND of bird does backward somersaults in flight?" A. The tumbler pigeon.

•

Q. "WHO WAS the actress who killed herself by jumping off the 'H' in the Mount Lee hillside 'Hollywood' sign?" A. Peg Enwhistle. On Sept. 16, 1932. A 50-foot drop, that.

MEN'S hats are coming back. Particularly the fedora. Sales figures indicate such.

Q. "WHY IS the 'macadamia nut' so called?" A. In honor of an Australian chemist named John Macadam.

•

Q. "WHAT'S THE 'After Five Club' all about?" A. A social group in Las Vegas, that one. For divorced men and women who've been married five or more times. They meet twice a year to compare matrimonial news.

Q. "WHAT'S THE difference between a 'schlemiel' and a 'schlemazel'?" A. The schlemiel is the guy who spills his beer, the schlemazel the guy he spills it on.

•

Q. "DIDN'T ACTOR Warren Oates, who died in 1982, leave all his estate to actor Peter Fonda?" A. Not property. They were close friends. Oates' will noted: "To Peter Fonda I leave nothing — but all my love."

YOU SAY you've never seen a green polar bear? They exist. When algae invades the hollow center of each hair follicle, the bear turns green, and stays green.

•

HARRY S. TRUMAN said, "No man should be allowed to be president who doesn't understand hogs." You can read something into that, if you like. Truman was better than Winston Churchill with the quaint generalities. Churchill said, "Any man who wears a brown suit is a cad." You can't read anything at all into that.

•

A CENTURY AGO, the great French naturalist, Professor Jean Henri Casimir Fabre, let women come to his science classes. Extraordinary! The Government of France awarded him the Legion of Honor, then canned him.

•

LONG BEFORE George Lucas produced "Star Wars," "The Empire Strikes Back," and "The Return of the Jedi," he made it through his last year at Modesto's Downey High School with a D-plus grade average.

HISTORY records that American Indians in colonial days bathed frequently. The same cannot be said of the settlers from Europe. It was the whites, not the Indians, who most easily could be tracked by hounds, I've read.

HISTORICAL footnotes show the cooks for King Charles VI of England ordered 200 sheep a week for the royal tables.

•

REMEMBER, the United States leads all the nations of the world in teenage motherhood.

•

IT'S NOT uncommon for a mother koala to put her misbehaving baby koala over her knees to spank the little rascal on its bottom.

MAGNETITE is a black iron oxide strongly attracted by magnets. It has been found in the heads of dolphins. And most of us unlearned amateurs immediately assume it has something to do with how they sense direction to navigate.

•

FEBRUARY once had 30 days, too. Julius Caesar swiped a day to put in his namesake, July. Emperor Augustus swiped a day to put in his namesake, August. February got robbed.

BRITISH NOVELIST John Creasey has published 564 books. But he didn't make his first sale until after he'd received 774 rejection slips.

•

GO DOWN lists of the world's most famous poets and soldiers, and you'll find a remarkably high number of men who worshipped their mothers and detested their fathers.

•

IN SOUTH AFRICA, it's against the law to sell a publication called "Western Areas Table Tennis Association Souvenir — 2nd Open Championship — 1983." But I don't know why.

•

TO THAT LIST of famous folk who never learned to drive a car, please add the name of British actor Sir John Gielgud.

•

THE LAW in Kansas City, Mo., prohibits the sale to children of cap guns but not of shotguns.

ANSWER DEPT.

Q. "NAME the only purple animal." A. The blesbok, a small South African antelope.

YOU HAVE TO cook duck longer than any other bird you might choose to eat.

Q. "I'VE READ that John Wayne in an early movie was the first singing cowboy. How come he didn't sing in any others?" A. He couldn't. He didn't sing in the first, for that matter. A songster named Smith Ballou actually did that early vocalizing for Wayne.

Q. "WHAT DO ostriches feed their young?" A. Eggs. The female ostrich lays maybe two dozen eggs. Some hatch early. To feed the first little birds, the mother cracks the unhatched eggs.

•

Q. "SOME OF the most popular hamburger franchises spray sugar on their french fries. Why?" A. To give those fries that golden color. The sugar carmelizes in the cooking, so turns the fries brown.

•

Q. "WHICH COUNTRY in Western Europe has the least murder?" A. Spain. One homicide per million people per year.

•

Q. "WHAT DOES 'Burgundy' on the label of an American wine tell you about it?" A. That it's red, nothing more.

•

Q. "ONE FAMOUS playwright wrote 12 of his greatest hits off duty while he worked full-time on the staff of a newsaper. Name him." A. George S. Kaufman. He started on the New York Times in 1917 and kept at it until 1930, collecting his $80 a week as drama critic.

"**H**OW WELL you slept last night is of little importance," contends one medical specialist. "We've learned that what matters is how well you think you slept."

•

THAT POLICE car known hereabouts as a "black-and-white" is identified in the jargon of Great Britain as a "panda."

•

IF YOU'RE sending a letter to Cold Harbour, England, be more specific than that. There are 170 places there called Cold Harbour.

•

VOLCANIC eruptions of the past are traced through the rings in trees.

•

ANOTHER WORD for left-handedness is "mancinism."

•

TO BE attractive to men, a woman needs to: 1. Look alive. 2. Forget her own shyness. 3. Be responsive. And 4. Ignore the men's faults. That's Item No. 633C in our Love and War Man's file.

UNDER the law of Indiana, any man who "habitually kisses human beings" cannot wear a mustache.

WHAT MAKES "unquestionably" a noteworthy word is it contains all five vowels plus the sometimes-vowel "y."

•

RATTLESNAKES kill about 20 people a year in this country.

•

SOME DANUBE catfish weigh 400 pounds.

•

THE CITIZEN of France uses two bars of soap a year, average.

MANY if not most restaurants in France invite customers to bring their dogs and even offer special menus with side dishes for said dogs.

•

YOU'VE SEEN pictures of President Ronald Reagan swinging an ax at his California ranch home. More to it than exercise. Only heat in that house comes from the sun and two fireplaces.

•

AMISH CHILDREN quit school after the eighth grade.

IT'S SAID human taste buds are more sensitive at sea level than at higher altitudes.

•

KILTS originated in France.

•

IN ROMANIA once, a man had to get a government permit to grow a beard.

•

A RADIO announcer in Oregon complied with the request of a high school principal to broadcast the names of absent students every morning. The truancy rate dropped 25 percent.

•

WORCESTERSHIRE sauce was created in India. By accident.

•

EACH DAY, on the average, the human mouth produces a quart of saliva and the human skin excretes two-and-a-half quarts of sweat, I'm told. Why I'm told is a mystery. I didn't want to know.

•

INSURANCE statisticians will tell you it's riskier to be a garbageman than either a policeman or a fireman.

THE LAW in Gurnee, Ill., specifically prohibits any woman weighing more than 200 pounds from riding a horse while wearing shorts.

ANSWER DEPT.

Q. "IS THERE anyplace on land in Central America where you can see both the Pacific and Atlantic oceans?" A. Only from atop Mt. Izaru — at 11,200 feet — in Costa Rica.

Q. "WHERE'D WE get the word 'bamboozle'?" A. It was common practice in the Orient once to whip cheaters, chiselers, con artists with bamboo sticks. Foreigners said those so whipped were "bamboozled." Eventually, for reasons unknown, the whippees instead of the whippers came to be known as the bamboozlers.

•

Q. "IS THERE any sort of bird that can fly immediately after hatching out of the shell?" A. One only — the mound builder of Australia. It breaks out fully feathered.

•

Q. "WHAT DO the French call a 'French kiss'?" A. An "English kiss."

•

Q. "HOW MANY gallons does a 10-gallon hat really hold?" A. About three-fourths of a gallon.

•

Q. "NAME the only one of the United States over which has never flown a foreign flag." A. Idaho.

•

Q. "WHAT DO sardine packers use to behead the sardines they pack?" A. Scissors.

MOST CHILD prodigies are first-born boys of middle-class parents beyond the usual child-bearing age.

•

DIVORCE GRANTED, said the Los Angeles judge, after the woman told him her husband made her unscrew the lightbulbs to turn them off in order to cut down wear on the switches.

•

RESEARCHERS commissioned by the perfume industry of France recently found out that French people bathe less frequently than citizens of any other country in Western Europe.

•

PATENT medicines aren't patented.

•

SALADS in Australia's Sydney are served warm. Containers on the salad bar rest not in ice but in hot water.

•

THERE WAS a time in your life — about four months before you were born — when you had more hair on your back than a grown gorilla.

HERE'S TO that most imaginative Los Angeles derelict, who recently declared himself the Official Wino of the 1984 Summer Olympics — clink!

MIGHT NOTE that 15 percent of the liquor drinkers drink 50 percent of the liquor.

•

THOSE WHO claim to know say more illegal aliens cross the Mexico-United States border in a day than cross the Canada-United States border in a year.

•

IF THOSE hard-boiled eggs won't peel, they were probably too fresh. Elderly eggs are easier to strip.

MEDICAL researchers counted broken necks to learn that 58 percent resulted from car smashups.

•

ONLY ONE citizen in 50 has an I.Q. over 140.

•

NOT JUST eels but all sorts of fish create electrical fields. Sharks possess small organs in their snouts to detect these fields. So a shark, it's claimed, can find a bottom fish buried in the mud.

SUGAR CANE is something else you won't find growing wild.

•

DUELING IS only legal in Uruguay if both participants are registered blood donors.

•

IN HONOLULU, the house is exactly "average" if its sale price is $139,983.

•

THE NARRATOR of Genesis was a good student of human psychology. He made it clear that Adam was more shocked by his nakedness than Eve was by hers. Quite so. A man is more modest than a woman, say the scholars.

CLAIM IS that 98 percent of all the species of plants and animals that ever inhabited the earth are extinct.

ANSWER DEPT.

Q. "WHAT COUNTRY has the fewest murders?" A. Norway long has claimed that distinction.

•

Q. "ONLY ONE man-made object becomes increasingly stronger structurally as its size is increased. Name it." A. The geodesic dome.

Q. "THE GREAT French poet Francois Villon — how did he die?" A. Nobody knows. He was into poetry and crime. He wrote much, stole habitually, and murdered, repeatedly. And he disappeared.

•

Q. "CAN veterinarians give heart pacemakers to dogs?" A. They can. And cornea transplants. And skin grafts. And psychological counseling.

Q. "IS THE Salvation Army a 'church'?" A. Not according to its members. No baptism. No Holy Communion. It calls itself a "movement" or "community."

•

Q. "IN OIL-FIELD movies, the drillers are filmed tasting the mud they bring out of a new well. What flavor are they trying to find?" A. Salt. That would show promise.

THIS METHOD of escape from jail is said to be as common as any other: The escapee just picks up a broom and sweeps his way out of the building.

●

SWOONING goes way back. Before Michael Jackson. Before the Beatles. Before Elvis. Before Sinatra. Women swooned at the piano recitals of Franz Liszt.

●

TO ENVIGORATE his power, the original Popeye cartoon character ate garlic, not spinach. Am glad he switched.

●

DID YOU know there are no left-handed polo players? Left-handers are barred from the game.

●

A CURIOUS California law makes it illegal to set a trap for a mouse without a hunting license.

●

SOME prizefighters toughen up the skin on their hands by soaking them 15 minutes a day in beef pickling brine.

WE'RE RAPIDLY running out of bluebirds. It has come to this: Most people in the United States have never even seen a bluebird.

FOREIGNERS from about 80 countries can enter Canada without a visa. Foreigners from only one country — Canada — can enter the United States without a visa. Legally, legally.

●

ON A CLEAR DAY in flat, open country, you can see 3.2 miles, if you're six feet tall and not too myopic.

●

IF THE SIGN on the door identifies the professional therein as a "phycologist," check the spelling. A phycologist studies seaweed.

EACH STAR has its unique color.

●

THE LETTER "e" is used five times more than any other letter in English.

●

IN MANITOBA'S Winnepeg, Carol Buttons was engaged to Bob Bowes at last report, and the pair were getting a little tired of cute comment.

●

A FOURTH of the bones in your body, about, are in your hands.

IN TODAY'S mail came the following question: "Why do we have to choose between disarmament and nuclear war? Can't we have both?"

•

HOW DO YOU account for the fact that men usually find it easier to quit smoking than women?

•

PLAY THE tape of a piano solo backwards and it sounds like an organ.

•

TRUCKERS with citizens band radios were not the first to join forces to avoid speeding tickets. The U.S. Automobile Association organized in 1905 specifically to spot police traps and warn its members of same.

ANSWER DEPT.

Q. "WHAT publication for doctors has the largest circulation?" A. "Physicians' Travel and Meeting Guide."

•

Q. "WHO WAS the first American playwright to make a living at it?" A. Howard Bronson. You say you never heard of him? He turned out "Saratoga" in 1870, and earned enough to get by.

DID YOU make 779 phone calls last year? That's said to be average.

Q. "WHAT WAS King Kong the king of?" A. Skull Island.

•

Q. "WHICH president was the tallest — George Washington, John Adams or Thomas Jefferson?" A. Jefferson at 6 feet 2½ inches. Washington was 6 feet 2. The widespread Adams at 5 feet 6 was known to some then as "His Rotundity."

Q. "WHY ARE a woman's 'Fallopian tubes' called by that name?" A. Because an Italian anatomy researcher named Gabriel Fallopus discovered them. He couldn't figure out what they were for, though. Took another three centuries before science realized their role in human fertilization.

•

Q. "WHAT WAS Albert Einstein doing for a living at the time he revolutionized physics with his three historic papers in 1905?" A. Clerking in a Swiss patent office. Took him another five years to get an underpaid professorship at the University of Zurich. But he never did sweat the money matters much.

•

Q. "THE SPARTANS of early Greece took young boys away from their mothers, did they not?" A. If said boys appeared healthy, they did. At age 7. To be brought up in barracks. If at birth the boys didn't appear healthy, they were simply abandoned to starvation.

•

Q. "WHAT DOES it cost to get a lawyer to execute an uncontested divorce?" A. About $150 an hour is typical now. Less than it would cost to execute the lawyer, at any rate.

THERE ARE dog trainers in Great Britain who make something of a living just teaching pups how to find lost golf balls.

•

CLAIM IS only about 150 computer programmers designed all the video games on the market, and most of these 150 have become multi-millionaires therefor.

•

MORE FLOWER seeds come from Lompoc, Calif., than from anyplace else in the world.

•

YOUNG LADY, if you insist on a gentleman friend who's at least 6 feet tall, you'll have to eliminate 82 percent of the candidates.

•

DID YOU EVER read Gustave Flaubert's "Madame Bovary"? Our Love and War Man notes the government of France has seen fit to give this great novel to all newlyweds there. Not sure a book about adultery is appropriate for the occasion. But it's the thought that counts, anyway.

BOTH THE TOMATO and the jellyfish, if typical, are 95 percent water.

BIRDS DON'T sing on the ground. At least, most birds. A few, maybe.

•

THE ANALYTICAL mind may wish to search for significance, too, in the fact that the typical family of four flushes the toilet 20 times a day.

•

IN 533 A.D., the Roman Empire and Persia signed a commitment known as "The Treaty of Endless Peace." Quite an accomplishment. They didn't go to war against each other again for seven years.

COLLEGE basketball teams typically win about two-thirds of their home games.

•

DON'T CALL yourself a skillful knitter if you can't make 100 stitches a minute.

•

CHRISTOPHER Columbus visited Iceland long before he ever set sail for America. The Vikings beat him there, too.

•

MEMBERS OF Congress get their packages wrapped free.

MOST OF the potatoes in Idaho come from potatoes in Montana.

•

THE WAGOGO tribespeople of South Africa will eat the chicken but never the chicken's heart. That, they think, would give them characteristics they don't want. Logically, they will eat a lion's heart.

•

ONE CITY only in this world routinely takes visitors on tours of its sewer system — Paris.

•

IN SHAKESPEARE'S "Julius Caesar," a character says he heard a clock strike. But the Romans had no clocks, only hour glasses. Poor Shakespeare! He did not have the advantage of a perfectionist on the copy desk.

•

NOBODY knows where dogs came from.

•

NOAH stocked beer on the Ark. At least, one Assyrian tablet indicates that.

•

ANOTHER PROVEN fact of nature is that it troubles shrimp when they get sand in their ears.

PEOPLE EAT more sharks than sharks eat people.

ANSWER DEPT.

Q. "WHAT ANIMAL runs backward in the dark by following its tail?" A. The gopher. With that sensitive tail as a feeler, a gopher can go backward through its tunnels as swiftly as forward. Unfortunately, not everybody cares.

Q. "WHICH QUEEN of England was only four feet tall?" A. You must mean Matilda of Flanders. That was her height. She was the wife of William the Conqueror, and he was a King of England. It was William who first came up with the bright idea to put animals on display in public zoos.

•

Q. "WHAT WAS the first food cooked?" A. The boiled egg. Or so some theorists think

•

Q. "CAN A cockroach live without its head?" A. For up to seven hours, it can.

•

Q. "HOW MANY of those Mobile Army Surgical Hospitals — as in 'M*A*S*H' — does the U.S. Army have, anyhow?" A. One. In South Korea, still.

•

Q. "REMEMBER that show called 'The Elephant Man'? What was the name of the leading character's physical ailment?" A. Multiple neurofibromathosis. Also known as Van Recklinghausen's disease. It's not so uncommon. Occurs about once in every 3,000 births.

FIVE HUNDRED square feet of solid silver seven inches thick — can you imagine that? Such is the foundation of the Ruwanweli Pagoda in Anuradhapura, Sri Lanka, the island we used to call Ceylon.

•

TAKES THAT saguaro cactus 30 years just to form one branch.

•

THE ONLY cells in the human body that don't reproduce are the brain cells. I've noticed.

•

WHY DON'T you pay attention when I tell you the rings of Saturn are no more than 50 meters thick?

•

THE UNICORN was dreamed up long ago by somebody who saw that African animal called the oryx. Or so the scholars believe. Almost extinct, the oryx. Possibly because the Arabs believed the eating of Oryx meat heightened their virility.

•

THE SUNFLOWER is not one big bloom but a whole bunch of little ones.

THOSE SICKENING bacteria called salmonella got their name not from a fish but from the 19th century American veterinarian David E. Salmon.

IN 1938, the late Howard Hughes set the around-the-world speed record in an airplane filled with ping pong balls. So it would float, if he had to ditch it.

•

THE TWO MOST lethal weapons are guns and cars. One man did more than any other to quiet these killers. Hiram Percy Maxim invented both the silencer and the muffler.

•

NO VOTER should forget the fact that Adolf Hitler managed to get himself elected to the leadership of the Nazi party in 1921 by a single ballot.

THE SUN isn't round. Not quite. It, too, is fatter at the poles.

•

TV COMMERCIALS pay 52 percent of the money earned by members of the Screen Actors Guild.

•

CALIFORNIA LAW is such that a woman can't legally drive a car in the state while wearing a housecoat.

•

THE RECORD shows Abe Lincoln's favorite dessert was a concoction called molasses pie.

IN WHICH state is the Statue of Liberty? Come on, say New Jersey.

•

MOST COMMON cosmetic surgery on men now is the hair transplant.

•

MARK TWAIN'S wife Olivia was his copyreader. After their marriage, nothing he wrote went out of his hands without her editing. He often rewrote at her suggestion.

•

AVERAGE IQ of Japanese children now is 11 points higher than the average IQ of American children, the education researchers say.

•

MOST DINOSAURS were the size of chickens.

•

THE FIRST iron-clad ships were built by the Koreans.

•

MARRIAGE CAN cost a lot of money in Africa, too. So engaged couples there have started to throw fund-raising parties. Much like wedding showers, but the gifts are cash.

IF YOU PUT end to end all the hens' eggs laid in America during one year, they'd encircle the earth 100 times.

ANSWER DEPT.

Q. IN THE U.S. flag, the stars represent states and the stripes represent the 13 original colonies. What do the colors stand for, if anything? A. Red, courage. White, purity. Blue, justice. That was the original plan, at any rate.

Q. DO YOU believe, as does Muhammad Ali, that he was the greatest fighter of all time? A. No, sir, a Greek boxer named Theogenes was tougher. Around 900 B.C., Theogenes fought, bare-fisted, 1425 opponents, winning all bouts, without draws, without split decisions, without TKOs or even KOs, as we know them. Theogenes just flat out beat everybody he fought — to death.

•

Q. YOU SAID China's Peking killed off 200,000 dogs. How many are killed off annually in American animal shelters? A. Five million cats and dogs combined is a fair guess.

•

Q. ARCHITECT FRANK Lloyd Wright designed a building to be 528 stories high. How come it was never built? No money? A. Fire officials thought it would be a nightmare. So did the window washers. Most other experts likewise nay-sayed it.

•

Q. WHERE'S THE next National Football League franchise going to be? A. Would have to guess either Phoenix or San Antonio. Those are the two biggest U.S. cities without NFL teams.

CHEWING burns calories. Celery offers few. It has been calculated that if you devote at least 16 minutes to the eating of one eight-inch stalk of celery, you'll use more energy than you'll gain.

•

UNDERSTAND NBA players this season will bounce around about $150,000 worth of new basketballs.

•

THOSE WHO know all about the penguin say that bird will starve itself to death, if necessary, to provide food for its offspring.

•

SOME MARKET researchers say the two words most influential in the moving of merchandise, in order, are "new" and "free."

•

FEMALE APHIDS are born pregnant.

•

DID YOU know that highway patrol officers nationwide hand out more traffic tickets at night than during the day?

THE LAW of Rochester, Minn., stipulates you can't go swimming in a public pool unless police first inspect your bathing suit.

AM TOLD the only animal with a straight backbone is the camel. Can that be right?

•

ASHES OF burned magnesium weigh more than the original metal. Explain the why of that.

•

TO GET a pound of pure dry insulin, the processors need the pancreases of 60,000 cattle. One cow's pancreas will give the average diabetic a two-day supply of insulin.

IN VANCOUVER, Wash., lives a man named Pepper Roni.

•

AVERAGE newspaper carrier in the United States earns a higher annual income than half the people on earth.

•

MOST ANY seasoned citizen will tell you the 60-year-old wears shoes a size larger than said soul wore at age 30. Or at least a size or two wider. Yes, our feet splay, too.

DID I SAY "temper" means to harden as well as to soften? Wrong! Metal men are quick to report they temper steel to take some hardness out of it for specific purposes. Tempering softens it, in fact.

ANSWER DEPT.

Q. "YOU said VA records list somebody named Love'n Kisses Love. During World War II at Fort Mason in San Francisco, I fingerprinted a man named Love'n Kisses Love. Wouldn't it be amazing if that were the same person?" A. It'd be amazing if it weren't, what?

•

Q. "I REALIZE chop suey was first concocted in the United States. But I don't know what the name 'chop suey' means." A. "Odds and ends."

•

Q. "WHAT CAUSED actor Lorne Greene to have to wear hearing aids in both ears?" A. Gunfire during filming of "Bonanza" shows, he reports.

•

Q. "WHAT'S a cowhide worth now?" A. About $37, if properly trimmed and brine-cured.

YE OLDE knights wore headgear decorated to identify the gallants therein. If such a horse-fighter wanted to pose as another, it was a simple matter to don a different helmet. This is the origin of our word "falsehood."

Q. "WHAT'S the only animal, besides man, that can be trained to stand on its head?" A. The only one with four knees, isn't it? The elephant? Think so.

Q. "YOU SAID the five interlocking Olympic rings are black, blue, red, white and yellow. Why these colors?" A. Because at least one of them appears on every national flag.

•

Q. "ARE X-rated movies shown in China?" A. Only rarely. First such was a Japanese film about a girl sold into prostitution in 1978. It stirred some debate.

•

Q. "HOW MUCH money does an English nanny get these days?" A. The equivalent of $100 a week, or thereabouts, plus board and room.

•

Q. "WHAT WAS the first American-made car with the steering wheel on the left?" A. The Model T Ford.

•

Q. "WHERE WAS Queen Elizabeth II when she received the news of her father's death, which made her the new monarch of the British Empire?" A. In a tree house. About 100 miles east of Nairobi in Africa's Kenya. Some tree house. A plush observation post called The Treetops where VIPs watched the wild game.

IN JAPAN NOW, you can buy a can of beer that whistles when you pour. Not every drinker chooses to call attention to himself as he pours another, but some do, evidently.

•

OUR LANGUAGE man contends the reason people say the world is round when it's not is because it's too much trouble to say it's "an oblate spheroid flattened at the poles and bulging at the equator."

•

NOT EVERYBODY knows the first Frankenstein movie was made by Thomas Edison in 1910.

•

AM NOW informed Frankenstein's monster did indeed have a name: Adam.

•

WHY THE CITY of Riverside in California saw fit to pass an ordinance to outlaw the carrying of lunch buckets on the streets there I do not know.

•

DOGS BARK, wolves don't. Nobody knows why this difference.

ONE ORDINANCE of Clawson City, Mich., specifically permits residents there to sleep with their pigs.

NEW YORK CITY now is said to have 36,000 street people who bed down wherever.

•

REMEMBER, "Swahili" is just an Anglicized corruption of the real name of that African language, "Kiswahili." A "Mswahili" told me so.

•

FIX THAT: Who said the Salvation Army is not a church? On the contrary, top dignitaries of that dedicated body say yes, absolutely, it's a church.

LATEST COUNT of America's homeless is about 2,000,000.

•

AM TOLD MANY a parakeet has been shocked to death by the sound of firecrackers on the Fourth of July.

•

A RAT CAN go longer without water than a camel can.

•

THIRTY-TWO percent of the employees of Italy's postal service are absent at any given time. Except in the summer. Then, it's often 50 percent.

"THE QUALITY of life," said the philosopher on the bar stool, "depends on the liver."

•

WHAT MUSICIANS call "groupies" — those clusters of girls in the vicinity of the bandstand — have their counterparts in auto racing. Drivers call them "pit poppies."

•

IN THE CASINOS of Atlantic City, 24.4 percent of the wins occur in the blackjack hands, and 19.3 percent show up in the craps tosses. But 28.2 percent come from the slots.

•

A BARNACLE'S ovaries are in its head.

•

WITH 6 percent of the world's population, the United States has 66 percent of the world's lawyers.

•

WHAT SORT of food would you keep in your bomb shelter, if such you possessed? The Swedish government has a bomb shelter. Several, in fact. Deep caves in the mountains. Therein is an enormous supply of pickled herring.

CURSES! FOILED AGAIN

YOU'VE SEEN that foil cover around the cork in wine bottles. It's there to protect the cork from brown moths. They chew up cork. Love it. Better than the wine, that cork.

ANSWER DEPT.

Q. "HOW LONG have the Girl Scouts been selling cookies?" A. Since 1934. In Washington, D.C., they accept Visa and MasterCard for their cookies, incidentally.

Q. "TWINS DON'T usually learn to talk as early as single children, right?" A. They talk as early. But not with as many words, usually. Twins speak to each other a lot, naturally, so they teach each other less than they'd learn if they talked more with older people. They soon catch up in school, however.

•

Q. "ALBERT EINSTEIN wanted no tombstone or other monument to himself, I've read. Does this mean none exists?" A. No, sir, there's a sculpture of him outside the National Academy of Sciences in Washington, D.C.

•

Q. "DO HORSES have fleas?" A. No, and neither do people around horses a lot. Horse odors drive off fleas.

•

Q. "AREN'T OBESE people more than normally susceptible to most all causes of death?" A. Most all except suicide, according to the medical statisticians.

•

Q. "WHY IS a 'cataract' in one's eye called by that name?" A. Things look as though you're peering through falling water, a cataract, that's all.

THAT U.S. CITY wherein the most people per capita read girlie magazines is Des Moines, Iowa. One out of every 12 people there buys one of the two leading nude-photo publications.

•

IT'S KNOWN that unnoticed sounds pitched too low for the ear to recognize still can make people sad.

•

"ATHLETICS have become professionalized," said Socrates, sadly, in 319 B.C.

•

SARASOTA, Fla., has the oldest population in the country. Median age there is 50 years.

•

MORE THAN four out of five college students drink — and one out of five of those gets into it in a heavy manner.

•

OWNER OF a small factory in New Orleans offered a $25 bonus to employees for money-saving ideas. First winner paid was the man who suggested the bonus be cut to $10.

THE CITY DOG lives on average 11 years, while the country dog lives on average only eight years.

IN INDIA'S Delhi is an iron pillar 23 feet high. Though exposed to the weather, it has not rusted in 1500 years. But nobody knows why.

•

DID I tell you that "He leadeth me beside the still waters" alludes to the fact that sheep won't drink from running streams?

•

UNDER THE LAW of Idaho Falls, Idaho, you have to stop riding your motorcycle after age 88.

THOSE WHO propose the United States "rent" the Israeli armed forces to resolve the Middle East crises have come up with nothing original. President James Madison realized war with England was imminent. And he knew this country couldn't afford to build a big navy. So he proposed we rent Portugal's.

•

A WOMAN with a four-year college education earns on the average about the same salary as a man with a ninth-grade education.

NO DOUBT it's due to archaic legislation no longer observed, but in Alabama, books about outlaws are supposed to be banned.

•

THERE WAS a time when newspaper reporters in trolley towns were allowed to ride all the streetcars free.

•

THE BANANA, I'm told, is free of both salt and sugar.

•

A JACKRABBIT has its turf. If pursued by a coyote, it will run to the edge of its territory, then turn and run again, staying within its personal boundaries. You can't chase a rabbit beyond what it senses to be its own property line. Or so a hunter of lengthy experience tells me.

•

LOUISIANA law specifically upholds your right to grow as tall as you can.

•

AM ASKED why the catfish in the Nile River swim upside down. To feed on what's afloat.

SIR WALTER Raleigh requested his coffin be lined with his old cigar boxes.

ANSWER DEPT.

Q. "IN JAPAN'S business jargon, what's a 'Supreme Adviser'?" A. The title usually given corporate presidents and board chairmen when they retire. It's a variation of "Consultant."

•

Q. "DOES CHINA execute criminals? If so, how?" A. Yes, by a bullet to the back of the head. About 5000 people convicted of capital crimes are expected to be so shot in 1984.

•

Q. "YOU SAID writers pay no taxes in Ireland. How about painters of pictures?" A. Likewise, and photographers, too. The key to exemption there is "works of art."

•

Q. "WHICH OF OUR states has the lowest divorce rate? The highest?" A. Lowest, Vermont. Highest, California. Incidentally, the divorce rate is down nationwide. It has been dropping off for a couple of years.

•

Q. "I'VE HEARD that West Berlin is the homosexual capital of Europe. Does Australia have a city with a similar reputation?" A. Sydney is said to be the South Pacific's center for such. Estimated gay population there now: 200,000.

•

Q. "WHAT WAS the name of the most famous bordello in Chicago?" A. The Everleigh Club? You have to go back a long way for that one. A 50-room mansion frequented by society bigwigs, the city closed it down in 1911.

IN NO society in the history of mankind have men and women been treated alike. Nor have they dressed alike. Nor have they done the same sorts of work. So wrote Vance Packard.

•

HOW MANY is "a few"? In the New Testament, St. Peter says it's eight.

•

IN MICHIGAN'S Sault Sainte Marie, it's not only unwise but illegal to spit against the wind.

•

THE ORIGINAL Harvard College of 1636 was surrounded by a high stockade to keep out wolves and Indians.

•

ANOTHER THING about hitting age 50, your taste buds get less acute and the growth of your thumbnails slows down. Think you can adjust to that?

•

DIAMONDS, rubies, sapphires and emeralds are never found in the same beds. Which is more than you can say for . . . Never mind.

AN INVENTOR named James Puckle in 1718 patented a gun designed to shoot round bullets at Christians and square bullets at Turks.

IF THAT 3-year-old is typical, said toddler eats more canned baby food annually than it weighs.

•

CATHOLIC PRIESTS don't smoke cigars during mass anymore. But they did. Long, long, long ago. Pope Urban VIII stopped it.

AMONG TURTLES, remember, males grunt, females hiss.

•

COFFEE DRINKING is off. Way off. Per capita, it's down 50 percent in the United States since 1950. It's not so much that oldsters are quitting as that youngsters aren't starting.